REVEALING TRIMONTIUM

REVEALING TRIMONTIUM

The Correspondence of James Curle of Melrose, Excavator of Newstead Roman Fort

Edited by

Donald Gordon, Fraser Hunter
and Phil Freeman

ARCHAEOLOGICAL LIVES

ARCHAEOPRESS PUBLISHING LTD
Summertown Pavilion
18-24 Middle Way
Summertown
Oxford OX2 7LG
www.archaeopress.com

ISBN 978-1-80327-515-4
ISBN 978-1-80327-516-1 (e-Pdf)

Archaeological Lives

Cover: James Curle later in life. © Courtesy of HES. Mary Curle Album.
Assorted letters sent to Curle.
Graffiti of Dometius Atticus on the backing plates of military decorations. Photo by Neil McLean, © National Museums Scotland (X.FRA 129).

Frontispiece: One of Curle's letters. Photo by Neil McLean, © National Museums Scotland

This book is available direct from Archaeopress or from our website www.archaeopress.com

Contents

List of Figures and Tables

Curle and Haverfield

James Curle: A Man of Melrose

Glimpses of the *Dramatis Personae*

Letters to Hercules

Foreword

As one of James Curle's grandchildren growing up in Melrose I was always aware of the Roman camp and his part in its excavation. It was only later, on finding bundles of his letters, that I began to understand the extent of his correspondence and his enthusiasm for learning. His passport, which I possess, shows the extent of his travels in the pursuit of such knowledge, even the smallest detail.

His great love of the Borders and of Melrose made him the man that he was. But the fort at Newstead was the overriding interest of his life as the Report on the excavation shows.

I am delighted that the publication of the letters will add to the appreciation of the wide interest he showed in many aspects of archaeology.

Lady Jean Cameron of Lochbroom

Acknowledgments

We are very grateful to many people for their encouragement, forbearance, and skill in bringing together these groups of letters. Donald Gordon would like to thank his co-editors: Dr Fraser Hunter, National Museums Scotland, an old friend and enthusiast who saw the possibilities and led the way; and Dr Phil Freeman of Liverpool University, who knows his Haverfield and far, far more. He also thanks Mike Bishop, archaeologist, busy publisher and site guide and lecturer in days of yore; Lady Jean Cameron of Lochbroom for her constant encouragement and support; Professor Lawrence Keppie; all the translators – Mrs Elfriede Mackay, Mrs Ishbel Gordon, ever tolerant of domestic disruption, Dr Connie and Mr Brian Martin; the Old Gala Club and Sutherland Masons Archive for photographs; the British Museum authorities and staff, in particular Francesca Hillier (Senior Archivist) and Thomas Kiely; Alain Wright of the Royal Highland and Agricultural Society of Scotland; and the Trustees of the Haverfield Bequest. Fraser Hunter is grateful to Tori Adams, Alice Blackwell, David Clarke, James Graham-Campbell, Julie Holder, Stefanie Hoss, Dan Potter, Louis Swinkels, Friederike Voigt, Colin Wallace, and Marenne Zandstra for assistance with journeys down assorted antiquarian rabbit holes. The Trimontium Trust readily gave permission to republish material previously published under their aegis. We thank Alan Braby for his fine re-drawings of Curle's sketches, and the staff at *Archaeopress* for their attention in preparing the publication.

Chapter 1
Introduction

We gather here some of the key groups of correspondence by and to James Curle, a solicitor in Melrose in the Scottish Borders and a prominent antiquary (Figures 1.1–1.2). He is best known today for his excavation and seminal publication of the Roman fort of Newstead (*Trimontium*), near Melrose,[1] the results of which still influence scholarship to this day, but some of his wider interests have been recognised by scholars assessing his Swedish antiquarian work.[2] Four main groups of correspondence totalling 156 letters or notes, published here with accompanying critical apparatus, are used to illustrate his working methods around the Newstead excavations and on other antiquarian topics. One set is his correspondence with various staff members in the Department of British and Medieval Antiquities at the British Museum, primarily Charles Hercules Read and Reginald Smith; a second, smaller set comprises the surviving correspondence with curators in the same museum's Department of Greek and Roman Antiquities; a third series was to Francis Haverfield, the foremost Romanist of his

Figure 1.1. James Curle later in life.
© Courtesy of HES. Mary Curle Album

day in Britain; and a fourth, more eclectic set illustrates wider links, especially to continental scholars.[3] As discussed below, the archive history of these four sets gives each a coherence. To this we have added other relevant letters that have come our way. Curle was an inveterate correspondent, and there will undoubtedly be more archive material – his correspondence with other Scottish antiquaries is poorly represented in this collection – but what is presented here seems to us a representative sample that allows broader assessment of his important work on Roman topics and selected other aspects.

The other key archive source for his Newstead work is his set of excavation notebooks, now held in the archive collections of the National Record of the Historic Environment in Edinburgh. We have consulted them in the course of this work but have not attempted a

---

[1] Curle 1911a. See Chapter 3.

[2] Kidd and Thunmark-Nylén 1990; Kidd 1994.

[3] The first and third sets have been published previously (Gordon 2005; 2008); here we offer more extended critical apparatus and context.

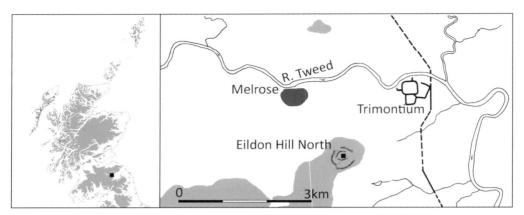

Figure 1.2. Map locating Melrose and Trimontium.
Ground over 250m is shaded.

critical edition of them; this would add great value to the existing archive of *Trimontium* but is beyond what we can attempt here. There are two sets of notebooks. One contains a mixture of field observations (fair copies, not the original field notes which do not survive), artefact descriptions (with lists and drawings of material before it went to the National Museum of Antiquities of Scotland [NMAS] in Edinburgh), and notes from his reading and travels. The other is a series of thematic notebooks where he gathered and sorted information ready for the publication: one can see in these the structure and often the very wording that appeared in print, with plentiful sketches that served as an aide memoire. Curle was a very competent draughtsman, and this was clearly a key element in his scholarly apparatus; one finds in the notebooks and letters sketches of comparative material as well as his own finds, a critical tool in the days before photocopiers and scanners.

We are also fortunate in being able to draw on personal collections and family archive from the descendants of James Curle, and have used this where appropriate to add to the picture of the man.

A series of introductory essays look at Curle himself (Chapter 2), his work as an antiquary (Chapter 4), his connections to Francis Haverfield (Chapter 5), and his life as a key part of Melrose society (Chapter 6); his writing and travels took him far and wide, but he was at heart a Borderer. The groups of letters are provided with a critical apparatus in footnotes. Key individuals who are mentioned in the letters as contacts of Curle's appear in a cast of *dramatis personae* (Chapter 7); if an individual is not footnoted, this is where to find them. Figure 1.3 locates the main British and Irish places mentioned in the Letters; Table 2.1 lists his wider travels.

We have inevitably found loose ends that we cannot currently resolve, and would be delighted to hear of further leads and letters to illuminate this fascinating man.

Conventions

Footnotes seek to clarify the contents of letters and their context, focusing on aspects important to archaeology. Deletions by Curle are retained but struck through, ~~thus~~. Curle frequently illustrated his letters with ink sketches. Available copies were hard to reproduce; they have been redrawn by Alan Braby. Works by James Curle referenced in footnotes are quoted simply as Curle xxxx; those of other Curles include initials to differentiate them.

Abbreviations

BM   British Museum
NMAS   National Museum of Antiquities of Scotland (now part of National Museums Scotland)
RMS   Royal Museum of Scotland (now part of National Museums Scotland)

Table 1.1: significant places in Britain and Ireland mentioned in the Letters; the numbers correlate with Figure 1.3.

1	Ambleside	22	Cirencester	43	Lochlee
2	Ardvouray	23	Colchester	44	London
3	Aylesford	24	Corbridge	45	Middlebie
4	Balmuildy	25	Cramond	46	Milsington
5	Bar Hill	26	Croy	47	Oronsay
6	Bertha	27	Dorchester	48	Polden Hill
7	Bhaltos	28	Dowkerbottom Cave	49	Porth Dafarch, Holyhead
8	Birdoswald	29	Dublin	50	Pudding Pan Rock
9	Birrens	30	Edinshall	51	Ribchester
10	Borness Cave	31	Eildon Hill North	52	Richborough
11	Bosham	32	Erickstanebrae	53	Rough Castle
12	Bow	33	Ewell	54	Santon Downham
13	*Bremenium*	34	Glastonbury	55	Settle
14	Brentford	35	Glenmailen	56	Silchester
15	Broighter	36	Great Chesters	57	Stanwick
16	Burrian	37	Grimthorpe	58	Taplow
17	Camelon	38	Guisborough	59	Torrs
18	Cappuck	39	Hod Hill	60	Torwoodlee
19	Castlecary	40	Housesteads	61	*Trimontium*
20	Chesters	41	Inveresk	62	*Vindolanda*
21	Chew Green	42	Lincoln	63	Welwyn

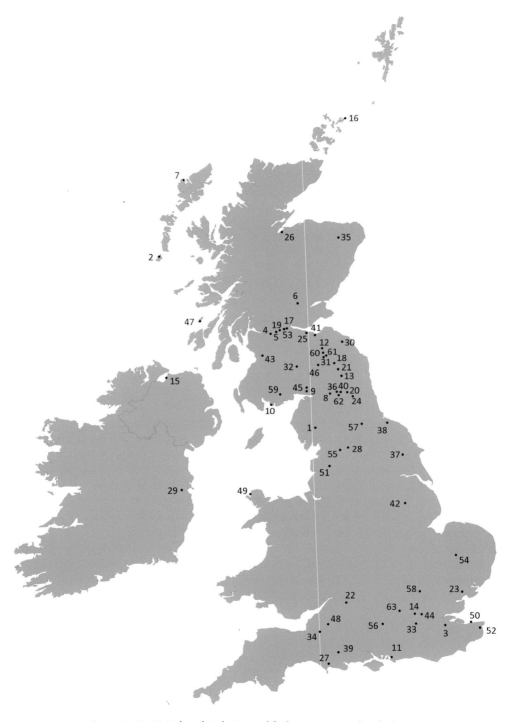

Figure 1.3. Key British and Irish sites and findspots mentioned in the letters.

Chapter 2
James Curle and his Letters
Donald Gordon

'I hope to hear from you one day soon, if you have not abandoned the custom of writing letters.' (Letter 1.7)

'Please excuse my inflicting such a long letter upon you.' (Letter 1.24)

James Curle (1862–1944; Figures 1.1, 2.1) was a lawyer by profession, but his interest in archaeology led to his excavating and publishing the Roman fort of Newstead (*Trimontium*), a landmark excavation which remains oft-quoted across Roman scholarship today.[1] His correspondence, much of which is drawn together here in four groups, gives insights into Curle's network of contacts which enabled this great work, and displays his wider antiquarian interests.

Curle was the eldest son of a legal family in the small town of Melrose on the River Tweed in the Scottish Borders, some 56 km south of Edinburgh. The three Eildon Hills, *c.*400 m high, form a dominant landmass and backdrop to the town on the south (Figure 2.2). The Latin name *Trimontium* – the Place of the Three Hills – became the title of the large 1st- and 2nd-century AD Roman fort and settlement which grew up a mile east of what is now Melrose, in the lee of the hills, at the village of Newstead

Figure 2.1. James Curle as a young man, c. 1890. By courtesy of the family.

(Figure 3.6). It was one of the largest and longest-occupied Roman settlements in Scotland.

James's grandfather had been Sir Walter Scott's 'man of business', a fact of which the family was very proud (Abbotsford, Sir Walter's estate, is 6.5 km west of Melrose).[2] The extended Curle family had antiquarian interests. Alexander, father of James, introduced him and his brother Alexander (A.O.) to the National Museum of Antiquities in Edinburgh as boys.[3] A.O. Curle became a noted professional archaeologist,[4] and his son, Alexander Tancred (Sandy; 1900–1986) researched and collected archaeological matters while working in east Africa.[5] Sandy's second wife, Cecil Louisa Mowbray (1901–1987), was a renowned archaeologist in her

---

[1] Curle 1911a.
[2] Sir Walter Scott (1771–1832) was the greatest novelist of his age, poet, playwright and something of an antiquary in his own right. See Brown 2003; Kelly 2011.
[3] See Chapter 4..
[4] See *Dramatis personae*.
[5] See C. Curle (ed.) 2008: 14, 19, 41, 63, 73, 80, 82, 122, 130–131, 143–144, 166, 171, 176, 193, 247; A.T. Curle 1937a and b. He was also a Fellow of the Society of Antiquaries of Scotland.

Figure 2.2. The three Eildon hills which gave the fort its Latin name Trimontium, viewed from the east.
© Lawrence Keppie.

own right, publishing on her excavations in Shetland, on Pictish monuments, and on the early medieval finds from Birsay in Orkney.[6] A distant cousin, R.A. Curle of Overwells, Jedburgh, donated a Roman intaglio from Cappuck to NMAS[7] and was a member of the Berwickshire Naturalists' Club for a short time before moving south.

James's solicitor father, Alexander (a 'Writer' to the Signet, in Scots terminology; 1819–1897) had a large Victorian family of three sons (educated at Fettes College, Edinburgh) and four daughters. As the eldest son, James (signing himself as James Curle Jr during his grandfather's lifetime) had to forego University for a career in the family firm, training as a Writer to the Signet,[8] while brother Alexander Ormiston Curle went to Cambridge University, later to work for the Royal Commission on the Ancient and Historical Monuments of Scotland, become a Museum Director and be known for excavations at Traprain Law in East Lothian and Jarlshof, in Shetland, *inter alia*. Both became Fellows (and office bearers) of the Society of Antiquaries of Scotland, like their friend Mr, later Sir, George Macdonald, another of the great names of Roman archaeology in Scotland.[9]

---

[6] Mowbray 1936a; 1936b; C.L. Curle 1940; 1982.
[7] *Proceedings of the Society of Antiquaries of Scotland* 49 (1914–1915): 12; Stevenson and Miller 1912: 476 n.1.
[8] This involved serving a five-year apprenticeship with a law firm and attending courses at Edinburgh University in Civil / Roman Law, Conveyancing and Scots Law, but was examined by the Society of Writers to Her Majesty's Signet, the incorporated body of Scottish lawyers, not by the University. We are grateful to Mr James Hamilton, Research Principal of the Society, for this information.
[9] See *Dramatis personae*.

In the 1890s and the first decade of the 20th century there was an upsurge in the excavation of Roman forts in Scotland, driven by the Society of Antiquaries of Scotland, and James Curle took charge of the excavation of Newstead between 1905 and 1910.[10] In 1911 he published a 450-page magisterial Report *A Roman frontier post and its people: the fort of Newstead in the parish of Melrose* (Figure 2.3),[11] documenting a sensational series of military and civilian finds from this large fort based at the River Tweed crossing point of the Roman Great North Road, called by its medieval name of Dere Street. These remarkable survivals come from over 100 waterlogged pits, which are the internationally known feature and enigma of Newstead.

Letters to Hercules

Curle conducted an ongoing correspondence on finds and comparanda with eminent figures in

Figure 2.3. The two-volume edition of Curle's 1911 Report. Photo by Neil McLean, © National Museums Scotland

the British Museum, from 1891 to 1931 (Gordon 2008). The title for that extensive group of letters is **Letters to Hercules**, a gesture to Sir Charles Hercules Read, Keeper of the Department of British and Medieval Antiquities at the Museum (Figure 2.4); they are reprinted here with additional letters and expanded notes.

The gathering of this correspondence in London was an adventure in itself, well worth describing. During the consultation of aerial photographs of the Roman site at Newstead (*Trimontium*) in the National Monuments Record in Edinburgh[12] it was noticed that Mr Dafydd Kidd of the British Museum had forwarded, for interest and for the record, copies of James Curle letters to the BM, particularly in relation to Curle's extensive personal collection of Gotlandic bronzes, which the BM had sent a clerk to arrange systematically in Melrose and which it purchased outright in 1921.[13]

---

[10] For background see D.V. Clarke 2012.

[11] In keeping with the classical education of his day James was familiar with the principles of Latin and Greek prose and verse, and exercises in speaking aloud (declamation) and composition, which influenced his own writing style in English. Whether through conscious use or otherwise, this can be seen in the construction of the two-part title of the 1911 Report. The writer considers that *A Roman Frontier Post and its People* reveals a line of five 'beats' or 'feet' (a pentameter), while *The fort of Newstead in the parish of Melrose* gives six 'beats' or 'feet' (a hexameter). Let the reader listen and decide.

[12] Now the National Record of the Historic Environment (NRHE), curated by Historic Environment Scotland.

[13] Kidd and Thunmark-Nylén 1990. See Letters 1.16, 1.79–1.84.

Figure 2.4. Charles Hercules Read, Keeper of the Department of British and Mediaeval Antiquities and Ethnography at the British Museum, and a regular correspondent of Curle's.
© Trustees of the British Museum

The writer, former Honorary Secretary of the Trimontium Trust which was set up in 1988 to encourage public interest in the site,[14] wondered if that seam of letters had been fully mined, and his pursuit of that enquiry over the years has added to the collection. An initial direct postal enquiry at the BM having proved unfruitful, Prof. Lawrence Keppie let drop the information that Mr Neil McGregor, Director of the Museum, was a Glasgow University graduate. Emboldened, the writer wrote to him for assistance, chancing his arm 'as one Glasgow graduate to another', and the process began. From an exchange of letters with archivist Francesca Hillier and staff member Sylvie Seton and the lists that they kindly sent, it became apparent that there were indeed more Curle letters to be seen. It was suggested that if I came to London I could see and copy them for myself.

There began a series of sporadic visits in the 2000s by early morning train from Edinburgh Waverley or Berwick-upon-Tweed to King's Cross, a brisk walk to Great Russell Street by 10am, a pre-arranged place in the Students' Room till about 4pm, broken by a statutory one-hour displacement for lunch in the Great Hall, with a fascinating day's work laid out before me in huge, annual, leather-clad and alphabetically-arranged correspondence volumes, with letters in the familiar James Curle handwriting in the 'Cu' section and, wondrous to see, a copy of the occasional reply from a BM correspondent inserted behind the Curle letter on a sheet of tissue paper. For one who had experience of few replies from Haverfield to Curle (see below), the finding of replies from Sir Charles Hercules Read and Reginald A. Smith was a treasure. Then came an energetic walk back to the station, a reflective return, usually to Berwick, and an hour's drive home.

From Greece and Rome

These letters came from the archives of what is now the Department of Prehistory & Europe; a letter in the *From Home and Abroad* collection opened up further avenues, as it came from the Keeper of the Department of Greek and Roman Antiquities (Letter 4.4). Further enquiries revealed a small group of letters which are often complementary to the first series, as Curle pursued additional lines of enquiry. The surviving letters are partial; it is clear that

---

[14] See Gordon 2012a.

Curle corresponded with H.B. Walters in this department, for instance, but none of this correspondence survives.[15]

My Dear Haverfield

During the 1905–10 excavations, Curle had sought advice, as a supplicant, from Francis Haverfield (1860–1919), Camden Professor of Ancient History at the University of Oxford, who was the guru of Romano-British studies and a dominant figure in archaeology (Figure 5.1). The existence of the letters in the Haverfield Archive in the Ashmolean (now Sackler) Library was reported to the writer by Professor Lawrence Keppie in the late 1990s when the ingathering of Curle's writings seemed a worthwhile project. An arranged visit to the Library in 1998 led to the transcription of the letters and permission to publish them in 2005 in booklet form[16] to accompany a Melrose lecture by Dr P.W.M. Freeman, the authority on Haverfield.[17] They are reprinted here with additional letters and expanded notes under Curle's eventual and growingly confident title of **My Dear Haverfield.** Curle's gratitude for Haverfield's help is acknowledged generously in the Report.[18]

From Home and Abroad

James was an international traveller both before and after his marriage in 1902, with the occasional friend or family member, all over Europe, especially Scandinavia, as well as North Africa and, in 1899, for two months in the USA (Table 2.1; Figure 2.5). He was accustomed to visit museums, assess the displays and discuss the conservation techniques of the day. This was revealed when a third group of letters came to light in 2011, found by granddaughter Lady Jean Cameron of Lochbroom. Many came from scholars on the Continent, congratulating Curle on his famous discoveries and extolling their visits to him, while others carried renewed queries from English scholars keen to continue the discussions. To reflect the contents this section is entitled **From Home and Abroad**.

Table 2.1. The travels of James Curle derived from his passport (in the family's possession, covering 1886–1903), Letters or other sources. It will be incomplete for the period after 1903. Letter 4.10 implies a visit to Switzerland prior to 1913 but subsequent to the 1889 trip.

Year	Countries	Notes/source
1886	Italy via France and Switzerland	
1887	Norway via Sweden and Denmark	
1888	Sweden	
1889	Austria and Hungary via Germany, Switzerland and Paris	
1890	Russia via Sweden and Denmark	

---

[15] Letter 3.19. Thomas Kiely, pers. comm.
[16] Gordon 2005.
[17] e.g. Freeman 2007.
[18] Curle 1911a: viii. 'Among those who have helped me, I must especially mention Professor Haverfield of Oxford and Mr George Macdonald, of Edinburgh. Professor Haverfield and Mr Macdonald have both read the proofs of this volume, and to their sympathy and encouragement throughout the whole undertaking, no less than to their scholarship, I cannot too fully express my indebtedness'.

1891	Sweden via Denmark	Letters 1.1, 1.2
1892	France via Channel Islands	
1892	Germany	Letters 1.4, 1.5
1893	Netherlands	
1893	Sweden via Denmark	
1894	Algeria and Tunisia via France	
1895	Spain via France	
1896	Sweden via Denmark and Germany	Letter 1.12
1897	France	Letter 1.12
1898	France	
1898	Austria via Belgium	
1899	France	
1899	USA	Letter 1.14
1900	France	
1901	Sweden	
1902	Italy via France (honeymoon)	Letter 1.16
1903	Sweden	
1904		
1905	Sweden	Letter 3.2
1906	Germany, Belgium	Letter 1.30
1907		
1908	Germany	Letters 1.48, 3.21
1909		
1910		
1911		
1912		
1913	Germany	Curle 1917a mentions this tour

a

b

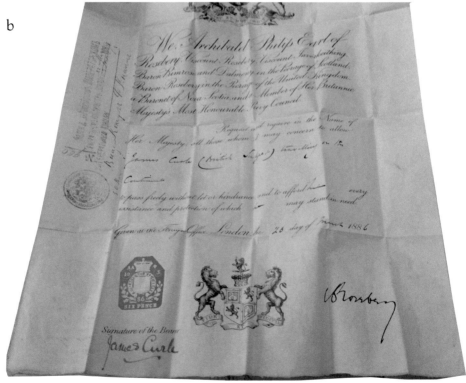

Figure 2.5. Curle's passport. a: folded into a wallet. b: unfolded.
The passport was authorised and signed by Viscount Rosebery, and signed by Curle bottom left.
Photos by Donald Gordon, reproduced by courtesy of the family.

Miscellanea

Other letters gathered over the years from outwith these major collections and to other correspondents are considered in a separate section, while a small group of letters between the British Museum and James's brother A.O. Curle is added as an Appendix. Five letters relating to Curle's links to the Society of Antiquaries of Scotland have been traced in NMS library archives; only one is relevant to his Roman interests, and is reproduced here (Letter 5.1).[19]

Curle considered

The place of James Curle and his youngest brother Alexander Ormiston Curle (A.O.) in the Scottish archaeological and society establishment was set out by J.N.G. Ritchie.[20] A member of many public bodies, James became a member of the monarch's ceremonial bodyguard in Scotland, the Royal Company of Archers in 1897 (Figure 6.2), and A.O. had a distinguished career in the National Museum (see *Dramatis personae*).

A detailed narrative of how James took on the project at Newstead[21] and an assessment of how highly his work should be regarded is given by Dr D.V. Clarke, who tackles the assumption that Curle was somehow a lesser figure than Macdonald or Haverfield: neither had Curle's experience of running a large excavation over several years.[22] Clarke indicates Curle's wide circle of friends and acquaintances in the archaeological world; his confidence in his own judgment of people and pride in his collection of bronzes; his ease in the company of senior academics; and the way he produced a Report unique in the annals of the Scottish Antiquaries. Although Clarke does not go so far as to declare that the evidence is conclusive, he suggests that it demonstrates that Curle had carefully planned the work and its interpretation: 'If this is the case, [James Curle] deserves to be treated as a very significant figure in the history of Roman archaeology in Britain'.[23]

---

[19] The others relate to acquisitions which Curle's father had facilitated (SAS UC Ms. 17/505, 15 March 1887; Ms. 17/370, 1 June 1890); library business (Ms. 31/47, 12 June 1895); and a letter to Joseph Anderson (Ms. 25/135, 18 November 1895) that discusses designs, perhaps for a bookplate(?). Its context is too uncertain to merit inclusion.
[20] Ritchie 2002.
[21] Like many scholars of the time he was shy of claiming it as *Trimontium*, although he used the term in later work, e.g. Curle 1929.
[22] D.V. Clarke 2012.
[23] D.V. Clarke 2012: 32.

Chapter 3

An Introduction to *Trimontium*

Donald Gordon and Fraser Hunter

James Curle described the site as a 'table land, tilted over to the south-east'.[1] You are looking east and the River Tweed is on your left side, flowing east until it curves gently to the south. The fort is lying up on your right side and it too spreads to the south and beyond its walls over the hollow in the ground, once a railway, now the A6091, and heads west out of your sight towards the three Eildon Hills before turning north behind you, heading to the river and completing the rectangle (Figures 3.1–3.2).

To arrive at that realisation took centuries. Local lore saw another abbey there of red sandstone, preserved in the field name 'Red Abbeystead' and reflecting the Roman sandstone foundations (Figure 3.3).[2] It was enlivened by chance finds of Roman altars in 1783 dedicated

Figure 3.1. Aerial photograph showing the fort in the bend of the river Tweed, with the Eildon Hills in the background. © Crown Copyright: HES.

---

[1] Curle 1911a: 1.
[2] Curle 1911a: 3–4. The famous abbey of Melrose lies close by.

Figure 3.2. The fort area today, approached from the west, sitting on the plateau where the line of trees runs.
© Fraser Hunter.

to the goddesses of the parade ground[3] and in 1830 to the god of hunting, Silvanus (Figure 12.1),[4] as well as the local parish minister's report[5] and the comments of General Roy in passing.[6] Only in 1846 did the laying down of the main line of the North British Railway lead to the opening up of a number of pits containing Roman material.[7]

Sixty years later, in the explosion of Roman fort excavations from *c.* 1890–1910,[8] the Society of Antiquaries of Scotland empowered James Curle to excavate this fort at Newstead (it took time for it to be recognised as *Trimontium,* the Place of the Three Hills).[9] James and Alexander Curle put the first spades in the ground, after drainage work by the tenant farmer in 1904 revealed areas of hard standing and possible walls.[10] This allowed James Curle and Alexander Mackie, the Clerk of Works who was experienced in excavating other Roman sites,[11] along

---

[3] RIB I: 2121.
[4] RIB I: 2124.
[5] Milne 1769: 6–7.
[6] Roy 1793: 115–117, pl. 21.
[7] Smith 1854; 1857. Drainage operations in the Fore Ends field in 1863 produced further finds (Smith 1864).
[8] The Society of Antiquaries of Scotland started a programme of excavations that covered the military complexes of Birrens, Burnswark and Lyne in southern Scotland, Castlecary and Rough Castle on the Antonine Wall, and Camelon, Ardoch and Inchtuthil north of the Wall, in the period 1895–1903 (Stevenson 1981: 177).
[9] Keppie 2012.
[10] Curle 1911a: 6. *The Scotsman* 26 August 1905: 6 shows that both brothers were involved.
[11] See *Dramatis personae.*

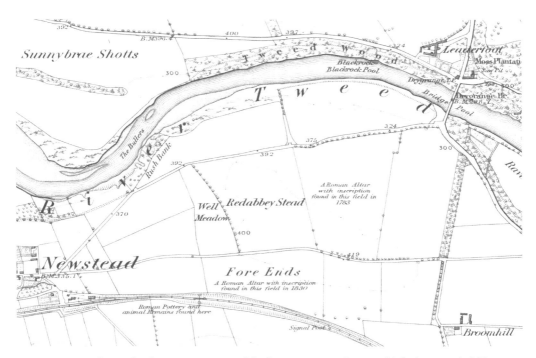

Figure 3.3. First-edition 6" Ordnance Survey map of the fort area, surveyed 1859, published 1863, with field names, the line of the 1846 railway, and stray Roman finds marked. Reproduced with the permission of the National Library of Scotland.

with some local workmen, to make a start, despite nothing being known 'of the extent, or indeed of the nature, of the site about to be explored'.[12]

A beginning was made by cutting a trench diagonally from west to east across the southern half of the Well Meadow, the field west of Red Abbeystead (Figure 3.3). Although the trench filled at first with water, the foundations of walls were seen underneath and by the end of the first week they had arrived at a bank of yellow clay, which proved to be the southern rampart of the fort.[13]

Curle kept notebooks of his digs and sketched his finds, dashing off a sketch to a correspondent in the middle of a letter to emphasise the point on which he was asking for information. On the ground he organised trenching to find walls and the pits for which the site became famous (Figure 3.4). Their details and contents are carefully recorded in his 1911 Report. He realised that he was excavating a large complex, not merely its buildings, and that required information about what lay outside the walls – the two sides of the coin were not to be separated. This was a major step forward, but one sadly missed by many later excavators.

Sir Ian Richmond had hoped to carry out a follow-up dig with Curle in 1939 to test the latter's suggested phasing of the fort, but that proved impossible with the imminence of war.

---

12 Curle 1911a: 6.
13 Curle 1911a: 6–7.

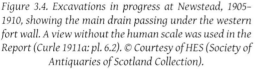

Figure 3.4. Excavations in progress at Newstead, 1905–1910, showing the main drain passing under the western fort wall. A view without the human scale was used in the Report (Curle 1911a: pl. 6.2). © Courtesy of HES (Society of Antiquaries of Scotland Collection).

Figure 3.5. Excavations by Bradford University within the fort, with Eildon Hill North in the background. © Fraser Hunter.

Richmond, with the aid of German prisoners of war, did it himself in 1947 and wrote it up 'as the dutiful fulfilment of a pledge' after Curle's death.[14]

The site then lay quiet for nearly two generations until Bradford University under Dr R.F.J. Jones did a third set of excavations from 1987 to 1998 (Figure 3.5). Their research work in the fort and annexes was augmented by complementary work on Iron Age sites and excavations along the old railway line through the Roman site in advance of the construction of a bypass. Although much information was obtained, the excavation has not yet been written up.[15]

In 2012 Fraser Hunter and Lawrence Keppie celebrated the centenary of James Curle's magisterial Report with an edited volume that rounded up work done since Curle's time and looked forward to remaining questions to which it would be helpful to find answers.[16]

The site lay at a key location, where the great road north, known in later times as Dere Street, crossed the river Tweed and another road running most likely from Berwick or Tweedmouth

---

[14] Richmond 1950; for commentary, see Hanson 2012: 64–65.
[15] Aspects of the work can be found in Clarke and Wise 1999; S. Clarke 2000; Dent 2012.
[16] Hunter and Keppie 2012.

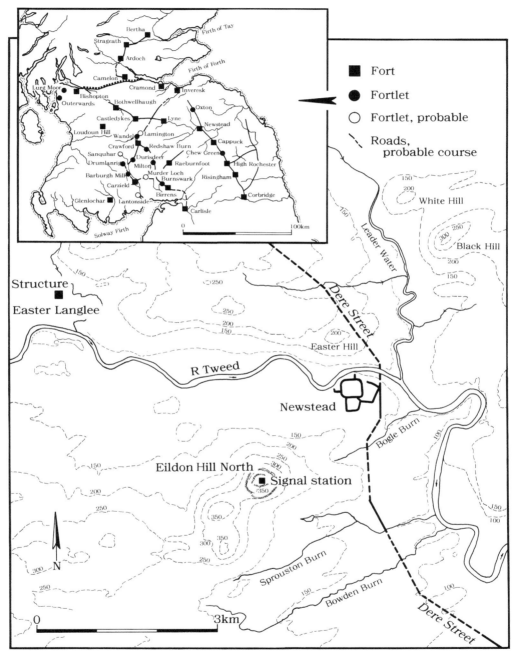

Figure 3.6. Location map; the inset shows the fort in the wider Antonine occupation. Drawn by Alan Braby, © National Museums Scotland.

The Roman Fort at Newstead

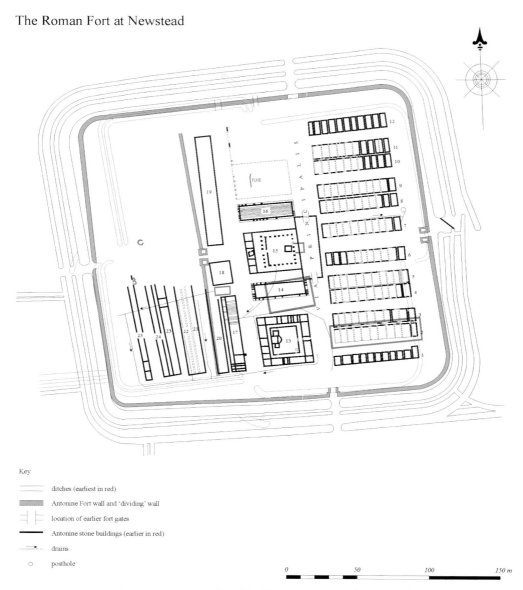

Key

— ditches (earliest in red)

▬ Antonine Fort wall and 'dividing' wall

╪╞ location of earlier fort gates

— Antonine stone buildings (earlier in red)

⟶ drains

○ posthole

0   50   100   150 m

*Figure 3.7. Composite plan of the fort remains that Curle uncovered
(drawn by Lorraine McEwan, after Curle 1911: plan facing p. 38)*

west along the river, ultimately to the Ayrshire coast (Figure 3.6).[17] It was one of the largest Roman military sites in Scotland, varying from 4.3–6.0 hectares over its ramparts,[18] and the fact that the only surviving milestone from Roman Scotland records its distance from *Trimontium* suggests the latter was *caput viae*, the head of the road system in the area from which all

---

[17] Margary 1973: 454–455, 473–476; much of its route at the eastern and western ends remains conjectural.
[18] Hanson 2012.

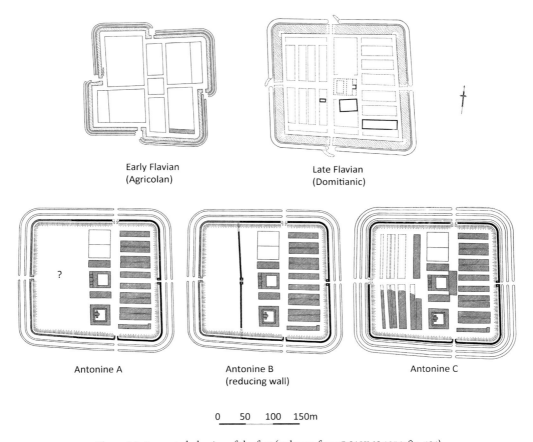

Early Flavian
(Agricolan)

Late Flavian
(Domitianic)

Antonine A

Antonine B
(reducing wall)

Antonine C

0   50   100   150m

Figure 3.8. Suggested phasing of the fort (redrawn from RCAHMS 1956: fig. 424)

distances were measured.[19] It was also placed on the doorstep of one of the largest Iron Age hillforts in the area, Eildon Hill North, which was a major central place.[20]

The fort sequence has seen continued and ongoing debate (Figures 3.7–3.8).[21] The most widely accepted phasing sees a Flavian fort of unusual form, with recessed entrances created by staggered ramparts, constructed under Agricola c. AD 78. This was rebuilt as a more conventional fort with a massive clay rampart under Domitian when the northern conquests were abandoned but southern Scotland was retained until the early Trajanic period. The site was then abandoned, to be reoccupied on the renewed invasion of southern Scotland on the orders of Antoninus Pius around AD 140. It is likely that the first Antonine fort adopted and renewed the lines of the Domitianic

---

[19] Keppie 2012: 12–14.
[20] Owen 1992.
[21] See Curle 1911a: 77–85; Letters 3.15–3.17 for debate between Curle and Haverfield; Dragendorff 1911, expressing his doubts about aspects of the sequence; Richmond 1950 and RCAHMS 1956: 312–320, presenting a four-phase model, broadly supported by Hanson 2012, though Manning (forthcoming) argues convincingly for the five-phase model, with the so-called reducing wall representing a separate phase early in the Antonine period. Simon Clarke (2012) saw further complexities within the sequence, based on the Bradford work and the postulated sequence of roads around the site.

Figure 3.9. The monument erected at the north-west corner of the fort in 1928; see also Figures 11.6–11.7. Photo by Neil McLean, © National Museums Scotland.

one, but with a stone wall fronting the rampart; this was quickly reduced to a rather smaller fort with a reducing wall cutting off the western end, suggestive of a rapidly changing security situation as the conquest proceeded. Probably on the abandonment of the Antonine Wall in the 160s, the fort was restored to full size for its new role as outpost rather than hinterland fort, being finally abandoned in the 180s under Commodus.[22] This suggests a five-phase sequence. The details remain a point of debate, but the outline is not so different from that inscribed on the memorial stone erected at the north-west corner of the fort in 1928 (Figure 3.9).

'Here once stood the fort of Trimontium, built by the troops of Agricola in the first century AD, abandoned at least twice by the Romans and ultimately lost by them after fully one hundred years of frontier warfare.'

The garrisons in each period are not entirely clear; they have been discussed in recent years by Bill Hanson and W.H. Manning, and their conclusions are followed here.[23] The garrison of the first Flavian fort is not known, though it was a large installation and most authors suggest it included cavalry. A cavalry unit is certainly attested in the second Flavian fort, with a legionary element also in garrison. The original Antonine plan and the reduced fort were most likely for an infantry unit. The final stage of the Antonine period included a component of legionaries from the Twentieth Legion alongside auxiliary cavalry, probably the *ala Augusta Vocontiorum* attested on the *Campestres* altar.[24]

Perhaps the most striking features of the site are the extensive evidence for settlement and activity beyond the ramparts (the first time this was recognised at a Scottish fort site), and the remarkable range of finds from the waterlogged pits, primarily in the annexes outside the site. The interpretation of these remains an unresolved cause of controversy.[25]

The site is one to which generations of scholars have returned, in the field and in print, from Britain and abroad. All build on the legacy of James Curle and his remarkable 1911 Report. It is the foundations of this work and the nature of this man's researches that we seek to explore in this volume.

---

[22] Breeze 2012: 118.
[23] Hanson 2012; Manning 2006a; Manning forthcoming.
[24] RIB I: 2121.
[25] For instance, Curle 1911a: 113–115; Ross and Feachem 1976; Clarke and Jones 1994; S. Clarke 2000; Manning 2006b; Bishop 2012a: 177.

Chapter 4

James Curle and his Archaeological World

Fraser Hunter

The antiquarian interests of James Curle have received extended treatment from other scholars. Graham Ritchie offered a thorough examination of his background and archaeological contributions, while David Clarke has provided a fine analysis of the context of his work at *Trimontium*; Dafydd Kidd and Lena Thunmark-Nylén thoroughly appraised his Scandinavian collecting interests, and in this volume Donald Gordon has looked at Curle's involvements in local society.[1] All have drawn on aspects of the letters published here. Yet there is still meat to be taken from these literary bones, assessing them primarily from the perspective of Curle's contribution to Roman and Iron Age studies. The letters, along with his wider archive and writings, allow us to explore aspects of his working practice and assess his research networks. The letters touch on a wide range of topics, but are strongly concentrated on areas and objects that Curle was actively researching at the time. Here I will consider how he developed his networks before focusing on the three key areas of his research: his Newstead excavations (and the continuing interests these gave him); the relationships between the Romans and the Iron Age communities of Scotland, and indeed of *Germania magna*; and Scandinavian material culture. From this develops a brief consideration of Curle as collector.

Curle's development of networks

James Curle came from a family with antiquarian interests: his father 'when he had a day in Edinburgh rarely failed to spend some time of it in conversation with Dr Joseph Anderson' at the National Museum of Antiquities, and James and A.O. Curle were indoctrinated by this early engagement.[2] Curle travelled frequently to Gotland between 1888 and 1903, and collected Gotlandic antiquities over this period.[3] The first indications of his interests in Scottish topics come from his involvement in the excavations of Torwoodlee broch near Galashiels in the Scottish Borders in 1891. He wrote this up, and his earliest letters to the British Museum are focused on parallels for Torwoodlee finds and a discussion of the dating of brochs. They show a good knowledge of the collections to hand in Edinburgh and a desire to ensure that he has captured relevant wider parallels.[4]

This desire for a broader perspective is clear in his correspondence, and in his travels. Most of his letters to the British Museum include some report of what he has been finding, but almost always feature a request for references or parallels, or an introduction to some museum he wanted to visit.[5] Both Hercules Read and Reginald Smith were unfailingly

---

[1] Ritchie 2002; D.V. Clarke 2012; Kidd and Thunmark-Nylén 1990; Kidd 1994; Chapter 6, infra.
[2] A.O. Curle *Journal*, quoted by Kidd 1994: 88; Ritchie 2002: 20–21. Anderson was the Keeper of the National Museum of Antiquities of Scotland; see *Dramatis personae*.
[3] Kidd 1994: 88; Ritchie 2002: 21.
[4] Letters 1.2 and 1.3.
[5] In some two-thirds of cases.

helpful; the tone that Read used to A.O. Curle when the latter wrote to him as director of the Royal Scottish Museum is notably more abrupt, one might say condescending,[6] and while this in part reflects James Curle's different status as a well-connected amateur, it must also be reflective of the fact that he held a prized collection of Gotlandic finds which were of great interest to the British Museum as a potential acquisition. In this they played a long game: the first surviving correspondence sees Curle sending a donation of brooches,[7] his collection appears at various other points in the correspondence,[8] and indeed in 1902 the BM despatched a staff member to help Curle with its arrangement,[9] but it was only thirty years later that it was successfully acquired. The BM database indicates other donations which do not feature in the surviving correspondence: a Romano-British brooch from Lavington, Wiltshire in 1901,[10] and two organic finds from Newstead in 1908.[11]

Curle's letter-writing was a key means by which he acquired knowledge, and the range of correspondents that we can glimpse shows something of how he used this tool. We have not systematically sought out Curle's correspondence in the papers of other antiquaries, but it is clear that he was corresponding widely: for instance Letter 5.2, preserved in the publications of H. St George Gray, offers an instance where Curle provided information on his finds to other antiquaries; Letter 1.6 mentions the renowned antiquary Canon Greenwell in Durham, while Letter 1.3 shows correspondence with 'Mr Evans', probably Arthur Evans. All three offer instances of Curle's connections with some of the foremost antiquaries of his day; Table 4.1 summarises the wider networks that can currently be seen.

Table 4.1. Antiquaries known to have corresponded with Curle, split by geographical area. For details, see Dramatis personae.

Person	Base or institution	Topic(s)
SCOTLAND		
Joseph Anderson	NMAS	Newstead
Gerard Baldwin Brown	Edinburgh University	Viking finds
Alexander Curle	RCAHMS/NMAS/RMS	Various
Peter Hume Brown	Edinburgh University	Newstead
George Macdonald	Edinburgh	Newstead, Roman Scotland
Alexander Mackie	Abernethy	Newstead, Balmuildy
Herbert Maxwell	Monreith	Newstead, Galoshins
William McDowell Selby	Port William	Galoshins, Newstead finds

[6] Letters A2–A4.
[7] Letter 1.1.
[8] e.g. Letters 1.2–1.4, 1.8, 1.9, 1.12, 1.13. Surviving correspondence over the collection drops off after 1898 apart from Letter 1.16 (1902), when Henry Oldland was in Melrose to work on the finds.
[9] Letter 1.16.
[10] Reg. no. 1901,1025.1.
[11] A leather patch and a wooden tent peg (reg. nos 1908, 0617.1–2).

Person	Base or institution	Topic(s)
WIDER UK		
George Gordon Coulton	Cambridge University	Melrose Abbey
Arthur Evans	Ashmolean Museum	Anglo-Saxon glass
Harold St George Gray	Taunton	Scale armour
Francis Haverfield	Oxford University	Newstead, Roman Society
William Henry St John Hope	Society of Antiquaries of London	Exhibition of finds
Thomas Athol Joyce	British Museum	Peruvian gold cup
Alexander Stuart Murray	British Museum	Glass vessels
Charles Reed Peers	Society of Antiquaries of London	Gotland finds
Charles Hercules Read	British Museum	Newstead, Gotland, continental museums
Cecil Harcourt Smith	British Museum	Roman finds
Reginald Allender Smith	British Museum	Newstead, Iron Age and Roman finds
Margerie Taylor	Oxford University / Roman Society	George Macdonald
Henry Beauchamp Walters	British Museum	Roman pottery
CONTINENTAL EUROPE		
Joseph Déchelette	Roanne Museum	Samian
Hans Dragendorff	German Archaeological Institute	Membership of the Institute / reviewer of the Report
Ernst Fabricius	Freiburg University	Visits to Melrose
Leopold Frölich	Königsfelden Health & Care Institute	Finds from Vindonissa, especially samian
Viktor Hoffiller	Croatian National Museum	Weaponry from Newstead
Gerard Marius Kam	Nijmegen	Roman helmets
Johanna Mestorf	Kiel Museum	Newstead finds
Emil Ritterling	Wiesbaden Museum	Roman excavations
Karl Schumacher	Römisch-Germanisches Zentralmuseum Mainz	Roman helmets

Person	Base or institution	Topic(s)
SCANDINAVIA		
Oscar Almgren	Uppsala University	Newstead (brooches, helmets)
Hans Hildebrand	State Historical Museum, Stockholm	Swedish finds
Oscar Montelius	State Historical Museum, Stockholm	Swedish finds
Bernhard Salin	Various roles in Stockholm	Gotland finds, oval brooches

Curle also read widely. He had a good personal library[12] and access to the excellent library of the Society of Antiquaries of Scotland, the best research library north of Oxbridge for temperate European archaeology, and one for which he acted as librarian for over a decade; Letter 1.14 shows him seeking recommendations from Read for purchases. We also see him giving and receiving offprints and books: in Letter 1.66 he thanks Smith for an offprint, while in Letters 4.2 and 4.3 Oscar Almgren and Johanna Mestorf thank him for copies of a paper on the site,[13] while he sent his note on the Roman bronze leg from Milsington to the local farmer.[14] Hercules Read sent him a copy of a catalogue of ancient glass, and he was also sent a complimentary copy of the BM pottery catalogue;[15] Letter 5.4 shows Curle in turn sending a copy of his Report to Thomas Hardy, though this was more a cultural than academic interchange.

The other key aspect was his travels to view comparanda. He could access the collections of NMAS, and clearly did so;[16] but he was also aware of its limits, commenting to Read that 'I must come and see your Roman pots on the first opportunity as there is nothing to study here'.[17] He travelled regularly to London, and there are indications of other study visits within Britain: he had visited the Mayer collection in Liverpool,[18] and planned to visit Peterborough and Northampton to study pottery,[19] though Letter 3.17 shows that by 1907 he had still not visited the museums in Carlisle or Newcastle.

His early travels in Sweden[20] gave him a wide knowledge of the antiquities of the area and of the relevant experts (he knew and corresponded with key Swedish antiquaries, notably Oscar Almgren, Hans Hildebrand, Oscar Montelius and Bernhard Salin)[21] as well as antiquities dealers, while Salin and Montelius visited his collection.[22] But the focus of his travels shifted: during his work on Newstead he travelled in the Rhineland, France and Belgium in search

---

[12] Much of it donated to the Society of Antiquaries of Scotland after his death; *Proceedings of the Society of Antiquaries of Scotland* 80 (1945–1946): 162. Cf. Letter 1.34, 'I am writing away from my books'.
[13] Possibly Curle 1906; more likely Curle 1907b.
[14] Curle 1936; Letter 5.8.
[15] Letters 1.17, 1.55.
[16] e.g. Letters 1.2, 1.3.
[17] Letter 1.19.
[18] Curle 1892: 76, 78.
[19] Letter 1.34.
[20] He also travelled to Denmark: Letter 1.8 references his notes from the museum in Copenhagen; in Letter 1.77 he mentioned he was not particularly familiar with Norwegian material.
[21] See *Dramatis personae*.
[22] Kidd 1994: 91; Ritchie 2002: 21.

of parallels, particularly for pottery and armour (see Table 2.1).[23] Curle was not initially conversant in German, though he had a good grasp of French,[24] but his publications indicate he became a competent linguist with academic literature in both languages.

Curle was also embedded in key antiquarian systems of the time. He was elected a Fellow of the Society of Antiquaries of Scotland in 1889 and rapidly became an office-bearer. He served on Council in 1893/4, was asked to act as Librarian from 1894/5 to 1907/8, and was one of the Curators of the Museum from 1908/9 to 1941/42; he was then elected a vice-president, a role he held until his death.[25] The honorary role of Curator (of which there were two at any one time) is ill-defined,[26] but I am grateful to David Clarke for researching the topic. He notes that the Society's Purchase Committee was chaired by one of the Curators, suggesting a clear desire for office bearers rather than paid staff (the Keeper) to be seen as those responsible for developing the collection. This would have given Curle considerable influence over the collection's development.[27] In several letters he wrote to the British Museum in his capacity as an office-bearer of the Society.[28]

Curle was an active participant in the Society's activities, especially in later years. He published a series of papers in the Society's *Proceedings*,[29] exhibited Swedish finds at Society meetings on three occasions over the period when he was building his Gotlandic collection,[30] and donated a wide range of items. His earliest donation was 'Midside Maggie's Girdle', a remarkable early 17th-century silver chain with a well-recorded historical tradition. Curle could trace his descent from Margaret Hardie, 'Midside Maggie', and he and another relation presented the find in memory of his father.[31] He gave models of Roman locks and keys during the course of his Newstead work, and from 1921 (after he had sold his Gotland collection to the British Museum) he regularly donated material, some with Borders associations, others representing a much broader collecting habit stretching from prehistoric to post-medieval finds.[32] As noted below, this included some Newstead material he had seemingly retained. He also found ways to broaden the Society's international reach in the course of thanking people who helped

---

[23] Letter 1.30.
[24] Letter 1.30.
[25] *Proceedings of the Society of Antiquaries of Scotland* 77 (1942–1943): 1.
[26] There is little mention of it in Stevenson's otherwise encyclopaedic treatment of 1981.
[27] For several years (1919/1920 until 1924/1925), the other Curator was his brother, giving the two a remarkable control over the collection. Curle on occasion published curious items that the Museum acquired (e.g. Curle 1925).
[28] Letters 1.12–1.14, 1.65.
[29] Curle 1892; 1895; 1913a; 1914; 1917a; 1917b; 1925; 1932a.
[30] *Proceedings of the Society of Antiquaries of Scotland* 24 (1889–1890): 381, Gotlandic antiquities; 26 (1891–1892): 214, a Swedish 'prime staff' purchased in Stockholm in 1891 (published by Morland Simpson in that volume); 36 (1901–1902): 245, a Swedish axe-hammer.
[31] Romanes and Curle 1898; Dalgleish and Fothringham 2008: 41, no. 3.16.
[32] *Proceedings of the Society of Antiquaries of Scotland* 43 (1908–1909): 269, models of Roman locks and keys; 56 (1921–1922): 169, two early Bronze Age flat axes, old finds from the Nairn area; 59 (1924–1925): 73, the hafted item from Bogancloch, Aberdeenshire, discussed in Curle 1925; 60 (1925–1926): 14, 96, a fishing reel and wooden quaich from Bemersyde, Borders; 63 (1928–1929): 323, 362–363, handles from Newstead, wide range of prehistoric and medieval material ranging from flint axeheads to a corbel from Old Melrose; 64 (1929–30): 11, two medieval ceramic pitchers from Whitton, Borders; 65 (1930–1931): 412, a fire plate of the Caledonian Insurance Company; 69 (1934–1935): 323, two early 19th-century autograph letters; 70 (1935–1936): 18–19, 360, Newstead finds, medieval lead badge from Melrose Abbey; 71 (1936–1937), coin of Vespasian, an old find from Ruberslaw, Borders; 72 (1937–1938): 14, Newstead finds.

him: Robert Stevenson observed that five foreign scholars were made Honorary Fellows of the Society on the back of their assistance with Newstead.[33]

Curle was also a regular contributor to the *Scottish Historical Review*, which carried articles, notes of recent work, and book reviews. His work on Newstead featured regularly,[34] and he was also a reviewer for them, on Roman topics and of Swedish literature.[35]

Although he was elected a Fellow of the Society of Antiquaries of London on 18 May 1893,[36] attended at least some of their lectures,[37] and exhibited material on two instances via Hercules Read at the British Museum,[38] he did not participate extensively in their work, although he was regularly in the city. His principal London network was the Society for the Promotion of Roman Studies: he was one of the first members when it was formed in 1910, influenced no doubt by his strong links to Haverfield, the founding President. Curle was a Council member for two years upon the Society's foundation and served three further three-year terms.[39] He was subsequently elected as one of the Vice-Presidents from 1935–36 until his death.[40] He lectured to the Society twice, on three separate topics (a parade helmet from Nijmegen, samian ware, and the Romans in the upper Rhine),[41] reviewed books for them,[42] and donated books to the Library.[43]

Curle engaged in more local antiquarian networks as well, speaking for instance to the Scottish branch of the Classical Association (on the Romans in Scotland),[44] the Tweeddale

---

[33] Stevenson 1981: 179. *Proceedings of the Society of Antiquaries of Scotland* 42 (1907–1908): xli records five relevant appointments in 1908: Salomon Reinach (Musée des Antiquités Nationales, St-Germain-en-Laye), Hans Dragendorff (Director of the Römisch-Germanisch Kommission), Emil Ritterling (Wiesbaden Museum), Ludwig Jacobi (Saalburg Museum) and Joseph Déchelette (Roanne Museum).

[34] Curle 1906; 1907a; *Scottish Historical Review* 4 (1906–1907): 364 (note of appeal for funds, and recent finds); 5 (1907–1908): 372–376 (appeal for funds, results of 1907 season, and report on Macdonald's [1908] article in the *Scotsman* on parade helmets); 5 (1907–1908): 510–511 (report on Rhind lectures).

[35] *Scottish Historical Review* 9 (1911–1912): 197–199 (recent Swedish journals); 18 (1920–1921): 214–215 (May and Linnaeus 1917, on Roman pottery from Carlisle); 14 (1916–1917): 380–381 (Macdonald 1916a, on coinage); 18 (1920–1921): 302–303 (recent Swedish journal); 22 (1924–1925): 127–129 (Haverfield and Macdonald 1924, on Roman Britain); 23 (1925–1926): 298–300 (Home 1926, on Roman London, received badly); 25 (1927–1928): 126–127 (Collingwood 1927, on Northumbrian crosses); and Curle 1923, a review article on Balmuildy Roman fort (Miller 1922).

[36] Letters 1.5, 1.6.

[37] This can be inferred since he was formally admitted to the Society on 17 January 1895, which requires attendance at a meeting; *Proceedings of the Society of Antiquaries of London* (2nd series) 14 (1891–1893): 356.

[38] Some Gotlandic gaming pieces and a Byzantine spoon on 17 January 1895 (see preceding note); some of the Newstead finds on 2 May 1907 (Letter 1.36).

[39] 1914–15 until 1916–17; 1918–19 until 1920–21; 1922–23 until 1924–25. There are some inconsistencies in how information on office bearers was presented during the two World Wars in the *Journal of Roman Studies*; the second stint is poorly attested but appears to be correct.

[40] The note of his death in *Journal of Roman Studies* 35 (1945): 150 said he had been Vice-President since 1934, but this seems to be an error.

[41] 2 March 1915: spoke on the Nijmegen visor helmet (published in the journal as Curle 1915) and on the development of samian ware (*Journal of Roman Studies* 5 [1915]: 251–252). 16 March 1926: spoke on 'The Romans on the Upper Rhine' (*Journal of Roman Studies* 15 [1925]: 299; 16 [1926]: 286).

[42] *Journal of Roman Studies* 1 (1911): 128, reviewed Macdonald 1911; *Journal of Roman Studies* 6 (1916): 208–9, reviewed Atkinson 1916; *Journal of Roman Studies* 21 (1931): 302–303, reviewed Koepp *et al.* 1924–1930.

[43] *Journal of Roman Studies* 10 (1920): 192, gift of 18 Loeb editions of classical texts; *Journal of Roman Studies* 12 (1922): 317, thanked for continuing his generous gift of Loebs to the library; *Journal of Roman Studies* 14 (1924): 289, gave further unspecified books.

[44] Curle 1913c; Letter 1.70

Society (on the Romans in the Borders),[45] the Glasgow Archaeological Society (on Newstead),[46] the Edinburgh branch of the Historical Association (on the Romans in the Borders),[47] and the Dumfriesshire and Galloway Natural History and Antiquarian Society (on the Roman road from Tyne to Tweed).[48] He also contributed a short piece on Newstead to a 1929 guidebook on Melrose and district.[49] However, his most regular contributions were to the Berwickshire Naturalists' Club. He was admitted to the Club in 1893, following in the footsteps of his father,[50] although he played little active part in it apart from guiding them around the Newstead excavations until he was elected President for 1913.[51] In the following years, he regularly guided the Club on their excursions and talked to them in the field on the Roman fort at Cappuck, the abbeys of Jedburgh and Melrose, and Walter Scott's house at Abbotsford.[52] In these more local networks he was disseminating the information he had acquired; it was the national societies, the letter-writing and the travels which brought him the information needed for his work.[53]

Curle's three key research foci were the Romans (particularly in Scotland), Scandinavian antiquities (especially the long Iron Age, up to and including the Viking period), and relations between the Romans and the peoples beyond the frontier, seen in both his Scottish and Scandinavian interests. We shall review these in turn, focusing in the first on his Newstead work.

Curle's Newstead networks

'We have really been most lucky at Newstead.' (Letter 1.24)

David Clarke has provided an authoritative overview of Curle's work at Newstead,[54] but further aspects can be teased out. In what follows, I will touch on what can be gleaned of

---

[45] On 19 November 1913; recorded on a poster for the event in Scottish Borders archives (SBA/411/2).

[46] To their AGM on 18 November 1909, reported in *The Scotsman* 19 November 1909: 4.

[47] *The Scotsman* 13 February 1920: 5; the report makes it clear that he used the Romans along Dere St as his focus, which was a common structure for his talks; see the following note.

[48] *Transactions of the Dumfriesshire and Galloway Natural History and Antiquarian Society* (third series) 17 (1930–1931): 43. The talk was not published; the topic sounds very similar to his presidential address to the Berwickshire Naturalists some twenty years previously (Curle 1913d), and was clearly a long-term research interest. He gave a similar talk to the Cambridge Antiquarian Society (of which he was an honorary member) on 8 May 1922 on 'A Roman road across the Scottish Border' (*Proceedings of the Cambridge Antiquarian Society* 24 [1921–1922]: 14–15).

[49] Curle 1929.

[50] Whose tombstone describes him as 'of East Morriston and Melrose', the former location a Berwickshire farm in Legerwood parish, some 10 km north-east of Melrose.

[51] *History of the Berwickshire Naturalists' Club* 14.2 (1893): 253; 19.3 (1905): 265–267 (Newstead visit); 20.2 (1907): 169–173 (Newstead visit); Curle 1913d (Presidential address).

[52] *History of the Berwickshire Naturalists' Club* 23.1 (1916): 37–46 (Abbotsford); 25.1 (1923): 49 (Melrose Abbey); 28.2 (1933): 138–139 (Cappuck); 30.1 (1938): 17 (Jedburgh Abbey). He also spoke to the Club on the occasion of the unveiling of a view indicator as the Club's centenary memorial; *History of the Berwickshire Naturalists' Club* 27.3 (1931): 307–311. It is perhaps noteworthy that he was not a member of the Hawick Archaeological Society (though he did show them around the Newstead excavations; *Transactions of the Hawick Archaeological Society for 1905*: 47–48), whereas his brother A.O. Curle was a member and regular contributor to the latter but never joined the Berwickshire Naturalists, although he surveyed the area for the first volume of the Royal Commission on Ancient and Historical Monuments' *Inventory of ancient monuments* (RCAHMS 1909; revised 1915).

[53] He acquired a wide range of other committee roles and honorifics, but these are of less relevance in the current context. See Ritchie 2002: 27.

[54] D.V. Clarke 2012.

the excavation process before focusing on the key areas of artefact research to which Curle devoted attention in his letters.

Curle's comments on Newstead in his report on the Torwoodlee broch excavations now seem prescient: 'no systematic excavations, as far as I am aware, have ever been undertaken, and our chief knowledge of it is derived from remains brought to light when the railway cut through part of it in 1846'. From the stray coins he suggested 'we may infer that the occupation was probably continued at least to the end of the fourth century'.[55]

The letters show Curle engaging with both British Museum colleagues and with Francis Haverfield over particular topics of concern to him. They provide some insights also into what he was digging at particular dates (the sequence of numbered pits shows this too); this is an area that would be much clearer from analysis of his notebooks.

With the British Museum colleagues, Curle was mostly seeking parallels and references. With Haverfield, there was much more debate. Curle originally sought advice from him, and Letter 3.7 indicates that Haverfield's views were guiding field strategy in the first season,[56] but subsequently there was notable debate, especially over the sequence of occupation.[57] The two men also met in person, when they must have discussed and debated issues invisible on the written page. As Donald Gordon has noted, the relationship shifted visibly over time, as tracked in the changing modes of address (from 'Dear Mr Haverfield' to 'My Dear Haverfield')[58] and in the content, with Haverfield seeking Curle's advice on pottery and using information he provided in his own publications.[59] Some topics were explored in a provisional fashion with Haverfield before approaching the British Museum, such as the scale armour from the *principia* well: the Haverfield correspondence shows the initial excitement at a find of gold transforming to one of brass as more work was done, but the first discussions of the topic with the British Museum only occurred after the metal identification was confirmed.[60] Curle clearly valued the insights and connections that Haverfield offered: he commented in the course of a review that 'the influence, not only of his written work, but his personal encouragement and help to younger men, cannot be overrated', and this rings of specific experience.[61]

Curle's correspondence was highly focused and highly efficient: it consisted of finds he had just made and was actively researching. This must reflect his means of working, where he was preparing publication-quality notes on the finds as he went along (aided by his sketches, as the finds themselves were dispatched at regular intervals to NMAS). This is reflected also in the notebooks, which contain what are in essence final drafts of the published text.

---

[55] Curle 1892, 82. This was not a conclusion he supported after the excavations (Curle 1911a: 342).

[56] Letter 3.7, from George Macdonald to Haverfield: 'The men have now started cuttings on the lines you suggested'.

[57] See in particular Letters 3.15–3.17.

[58] Gordon 2005; 2012b: 35.

[59] Haverfield 1909: 411 (quoting Curle's interpretation of the samian potter Divixtus), 419 (Curle's comments on coarse wares from Corbridge).

[60] Compare Letters 3.8 and 3.9 to Letter 1.18.

[61] *Scottish Historical Review* 22 (1924–1925): 510–511, reviewing Haverfield and Macdonald 1924.

Excavating Newstead

The excavations ran continuously from 13 February 1905 to 19 May 1909 (Figure 4.1). After a break of some months, they restarted on 22 December 1909 and ran until mid-September 1910.[62] Yet the Letters show that there were variations in scale and pace over this time: 'we have been busy filling in';[63] there had been very few finds recently as 'most of the time we have been filling in';[64] 'still finding a few things, though we are working on a small scale';[65] 'I have been digging again at Newstead'.[66]

Curle was clearly working around the agricultural cycle, and trying to avoid inconveniencing the farm tenants. 'The reducing wall has not yet been traced to its junction with the main wall on the S. As soon as the hay is cut we shall do it'.[67] 'I am being much harassed in dealing with the farm tenants who, as usual, make absurd demands'.[68] Indeed, a letter to *The Scotsman* from the President of the Society of Antiquaries of Scotland, Sir Herbert Maxwell, in July 1905

Figure 4.1. Excavation of the titulus outside the west gate of the fort, 1905–1910. © Courtesy of HES (Society of Antiquaries of Scotland Collection).

specifically noted the need for funds to indemnify the tenant against damage to the crop.[69] Funds were always a concern: in December 1907, Curle wrote 'funds are running out and I don't know if we shall see much more'.[70] Several of the Letters are concerned with aspects of fund-raising; letters to newspapers were a key strategy.[71]

Early in the excavation, Macdonald's letter to Haverfield indicates the latter had in part guided the strategy: 'The men have now started cuttings on the lines you [Haverfield] suggested',[72] but it is clear that Curle developed his own approach as his questions around the site grew, though he was aware of the limitations: 'So far we have not cleaned out any of the buildings and I

---

[62] Curle 1911a: vii; 1913a: 384: 'The excavation carried out in the South Annexe at Newstead during the first half of the year 1910 was in some measure the result of an afterthought'.
[63] Letter 3.18, 10 December 1907.
[64] Letter 1.44, 21 February 1908.
[65] Letter 1.47, 8 May 1908.
[66] Letter 1.60, 18 February 1910.
[67] Letter 3.16, 16 July 1907.
[68] Letter 3.11, 20 November 1905.
[69] *The Scotsman* 12 July 1905: 11.
[70] Letter 3.18, 10 December 1907.
[71] e.g. Letters 3.8, 3.14, 3.18 n.100.
[72] Letter 3.7, 23 September 1905.

doubt whether funds and time will permit of our doing much more than trace out the walls, which is unsatisfactory'.[73] Once the potential of the pits was realised, they naturally became a particular focus: 'I have just started pit-hunting again S of the railway'.[74] Yet Curle was not just seeking rich finds, though his disappointment at barren pits is clear;[75] the detailed field observations he used in his arguments with Haverfield over the site sequence show a clear focus on disentangling the series of forts on the site.[76]

A search of the archives of *The Scotsman* newspaper over the period of the excavations reveals more of his working methods. The pages of the paper saw an appeal for funds in 1905[77] and regular updates on progress, some by Curle, some unsigned,[78] while there was an extended discussion of the face-mask helmets by George Macdonald.[79] The paper also records a series of visits, no doubt only a selection but indicative of the interest, from the Hawick Archaeological Society,[80] the Edinburgh Field Naturalists and Microscope Society,[81] and Durham and Northumberland Archaeological Society.[82] Some of the finds were kept in the site sheds, so could be shown to visitors,[83] while intriguingly one progress report, in describing the baths, noted that 'The buildings are open for inspection now, and are well worth the visit',[84] indicating a clear desire to encourage visitors.

Helmets and armour

While a variety of finds are mentioned, two topics dominate: military equipment and pottery.[85] With the former, Curle was clearly aware of the importance of what he found: 'I fancy this must be one of the best armour finds ever made in this country'.[86] There are flurries of letters concerning the brass ('gold') scale armour from the *principia* (Figure 10.2)[87] and the problematical 'shoulder pieces', in truth saddle stiffeners, which continued to puzzle Curle in his Report, and which he exhibited to the Society of Antiquaries of London in hope of a solution (Figure 8.9).[88]

But it was the three face-mask helmets which were Curle's main focus – unsurprisingly, as they are among the most remarkable finds from the site (Figures 8.8, 8.10, 8.11). Much of Curle's correspondence was consumed with seeking parallels and references. He wrote to Smith and Read at the British Museum repeatedly on the topic, and also corresponded more widely: Letter 1.61 shows that he wrote to Karl Schumacher at the Römisch-Germanisches

[73] Letter 3.2, 10 August 1905.
[74] Letter 3.18, 10 December 1907.
[75] e.g. Letter 1.30; 'We are working away but have had no luck for some weeks'; Letter 1.34, 'We … have cleared out three pits without any result, which is disappointing'.
[76] Letters 3.16, 3.17.
[77] *The Scotsman* 12 July 1905: 11.
[78] *The Scotsman* 28 October 1905: 9; 12 August 1907: 6
[79] Macdonald 1908.
[80] *The Scotsman* 26 August 1905: 6.
[81] *The Scotsman* 9 July 1906: 6.
[82] *The Scotsman* 20 July 1907: 8.
[83] *The Scotsman* 15 July 1905: 11.
[84] *The Scotsman* 12 August 1907: 6.
[85] Letter 1.30.
[86] Letter 1.21.
[87] Letters 1.18. 3.7–3.9, 5.2.
[88] Letter 1.36.

Zentralmuseum in Mainz on the question, and in Letter 4.2 Oscar Almgren of Uppsala offered some parallels. Curle acquired an impressive grasp of the literature, and it clearly caught his interest: Letters 1.79 and 2.6 show his awareness of a new find from Palestine in the British Museum, post-dating his Report, and Letter 4.12 saw him corresponding over helmets with G.M. Kam in Nijmegen; he subsequently prepared a report on a new find from Nijmegen (Figure 11.5).[89]

Figure 4.2. Copy of the Newstead face-mask owned by James Curle. Photo by courtesy of the Trimontium Trust, © J. Reid.

The helmets also played a role in his Roman Society networks. In 1912 the Society issued a handlist of casts which could be purchased, the idea being to disseminate knowledge of Romano-British art, a topic Haverfield (the President), thought was key.[90] The published catalogue[91] included all three Newstead helmets: item 18 is the iron helmet, 'Probably the finest piece of Roman work in iron yet discovered in any part of the Roman Empire' (available in bronze, at £7 18s or plaster, £1 5s); 19 is the bronze mask (likewise in bronze or plaster), and item 20 the brass helmet (in hammered brass sheet, or plaster). It is interesting that item 19 is noted as by permission of the Society of Antiquaries of Scotland <u>and</u> of Curle, whereas the others were simply granted by the former. Curle seems to have had an affinity for this mask, as he owned a copy of it himself (Figure 4.2).[92]

The helmets caught the wider imagination, too. The Border poet, Will H. Ogilvie, composed a poem about the iron helmet,[93] and when King George V visited Edinburgh in May 1911, he 'expressed a desire to have an opportunity of personally examining the Roman helmets from Newstead'; Curle showed him 'the helmets and one or two other interesting objects from that camp'.[94] A month later Curle had an audience with the German Kaiser Wilhelm II, who had a strong interest in Roman archaeology.[95]

---

[89] Curle 1915.
[90] *Journal of Roman Studies* 3 (1913): 336–337; the sculpture itself was presented by Haverfield and Jones 1912 but the helmets were not discussed.
[91] Anon. 1912.
[92] Now in the collections of the Trimontium Trust. It is unclear who made the replica, although one may suspect it was Brook and Son of George St, Edinburgh, who made other replicas and did restorations for the Society (see Dalgleish 2022). The *Journal of Roman Studies* 3 (1913): 336–337 noted that 'local contractors' were involved; most of the 'moulds and store-casts' were stored in the British Museum (*Journal of Roman Studies* 4 [1914]: 247).
[93] The first publication of the poem seems to be in *The Scotsman* 21 May 1907: 5. See Gordon 2012c: 231–232, and 236 n.16 (the information in this footnote on its first publication is superseded by this 1907 *Scotsman* reference).
[94] *The Scotsman* 21 July 1911: 8.
[95] *The Scotsman* 21 August 1911: 4; 22 August 1911: 6.

Pottery

Curle's work on the Newstead pottery was of wide-ranging importance.[96] His main interest was in the samian ware (*terra sigillata*), a topic on which he made himself an expert (Figure 4.3). His well-recorded sequence offered the chance to query the dating that others had offered,[97] and he provided the first full description of certain types. It was a topic he returned to regularly after publishing the Report. The Letters show that he spoke to students in Glasgow on the topic in 1913[98] and to the Roman Society in 1915;[99] he also spoke to the Society of Antiquaries of Scotland on the topic of decorated bowls in 1917.[100]

Figure 4.3. Selection of samian ware from Newstead.
© National Museums Scotland.

He also had a grasp of ceramics more generally thanks to the well-stratified Newstead assemblage. Among the Letters we find him focused in particular on other fine wares: Castor ware was discussed repeatedly.[101] His expertise led to invitations to comment or report on finds from other excavations: F.A. Bruton sent him drawings of the finds from the Roman fort of Manchester and a sample of the pottery from Castleshaw (West Yorkshire), on the road from Chester to York; Curle's contributions are in the final reports.[102] Haverfield also sought his advice on coarse wares from Corbridge.[103]

Conservation

The conservation of the finds was clearly a major concern for Curle. There was at the time no facility for conservation in the National Museum, and the rather plaintive letter from Joseph Anderson over the inability to prevent much of the iron corroding highlights the problem.[104]

---

[96] Tyers 1996: 11, 'one of the key British publications of this period, and two of Curle's samian forms (15 and 21) have become the references for types that are not covered in the standard Dragendorff-Déchelette-Walters series'.
[97] e.g. Letters 1.34, 1.39–1.43, 1.46, 3.19, 3.21.
[98] Letters 1.71, 1.72.
[99] *Journal of Roman Studies* 5 (1915): 251–252.
[100] Curle 1917a.
[101] e.g. Letters 1.19, 1.32–1.34, 1.38, 1.58, 3.11, 3.25.
[102] Curle 1909a; 1911b.
[103] Haverfield 1909: 419 (comments on coarse wares).
[104] Letter 4.5.

Curle was unwilling to let the finds simply rot and took proactive steps, although not all his approaches would meet with approval today. Letter 1.24 sees him discussing the use of lemon juice to remove dirt and hammering a bronze vessel back into shape, while bemoaning that there is no-one in Edinburgh to fix the iron helmet; Read cautioned against trying to clean too much.[105] The reshaping of bronze items is seen also with the bronze mask: although the traces are very hard to spot today, he noted that 'It is somewhat doubled up but I have no doubt we can get it straight'(!).[106]

Curle looked beyond Edinburgh for help in conservation. Letters 1.33 and 1.35 show him using a private restorer linked to the British Museum for some Newstead pots, while Letter 1.64 mentions Mr Clinch[107] in connection with a plate. He also used, on Haverfield's recommendation, a restorer at the Ashmolean Museum in Oxford: brooches and 'a good many things' were sent to him.[108] This interest in conservation is reflected also in his notebooks, which have extensive notes on various means of conserving iron.[109] Yet he did manage to find local solutions as well. In Letter 3.14 to Haverfield he noted, rather plaintively: 'I rather wish I had full control over some of these objects. The battered bronze cap-looking helmet ought to be hammered out and the broken iron one, with its visor, like a human face, should be restored but I don't think there is anyone fit to do it in Edinburgh.' Yet a year later he was using William Brook, an Edinburgh goldsmith, for the work: 'Mr Brook has managed to pull into shape the bronze mask from the baths well. It is going to be fine when finished.'[110]

The success of Curle's efforts can be seen in the survival of the material to this day, but he and his brother also effected a long-term change of view at NMAS: the obituary of Arthur Edwards notes that a key part of his role when he was appointed to the museum in 1912 was to set up a conservation lab, and that this had been arranged by James and Alexander Curle.[111]

The Rhind lectures

It is clear that Curle's thinking in creating his 1908 Rhind lectures[112] came to shape the ultimate form of the Report. The contents of Curle's lectures were recorded in some detail in reports in *The Scotsman* (see Table 4.2).[113] The correlation with the published report is noteworthy; the Rhinds were a dry run for the structure of his book.

---

[105] Letter 1.28.
[106] Letter 1.41.
[107] Presumably a restorer, though he has not yet been traced.
[108] Letters 1.65, 3.18.
[109] It is a topic worthy of wider review in terms of the history of conservation approaches.
[110] Letter 3.18.
[111] Childe 1944.
[112] The Rhinds were a prestigious annual series of lectures organised by the Society of Antiquaries of Scotland using part of the bequest of Alexander Henry Rhind of Sybster, Caithness (on whom see Stuart 1864).
[113] *The Scotsman* 31 March 1908: 5; 2 April: 11; 6 April: 10; 7 April: 10; 9 April: 10; 11 April: 7. They were also summarised in the *Scottish Historical Review* 5 (1907–1908): 510–511.

Table 4.2. The contents of Curle's 1908 Rhind lectures, derived from reports in The Scotsman, and correlations with the published report.

Lecture	Date	Topics	Curle 1911a
1	30 March	Introduction to Roman Scotland; the roads near *Trimontium*; antiquarian work; the name *Trimontium*; the changing plan of the fort, and reconstruction of the walls.	Chapters 1 and 2
2	1 April	Literary references to camps, and the reliance on archaeology to understand forts; parallels for the fort plan; discussion of the buildings in the central block, and the barracks.	Chapters 2 (part), 3 and 4
3	3 April	The sequence of occupation; the annexes; the bath house; the pits; the occurrence of human remains.	Chapters 5–7
4	6 April	Arms and equipment. Representational evidence and archaeological evidence, then a discussion of different categories of find.	Chapters 9 and 10
5	8 April	Roman pottery in Scotland. Focus on samian (the term used in the newspaper report), and the value of the sequence from Newstead to understand change through time, placing the results in the context of other Scottish fort assemblages. More limited discussion of other forms of pottery, and passing mention of glass.	Chapters 11 and 12
6	10 April	The soldier as a craftworker. Evidence for vehicles; of iron tools and fittings; of domestic items such as lamps and locks; bronze vessels; Celtic influence; and personal ornaments. This was followed by a final summary, discussing the sequence but stressing the real value of the fort was in bringing life at Newstead alive.	Chapters 13–16

Curle and Roman Scotland

Curle's first recorded engagements with Roman Scotland were through artefacts in the museum collection or from recent excavations. Letter 1.2 shows him using NMAS collections to interpret pottery and glass finds from Torwoodlee, while he was asked to provide some notes on a glass beaker from the Birrens excavations in 1896 (Figure 4.4); here he drew on his impressive knowledge of Scandinavian evidence and wrote to Read for other parallels.[114] But Newstead was Curle's first direct field engagement with Roman Scotland, and his main focus until its publication. He returned to the topic subsequently, publishing additional finds from the site,[115] but also had a wider influence in research on Roman Scotland. Letters 3.7, 3.10 and 1.66 show him visiting excavations at Bar Hill and Balmuildy, while he played a formative role in the 1911–1912 excavations at Cappuck, which were framed very much as a comparison to the Newstead results.[116] One of the Cappuck excavators, G.H. Stevenson, spoke to the Roman Society on the results,[117] and one may suspect Curle's hand in this. It seems

---

[114] Christison *et al.* 1896: 190–191, and see Letters 1.10 and 1.11.
[115] Curle 1913a; 1917b.
[116] See Stevenson and Miller 1912: 476, 478, where the agenda for the excavation is defined in relation to Curle's Newstead sequence, and Curle is thanked for his assistance.
[117] *Journal of Roman Studies* 2 (1912): 289–291, reporting a lecture on 2 July 1912.

there were wider plans for subsequent work in the area: Letter 4.9 in October 1913 implies an intent to do something at the 'Cheviot camps'[118] with S.N. Miller, using Curle's old Clerk of Works, Alexander Mackie, but any such ideas were curtailed by war. He kept tabs on what was happening in northern England as well: Eric Birley's guest book at Chesterholm records James and Blanche Curle among a series of distinguished visitors in June 1934, visiting Birley's excavations at *Vindolanda* (Figure 4.5).[119]

It is clear there was an agenda behind these persistent interests. On several occasions Curle lectured or wrote on the Roman road from Tyne to Tweed,[120] but this was no mere description of the route of Dere Street. In each case he picked up the story of excavated sites from Corbridge north; he clearly wanted to see the Newstead sequence compared with others on the same road to understand the wider picture of the Roman invasions, a concern that comes through in some of the Letters.[121]

We noted above some of the lecturing that Curle was doing in Scotland which served to spread a wider interest in Roman Scotland, and this led to general articles on the topic.[122] He was also called upon to review volumes on the topic.[123] After Newstead, though, his main contribution was in studying the impact of Rome on the Iron Age population of Scotland.

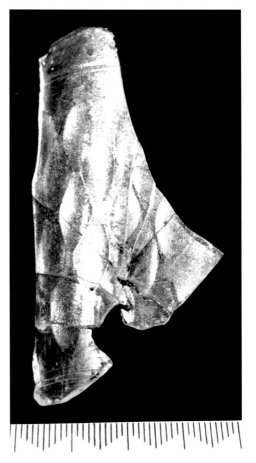

Figure 4.4. The facet-cut glass beaker fragment from Birrens which Curle wrote up. © National Museums Scotland (X.FP 245).

---

[118] Probably the camps at Pennymuir or the complex at Chew Green. See Letter 4.9 for discussion.

[119] The guest book is held by the Vindolanda Trust, and at the time of writing is on display in their museum. In the days either side of the Curles' visit, various luminaries of Roman Britain are recorded: F.G. Simpson, R.G. Collingwood, Ian Richmond (who later worked on the site), and R.C. Bosanquet. For the excavations, see Birley *et al.* 1936.

[120] Curle 1913d; *Proceedings of the Cambridge Antiquarian Society* 24 (1921–1922): 14–15; *Transactions of the Dumfriesshire and Galloway Natural History and Antiquarian Society* (third series) 17 (1930–1931): 43.

[121] e.g. Letter 3.16: '... hoping that some day the combined evidence gathered together from the forts of this Northern road will lead us to a truer state of knowledge.'

[122] Curle 1913c; 1913d.

[123] *Journal of Roman Studies* 1 (1911): 128 (reviewing Macdonald 1911); Curle 1923 (a review article on the Balmuildy excavations).

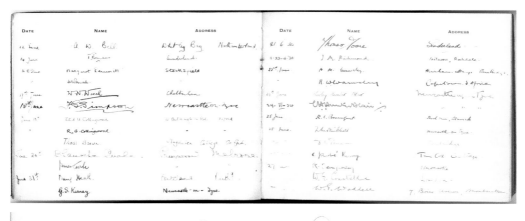

Figure 4.5. Signatures of Curle and his wife in the Chesterholm (Vindolanda) visitor book (bottom left).
a overall view; b detail. Two above Blanche Curle is R.G. Collingwood; two above him, F.G. Simpson.
Ian Richmond is second from top on the right. By courtesy of the Vindolanda Trust.

'Roman drift in Caledonia'[124]

Curle's interest in the relationship between the invading Roman armies and the local population is seen in his earliest letters to the British Museum. Letter 1.2 discussed the dating of brochs in relation to the Roman occupation, challenging Anderson's chronology, and also considered both Roman imports and Iron Age finds from the Torwoodlee site in an impressively broad context. His Scandinavian researches had informed him on the presence of a wide array of Roman imports there, and while he published nothing major on this topic his notes on cut glass beakers in the Birrens report[125] show an impressive grasp of continental scholarship on finds from *barbaricum*.[126] Dafydd Kidd and Lena Thunmark-Nylén argued that Curle's interests shifted from Scandinavian to Roman topics after his Italian honeymoon in 1902,[127] but the Torwoodlee and Birrens examples show a concern with Roman imports and their Iron Age influences long before then. It was a topic he presented a paper on in 1913 to the Third International Congress of Historical Studies in London, subsequently published in the *Journal of Roman Studies*.[128] The paper is particularly noteworthy in considering items of local manufacture from Roman sites as evidence for connections, an innovative approach developing from his Newstead discoveries which also served to clarify the chronology of Iron Age sites.

---

[124] The heading is taken from the title of Curle 1932b.
[125] Christison *et al.* 1896: 190–191.
[126] See also Letter 1.10.
[127] Kidd and Thunmark-Nylén 1990: 159–160.
[128] Curle 1913b. See Letter 1.69.

His greatest contribution in this field, however, was his corpus of Roman finds from 'sites not definitely associated with Roman constructions'.[129] This collated all then-known finds in a geographical gazetteer with comments often from personal inspection and a thoughtful analysis; it has laid the basis for all subsequent study. Its traces are only lightly observed in the correspondence after his initial discussions about the Torwoodlee finds, but Letter 1.85 shows Curle approaching Reginald Smith, apparently after a gap of some years, in pursuit of a tantalising loose end: the remarkable gold brooch from Erickstanebrae in Dumfriesshire,[130] which was then in private hands and was unfortunately subsequently sold to the Los Angeles County Museum.

Scandinavian research

Curle's interests in Sweden, in particular Gotland, are well known and have been thoroughly discussed;[131] we shall not duplicate that here. It is worth noting, however, that while he never published his collection, he did produce a valuable article in the early years of his collecting on the development of brooches in Gotland,[132] while, as noted, his publication of the Birrens glass beaker shows excellent knowledge of Scandinavian parallels.

His interest in Scandinavian finds clearly persisted even if his focus changed to Newstead and matters Roman. In the years after publishing Newstead he turned once more to the topic, albeit in a different form, publishing a series of Viking-period brooches found in Scotland,[133] and in the course of this discussing the wider development of the oval brooch style.[134]

Curle as collector: Gotland and beyond

Curle was actively collecting Gotlandic material in the period 1888–c.1903, both directly and through intermediaries. Letter 1.12 makes it clear that he was keen some of the finds did not come to the attention of the authorities (with whom he was well acquainted), aware that this would cause difficulties for the finders. It reflects a very different mindset from what archaeologists find acceptable today, though a lax approach to antiquarian legislation remains all too common now.[135] Curle's first surviving correspondence (Letters 1.1, 1.4) involves donating some Gotlandic brooches to the British Museum, though there must have been some communication before this. It is clear that he was proud of the quality of his collection,[136] and this quality was reflected in the British Museum's long-term pursuit of it.

Scandinavia was his main interest, but not his only one. Letters 1.67 and 1.68 discuss a remarkable 15th-century gold cup from Lambayeque in Peru which was in his collection (Figure 8.17).[137]

---

[129] Curle 1932a.
[130] Curle 1932a: 370–371; RIB II.3: 2421.43.
[131] Kidd and Thunmark-Nylén 1990; Kidd 1994.
[132] Curle 1895.
[133] Curle 1914; 1916; Macleod et al. 1916.
[134] See Letters 1.75, 1.77, 1.78.
[135] Fischer 2019: 99 n.18 offered a notably more hostile interpretation, but it is easy to critique the acts of previous generations; other finds he discussed which remained in private collections in Sweden are notably poor in contextual information (Fischer 2019: 97–98).
[136] For instance, Letter 1.13, a find 'which I think you will rather covet'; Letter 1.2 regarding a recent purchase of a glass beaker.
[137] It is now in the collections of National Museums Scotland, to whom it was sold by one of Curle's daughters in 1947; registration number A.1947.170.

Letter 1.9 refers to a Byzantine spoon exhibited to the Society of Antiquaries of London, which had been bought in Edinburgh (Figure 4.6). Curle also had a collection of other antiquities which has not seen full study and is now mostly dispersed.[138] After selling his Gotlandic material to the British Museum he seems to have decided to dispose of other items as well. He donated a wide range of material to NMAS, as discussed earlier, both Borders finds he is likely to have obtained from local contacts and much further-flung material, some of it old discoveries, indicating he was actively collecting. He gave a diverse range of items to the Royal Museum of Scotland in Edinburgh,[139] including a large collection of Swedish folk art items in 1937.[140] Some Roman finds were given by the family to the Trimontium Trust, comprising a collection of spoons, medical instruments, and a small figurine. Other items were sold; from the sale catalogues one may note a diverse selection, from Roman glass to Cypriot pottery and a Palaeolithic handaxe.[141] It suggests a rather eclectic collecting approach in contrast to the tight intellectual focus of his Scandinavian studies.

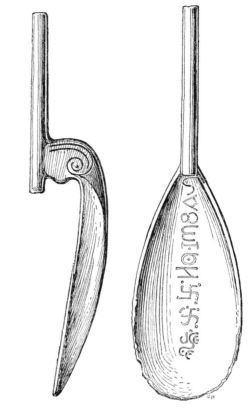

BRONZE BYZANTINE SPOON OF THE 5TH OR 6TH CENTURY.
(Full size.)

Figure 4.6. Drawing of a Byzantine spoon exhibited to the Society of Antiquaries of London by Curle in 1895. From the Proceedings of the Society of Antiquaries of London (second series) 15: 274.

---

[138] See Kidd and Thunmark-Nylén 1990: 155–156.

[139] For instance in 1924, a Roman glass flask probably from the eastern Mediterranean (A.1924.1) and a natural history specimen, a *Hyalonema* glass rope sponge 'from Japanese seas' (Z.1924.9); in 1930 two Maori stone adze heads (A.1930.759–760), and a sword (A.1930.766).

[140] '[T]he gift by Dr James Curle, Melrose, of an unusually interesting collection of old Swedish specimens has necessitated the almost entire rearrangement of the European Peasant Art Section'; Anon. 1938: 6–7. We are grateful to Julie Holder for drawing our attention to this material and its context. It included the two Swedish 'prime staffs' that he had previously exhibited to the Society of Antiquaries of Scotland (*Proceedings of the Society of Antiquaries of Scotland* 26 [1891–1892]: 214; A.1937.565–566).

[141] Lyon & Turnbull, *Antiques*, 9 May 2009: lots 125–139. Lots 125–129 were Scandinavian stone implements. Lot 130: five Neolithic implements including a stone axehead from Kemnay, Aberdeenshire, and a hand-axe from Mildenhall, Suffolk. Lots 131–132, Bronze Age bronzes with no findspot details. Lots 133–134, Cypriot pottery. Lots 135–139, Greek and Roman glass vessels.

Remarkably (to modern eyes), the records of donations to NMAS make it clear that Curle retained a sample of Newstead finds long after the excavation – including two of the four pairs of Niedermendig querns, and the altar erected by G. Arrius Domitianus which features regularly in the Letters.[142] These were only finally given to the museum in 1937![143]

Curle in context

Sir Ian Richmond described James Curle as one of the 'Big Three' of Scottish archaeology in the early twentieth century, emerging from the shadow of Joseph Anderson's long tenure of NMAS to dominate the scene along with his brother A.O. Curle and Sir George Macdonald.[144] A.O. Curle was a professional, with roles in RCAHMS, NMAS and RMS. James Curle and Macdonald were both amateurs in the strictest sense, Curle working as a solicitor all his life, Macdonald leaving a university post at Glasgow for the Civil Service.[145] But what James Curle's work reflects is detailed scholarship, engaged with what was happening in England in a way that Joseph Anderson had spurned, but retaining the wider connections to the continent that had given Scottish antiquarian studies such a distinctive course in the late 19th century.

There is a need for a broader historiographic review of Scottish archaeology over this period, but that goes beyond what is sensible in a volume focused on James Curle. What the Letters show is a well-connected antiquary, using these connections and his travels and reading to develop his knowledge, and with a sharp focus on the topic in hand; letters addressed topics which were soon followed up with a publication (Table 4.3), several of which were major landmarks. One obituary described his Newstead volume as 'one of the most valuable contributions ever made to the study of the Roman occupation of Britain';[146] his 1932 corpus of Roman finds from non-Roman sites was also a landmark study of lasting value. Curle did not publish major works often but he published well, and the Letters show the national and international networks and approaches which made this possible. They show him working with people over years, the relationship in many cases shifting from enquirer to friend.[147]

---

[142] e.g. Letters 3.4, 3.5.
[143] *Proceedings of the Society of Antiquaries of Scotland* 63 (1928–1929): 323, a pair of bronze handles; 70 (1935–1936): 18–19, a representative selection of small finds, along with samian ware from Vindonissa and Stockstadt; 72 (1937–1938): 14, the altar and querns. The altar had been registered in 1910, but apparently not dispatched from Priorwood.
[144] Richmond 1944: 145. Perhaps unsurprisingly, this was a very Romano-centric view.
[145] But with a formidable excavation and publication record in both Roman archaeology and Greek coinage; see Curle 1940.
[146] *Antiquaries Journal* 24 (1944): 177.
[147] Note the warmth of his last letter to Read (Letter 1.84), his reference to Smith as a friend in the context of the trauma of World War 1 (Letter 1.77), his reference to his friend Salin (Letter 1.7), his warm connections to Haverfield, etc.

Table 4.3. Summary of the Curle Letters published here, showing numbers of letters per year, source, key topics, and correlation with publications. SAS = Society of Antiquaries of Scotland.

Year	BM	Haverfield	Other	Key topics		Curle paper
1891	3			Gotland	Torwoodlee	1892
1892	5			Gotland	FSA election	
1893						
1894	3			Gotland		
1895	2			Gotland		1895
1896	2		2	Roman glass		Christison *et al.* 1896
1897	1			SAS – sale of items at Christies		
1898	1			SAS – collections from Oronsay	Gotland	
1899						
1900	1			SAS – advice on books for library		
1901						
1902	3			Gotland	Varia	
1903						
1904						
1905	1	11		Newstead		1911a
1906	14	3	2	Newstead		1911a
1907	17	4	4	Newstead		1911a
1908	13	4		Newstead		1911a
1909	3	1		Newstead		1911a
1910	5		2	Newstead		1911a
1911						
1912	2		1	SAS – appointment of assistant Keeper	Balmuildy	
1913	8		4	Roman/Iron Age	Varia	1913b
1914	2	2	1	Viking brooches	Roman Society	1914
1915			1	Helmet finds		1915
1916	2		1	Viking finds		1916
1917		1		General		
1918						
1919	1			Gotland – sale of collection		
1920	2					

Year	BM	Haverfield	Other	Key topics		Curle paper
1921	5		1	Gotland – sale of collection	SAS – sale of Torrs cap	
1922						
1923						
1924						
1925						
1926						
1927						
1928			2	General		
1929						
1930						
1931	1		1	Roman/Iron Age	Galoshins	1932a
1932						
1933						
1934			1	Melrose Abbey		1935
1935						
1936			1	Milsington leg		1936
1937						
1938						
1939			1	Fort in Romania		
1940						
1941			1	Death of G. Macdonald		
1942						
1943						
1944						

Chapter 5
Curle and Haverfield

P.W.M. Freeman[1]

With the benefit of hindsight it can be said that the decades either side of 1900 were an exciting time in the study of the archaeology of the Roman army. This was the time when the first attempts to work in a systematic fashion on Hadrian's Wall started. In north-west England a number of sites, including those in and around Manchester as well as at Ribchester and in south Wales were explored. At about the same time the Society of Antiquaries of Scotland, as well as the Glasgow Archaeological Society, initiated ambitious programmes on some of the forts along the Antonine Wall and elsewhere in Scotland. The explosion of work in Britain was part driven, part influenced by the work of the fledgling German Limes-Kommission whose work on the frontier along the Rhine was now starting to appear in print. This was a time when not only were excavations being started but when they were benefiting from new techniques for the dating and phasing of sites, not least by the use of *terra sigillata* or samian ware, the study of which was now becoming something of a science. It was in this vibrant period of exploration that between February 1905 and September 1910, James Curle became responsible for conducting an almost uninterrupted sequence of excavations on the site of the Roman fort at Newstead. The results were published in a lavish format as *A Roman Frontier Post and its People*.[2] Curle's excavations were widely admired at the time and continue to enjoy the same reputation today. The quality of the work and the range of the finds along with the exemplary way in which Curle managed to bring it to a definitive published format (in November 1910, only a few months after the excavations finally closed) are striking even today.[3]

The life of Curle (1862–1944), a resident of Melrose who lived just about a mile from the site and who ran the excavations on behalf of the Society of Antiquaries of Scotland, was described in a memoir authored by I.A. Richmond.[4] In this notice he explained the significance of Curle's work. As the excavations progressed, he entered into a correspondence with Professor Francis Haverfield (1860–1919; Figure 5.1), Camden Professor of Ancient History at the University of Oxford (1907–1919). Haverfield was then recognised as the leading Romano-British scholar, a reputation based in part on his intimate involvement in excavations along the western end of Hadrian's Wall (1894–1903) and at Corbridge (commencing from 1906). At the same time he was an internationally acknowledged authority on the epigraphy of Roman Britain as well as something akin to a sorting house for the receipt and dissemination of the fieldwork of lesser mortals.

---

[1] Most of the text here is a slightly revised correction of the original as published in *My Dear Haverfield* (Gordon 2005). In 2011 Donald Gordon came across four new Curle-Haverfield letters. Those 'new' letters are included here as 3.20, 3.23, 3.24 and 3.26. I have added some footnotes discussing aspects of their contents, and have also now included with the *My Dear Haverfield* (*MDH*) letters some additional footnotes clarifying points of detail in them or else highlighting particular issues. Fraser Hunter has included comments on the progress of the Newstead excavations which constitute the core of the letters, while I have concentrated on other issues.

[2] Curle 1911a.

[3] For the date, see notes to Letter 1.58. He published so fast that a supplementary paper was needed to present the final results; Curle 1913a.

[4] Richmond 1944.

The corpus of letters between Curle and Haverfield published here is small but important for all that. There is relatively little surviving Haverfield correspondence anywhere in this country. In the aftermath of his death, Haverfield's research papers were deposited in the Ashmolean Museum at Oxford, where they went through a process of editing and filtering before they came to form part of the Haverfield Archive. There are nineteen pertinent letters in the collection with seventeen of them from Curle addressed to Haverfield,[5] along with one from George Macdonald to Haverfield[6] and one Curle to Macdonald,[7] both of which contain matters relating to Newstead. The Haverfield Archive and so the collection of letters was subsequently relocated to the University of Oxford's Sackler Library. In addition to the 'Oxford' nineteen. Donald Gordon found three other letters in a Curle notebook in what was then the RCAHMS library (now part of Historic Environment Scotland) in Edinburgh.[8] Since the publication of that group of letters, four more appeared in the 'Home and Abroad' set, mostly from Haverfield to Curle. They are now incorporated here as Letters 3.20, 3.23, 3.24 and 3.26.

Figure 5.1. Francis Haverfield. By courtesy of P. Freeman.

There are some unavoidable drawbacks with the entire collection of letters. Its relatively slight size makes it difficult to draw out as clearly as one would like some of the issues in the correspondence as whole, a problem made doubly difficult by the fact that we do not have Haverfield's initial letters to Curle or his responses to Curle's writings and likewise for the four letters Haverfield sent to Curle. What is published here then often represents one side of a dialogue between the two. This in turn makes it difficult to assess the nature of their relationship. But there are certain features that might be indicated here which appear in Haverfield's letters to others. The following paragraphs are an admittedly rapid attempt to put into context some of the information preserved in the letters. Where appropriate more detailed comments are added as footnotes.

---

[5]   Numbered here Letters 3.2–3.6, 3.8–3.9, 3.11–3.14, 3.16–3.19, 3.21–3.22.
[6]   Letter 3.7.
[7]   Letter 3.10.
[8]   These were included in Gordon 2005 as Appendices 1.3 (Haverfield to Abercromby), 1.4 and 1.5 (Haverfield to Curle); here, Letters 3.1, 3.15 and 3.25.

The period covered by the letters is short. It ranges over the period April 1905 to July 1917 but with the majority relating to the time of the Newstead excavations. In that time Haverfield was involved, from mid-1906 (and down to 1914), with excavations at Corbridge on behalf of the Northumberland Excavation Committee and therefore should have been for at least short spells in each year close to Newstead. In a number of the letters Curle endeavoured to get Haverfield to visit his excavations. Haverfield did so in the spring of 1905[9] but apparently not subsequently on the letters published here,[10] which seems unlikely.

It is not now known how, when and why Curle first made Haverfield's acquaintance. Preserved in Letter 3.2 are allusions to Haverfield having seen the Newstead site before August 1905. In fact, from Letter 3.1 we learn that Haverfield had visited it sometime before 'Easter eve' of the same year, as he reported in a letter to Lord Abercromby, one of the Secretaries of the Society of Antiquaries of Scotland, and in which he suggested that Alexander Mackie, Curle's Clerk of Works, might not have been up to the job in hand. Easter eve that year fell on Saturday 23 April. One suspects Haverfield's visit to Newstead and the fact he was reporting to Abercromby was because he had been brought in as what would now be called an external advisor. Just as Haverfield may have reported his opinions to Abercromby, George Macdonald appears in the letters in the capacity as a fellow archaeologist, a leading member of the Scottish Antiquaries and in part as Haverfield's eyes and ears for work in Scotland.[11]

The thrust of the early letters involved Curle reporting on the most recent finds, assessing their significance and/or asking for help to preserve or otherwise to interpret them. The facts of these discoveries can be traced in his Report on the excavations. Perhaps the most interesting feature to emerge from the letters is the evolving nature of the way in which Curle addressed Haverfield, which in turn might say something about Curle's developing confidence as an archaeologist. From the start of their correspondence Curle appears as one asking Haverfield for advice, comparanda and support whilst at the same time reporting in a rather descriptive fashion the most recent discoveries. Clarification of the reading of the inscriptions is one example,[12] requesting the names of specialists another,[13] along with comments on comparative material from other excavation reports.[14] In this case it is noteworthy how important became the reading of the site's *terra sigillata*, of which more below, but this must have come from Haverfield who, with his established continental contacts, was already heavily immersed in its study. In such instances Haverfield was as much an advisor and sounding board as a *de facto* patron of the excavations.[15] In turn, one can imagine Haverfield was expected to use such information in his own publications reporting on recent finds in Roman Britain – as he did.[16] With time, however, we start to see Curle increasingly offering his own interpretations, which often challenged the authoritative assertions that Haverfield was wont to express.[17] Such a change in their relationship is partially reflected in the manner in which Curle addresses Haverfield. Up until May 1906 he was plain 'Mr Haverfield'. Thereafter

[9] Letter 3.1.
[10] Letters 3.2, 3.3, 3.17, 3.21 etc.
[11] Letter 3.7 where he seems to be confirming Curle's earlier description of recent finds.
[12] Letters 3.4, 3.5, 3.12, 3.14.
[13] Letters 3.14, 3.18.
[14] Letters 3.6, 3.11, 3.12, 3.17–3.19.
[15] Letters 3.2, 3.8, 3.10.
[16] e.g. Haverfield 1909.
[17] e.g. Letters 3.16, 3.17.

(with one exception)[18] he becomes 'Haverfield'. In turn, the growing confidence in Curle's writing reached the point where he could describe Haverfield as the Professor of History who approached the evidence in a different fashion to him, the archaeologist dealing with it from another perspective.[19] What is so striking in this is that it is a comment, if not an accusation, made by other Haverfield co-workers, notably on the Cumberland Excavation Committee and during the Corbridge seasons. Haverfield's propensity to dominate and dispute with his colleagues was in large measure based more on his status as an Oxford academic than his abilities as an excavating archaeologist. This impression is complemented by the general sense that Curle's questions and observations about the excavation become increasingly sophisticated as the letters progress. In this case however, Curle's independence of thought does not seem to have occasioned any (long-lasting) dislocation in their relationship. Indeed other than differences of opinion about how to interpret the archaeological evidence there is only the merest indication of other differences, as for instance in Curle's letter to Macdonald in October 1905.[20]

Other than the names already noted, the letters contain some references to a number of individuals who can still be recognised. Many of them are acknowledged in his Preface to *A Roman Frontier Post ...* Some of them, especially the continental names, are likely to come on Haverfield's recommendation as he is known to have corresponded closely with many of them.

Bearing in mind the time when the Newstead excavations were running and the Haverfield connection, it is not surprising that the names of some of the leading German workers on the Roman army appear in the correspondence. The Jacobi in Letter 3.7 (and obliquely in Letter 3.21) was Louis Jacobi, Director of the fort and museum at the Saalburg. Likewise Emil Ritterling (in Letter 3.22) was the excavator of Hofheim. His contact with Curle was with respect to his work at the fort at Wiesbaden. The Dr Anderson in Letter 3.9 is Joseph Anderson, Keeper of the National Museum of Antiquities in Edinburgh.[21]

The dating of the phases of Roman activity at Newstead became increasingly reliant on the *sigillata* that was excavated. While Haverfield had been trying to make progress on such material in Britain,[22] the lead work in the identification and dating of it was at this time being undertaken by German and French scholars. Josef Déchelette in Letter 3.11 was the author of *Les vases céramiques ornés de la Gaule romaine*.[23] Again as proof of his growing reputation, it seems that Curle came to be recognised as something of an authority on *sigillata*, not least when H.B. Walters of the British Museum asked him to review his catalogue of the pottery from the British Museum collection.[24]

In Letter 3.12, Curle acknowledges a reference to Benndorf provided to him by Smith. Otto Benndorf was the author of a detailed monograph which looked at the evolution of ancient

---

[18] Letter 3.17.
[19] Letter 3.16.
[20] Letter 3.10.
[21] For Anderson and Ritterling, see *Dramatis personae*.
[22] cf. Letters 3.11, 3.18–3.20.
[23] Déchelette 1904.
[24] Letter 3.19; Walters 1908. For the review, see Curle 1909b.

helmets,[25] including parade helmets of which, as is well known, Newstead had produced some remarkable examples. Reginald Smith, another acquaintance of Haverfield's, was at the British Museum.[26] The contribution of Mr Balfour of the Pitt-Rivers Museum at Oxford in Letter 3.19 is explained in more detail at p.313 in *A Roman Frontier Post....* The circumstances behind Curle's (and Macdonald's) visit to Bar Hill have been detailed by Lawrence Keppie.[27] The Mr Mackintosh (*sic*) of Barhill in Letter 3.10 is the head forester of Alexander Whitelaw of Gartshore upon whose land Bar Hill lay; McIntosh led the excavations there. Mr Brook of Letter 3.18 who worked on reconstructing one of the parade helmets was William Brook of Brook & Son, Goldsmiths in Edinburgh, a firm with a long association with the Society of Antiquaries of Scotland, and which went on to restore the Traprain Treasure.[28] The 'Galashiels authority' of Letter 3.14 was probably Bailie George Hope Tait, a councillor on the Galashiels Town Council, some 8 km west of Melrose, a local painter, watercolourist, poet and historian.[29]

As one would expect, the letters contain odd pieces of gossip and trivia that are instructive in themselves.[30] There is, for instance, Curle's initial reluctance to take up the invitation to deliver the Rhind Lectures in Edinburgh,[31] although he did subsequently do so in 1908. The Curles seem to have been sufficiently familiar with Haverfield that they knew his wife of 1907.[32] Indeed Curle seems to have stayed with them in Oxford.[33] In a set of striking revelations, Curle admits to Haverfield he had never visited Hadrian's Wall but would be pleased if he would be his guide.[34] Nor had he seen the museums at Carlisle and Newcastle.[35] The letters also add small but significant details relating to Haverfield's career and his field work. This includes the arrangements for the Corbridge seasons[36] and later in Scotland.[37] From Letter 3.23 we gain an insight to the personal circumstances in the process of his translation to the Camden Professorship in Ancient History at Brasenose College. Letter 3.26 may indicate something about Curle and his politics.

Although the bulk of correspondence published here ended in 1909, when the main Newstead excavations were drawing to a close, Curle and Haverfield were to remain in contact in the subsequent years, to the point that there is a degree of familiarity between the two. Curle was one of the original members of the Society for the Promotion of Roman Studies in 1910 while Haverfield was writing to him about related matters in December 1914.[38] In time, Curle was to contribute information for some of the obituaries of Haverfield after the latter's death in September 1919 and was to reflect on his importance to Romano-British studies in his own obituary of George Macdonald in the *Proceedings* of the Scottish Antiquaries.[39]

---

[25] Benndorf 1878.
[26] See *Dramatis personae.*
[27] Letters 3.7 and 3.10; Keppie 2002.
[28] See Dalgleish 2022.
[29] My thanks to Donald Gordon for information on these two figures.
[30] e.g. Letters 3.11, 3.14.
[31] Letter 3.16.
[32] Letters 3.19, 3.21.
[33] Presumably at their residence of Winshields out at Headington; Letter 3.24.
[34] Letter 3.3.
[35] Letter 3.17.
[36] e.g. Letters 3.15, 3.21, and implied in 3.2 and 3.3.
[37] e.g. Letter 3.23.
[38] Letter 3.25.
[39] Curle 1940.

What Curle and his group of workers achieved at Newstead was appreciated by his contemporaries. One has only to read Hans Dragendorff's review of *A Roman Frontier Post* to see this.[40] It is not an insignificant fact that Dragendorff was one of the acknowledged authorities on *sigillata*. It is therefore unfortunate that, other than for those who work on the archaeology of the Roman army in Britain, Curle's reputation is now not so widely appreciated. There are a number of reasons for this, not least in the way that George Macdonald came to dominate the subject in Scotland, a trend exemplified in Richmond's Curle memoir.[41] Hopefully the situation is, however, changing. There has been in recent years a surge of interest in the work of archaeologists of the early twentieth century and in turn in why and how the work of that time happened. There have, for instance, been published a number of historiographical studies looking at work on and along Hadrian's Wall and its Antonine counterpart further north and more work is imminent. The work of the Trimontium Trust has been significant in rekindling a fuller appreciation of Curle and his work. The letters published in this monograph are another contribution to our understanding of this important period in the history of British archaeology, for not only do they reveal something about what happened behind the scenes of the published version of one set of excavations, they also go some way to explaining why Curle and his work should be appreciated by a wider audience.

---

[40] Dragendorff 1911.
[41] Richmond 1944.

Chapter 6

James Curle: A Man of Melrose

Donald Gordon

'Never mis-treat a book: never be late – it makes the household staff late:
never buy anything in Galashiels.'[1]

James Curle had three daughters – Christian, Pamela, and Barbara – and the advice given above was one of the last's fond and oft-repeated recollections. James did not marry till he was forty and Barbara indicated that she felt he was more of a grandfather to his children. She was full of gentle tales like coming back from church through the garden and father with his stick 'tickling down' the plums for them. On one occasion Barbara had gone with a sister up on to the roof of Priorwood, the family house, in order to smoke. They had been discovered and, presumably in fear and trembling, were sent down to see father. He, Barbara would say, was a bit of a psychologist. He chided them for going up on to the roof. It was very, very dangerous. If they wanted to smoke they should come down to the Smoking Room (which, obviously, was the last thing on their minds). There was also a Billiards Room, and Barbara remembered as a child the odd stone from *Trimontium* temporarily lodged below the table en route to the Museum.

James married Blanchette Nepean in 1902[2] and through friends was introduced to the portrait painter Sir William B. Nicolson. Mrs Curle is depicted as a strikingly dressed hostess at the dinner table, in left profile, with arms poised on the table and hands raised together up to the tips of the fingers (Figure 6.1). Her husband, seated to face the painter, wears the dark green field dress of the Gentlemen of the Bodyguard in the Royal Company of Archers, the monarch's ceremonial bodyguard in Scotland. Gloved, he holds the longbow with relaxed string and the feathered bonnet, and wears the short sword (Figure 6.2).

In company with other towns in the Borders Melrose holds an annual Festival, with a young man to lead as The Melrosian and a primary schoolgirl as the Festival Queen, with her Court. The climax of the ceremony now involves an Oration, in the Abbey, in praise of Melrose and as an encouragement for the future, by a local speaker and also the crowning of the Queen by the speaker's wife or another lady. Mrs Curle performed the crowning in 1937 accompanied by her husband, but the Oration was not introduced till later. In 2012 Mrs Gordon performed the crowning and the writer, the then Orator, took the opportunity of telling the story of James and A.O. Curle (two famous archaeologists from the same small town) and the family, and how James, although denied a University place in his youth, had played the hand he was dealt, passed the archaeological 'examination' at Trimontium and was subsequently awarded the honorary degree of Doctor of Laws by Aberdeen University.[3] On the final day of the Festival

---

[1] Why? 'The shopkeepers in Melrose are our clients and we must do all we can to support them.'
[2] Letter 1.16.
[3] The laudation, recorded in the *Press and Journal* (2 April 1925: 4) is worth quoting in full. 'James Curle, W.S., member of Council of the Society of Antiquaries of Scotland. Mr Curle is, by general consent, one of Scotland's most prominent antiquaries, and for many years he has devoted himself to the study of questions connected with the

Figure 6.1. Portrait of Blanche Curle, by W.B. Nicolson. By courtesy of the family.

there is a popular tour of historic sites in Melrose and its villages. At the Trimontium Stone, erected in 1928 at the north-west corner of the fort (Figure 3.9), beside a suitably dressed

Roman occupation of Britain. In the field of exploration he has accomplished a work of the first importance. Under his supervision the Roman station of Trimontium, near Melrose, was excavated, and he has recorded the result of this elaborate undertaking in "A Roman Fort and its People" (1910). He has published his research in various other localities, and, in particular, his study of the so-called "Samian Way" [sic] is a model of minute and exhaustive treatment. His antiquarian interests, however, are not confined to Roman Britain. But for the chance that drew him to that subject, he would probably have attained equal eminence in the sphere of Scandinavian antiquities, to the study of which he devoted years of his life. As a striking example of disinterested passion for research, he has established a special claim on the regard of his fellow-countrymen, and we welcome the opportunity of showing appreciation of his labours in the field of Scottish history'. Our thanks to George Gordon for locating this.

Figure 6.2. Portrait of James Curle in the costume of a Royal Archer, by W.B. Nicolson. By courtesy of the family.

Roman soldier, the Melrosian pays tribute to 'the researches of our late townsman, the distinguished archaeologist James Curle'.

2005 was the hundredth anniversary of the start of James Curle's excavations, and a Curle Circuit of Melrose was devised to visit on foot a number of the places with which he had been associated.

On Saturday 7 May the tour started at his birthplace, Abbey Park House, now St Mary's School. Passing the Museum, we paused for a moment at Rosebank, his grandfather's house on Dingleton Brae (Curle signed himself as Junior during his grandfather's lifetime) to hear the story that James Snr had sold a part of his garden to the railway company on condition that every train would stop at Melrose. A nod to the Curle firm's office at the Bow on the edge of Melrose Square preceded a quick visit to the Curle-owned farm at Millmount, Newstead (which Curle used to pop out to each Sunday afternoon). Returning to Melrose we stopped at Harmony House (where he died in 1944; Figure 6.3) and Priorwood, the old family home where Curle spent most of his life, and the fine garden through which he would walk to work each morning (Figures 6.4–6.5). The garden wall fronting Abbey St was heightened in 1905 and Edwin Lutyens, future architect of New Delhi and of First World War memorials, was commissioned to design the five scoops on it, displaying iron representations of garden fruits (Figures 6.6–6.7). The lintel is dated 1905, with initials to the left JC and to the right BC, his wife Blanche (Figure 6.8). As we approached the Abbey to pay our respects at the Curle family tombstones, the Abbey bell rang out and David Murray, Curle's grandson, toasted his grandfather with the latter's silver christening mug.

Figure 6.3. James Curle at 'Harmony' with one of his grandchildren. By courtesy of the family.

James was a singer, an athlete and a sportsman. The school magazine, *The Fettesian*, recorded that James had run 'the hundred' in 12 seconds by the school clock.[4] He was a bowler and a member of the Melrose Curling Club, there being a pond at the base of Eildon Hill Mid, with wonderful Victorian group photographs showing the players kitted up in style to play and James himself on the ice (Figures 6.9–6.10).

In 1936 what is now The Royal Highland Show[5] with its established showground at Ingliston, near Edinburgh, came to Melrose. At that time it was peripatetic. Newspaper photographs show the long white tents filling the fields from Melrose to Newstead; Curle played a pivotal role, as accounts

---

[4] The hundred yards sprint. The school was Fettes in north Edinburgh. We owe this insight to his grandson, David Murray of Newstead.
[5] The premier agricultural show in Scotland.

Figure 6.4. 'Priorwood' with the Eildons behind. By courtesy of J.S. Crawford Contracts (Borders) Ltd.

Figure 6.5. 'Priorwood'. By courtesy of J.S. Crawford Contracts (Borders) Ltd.

Figure 6.6. The Abbey Street wall of 'Priorwood', rebuilt for Curle in 1905, showing the iron scoops designed by Lutyens, with the entrance towards the bottom by the modern sign.
© Fraser Hunter

Figure 6.7. Detail of one of the Lutyens-designed iron scoops. © Fraser Hunter.

Figure 6.8. Lintel over the entrance from the 'Priorwood' garden to Abbey Street. a: overall view. b: detail.
© Donald Gordon

Figure 6.9. Melrose Curling Club c. 1895–1900 depicts male sporting society – landowners, professionals, shopkeepers – and one girl. There is a Who's Who of attendees but the passage of time has not made it easy to clarify. An article in the Southern Reporter Annual by John Hart in 1952 offered identifications for many of those present with occasional ambiguities, though he stated he knew only one personally. Nos 1–3 are identified by Hart as James, Alexander and Robert Curle, and no. 4 as Ned Haig, the inventor of Rugby Sevens. Other views are tenable: it has been suggested that b and c are A.O. and Robert Curle and that d is Ned Haig, while the costume of the person marked a is more similar to that worn by James Curle in fig. 6.10. By courtesy of the Southern Reporter.

Figure 6.10. Curle the curler, c. 1900. By courtesy of the family.

of the meetings tell that the show used land that he owned.[6] It was too good an opportunity for a man proud of Melrose to miss, and he produced *A Little Book about Melrose* in time for the event.[7] Its two parts cover 'Some notes' on the history and development of the Abbey and then a section on 'The precinct wall of the monastery and the town' and how the latter grew.

James had a talent for light verse and it is said that the family engaged in verbal games. One of James's effusions has come down to us, sparked off by an *Edinburgh Evening News* article in September 1935, presumably about housebuilding at Inveresk. It reminded him of the Romans at Inveresk and goes on for nine verses. The second verse gives the tone:

And there they built them lordly halls
Facing the South where the ridge falls
Towards the river, and great walls
Against their foes
Where now the population sprawls........ in bungalows

[6] '... an excellent site was provided for the Show at The Annay, on fields belonging to Dr James Curle of Priorwood, Melrose'; information from the Transactions Book 1937 of the Royal Highland and Agricultural Society of Scotland, kindly provided by their House and Heritage Officer, Alain Wright.
[7] The booklet is not dated; the two papers it contains were first published in 1935, so it is likely it appeared in late 1935 (as an annotation on the copy in the library of National Museums Scotland suggests) or 1936.

After the 2005 Festival Walk round the Curle family locations in Newstead and Melrose, permission was obtained to erect a plaque on the garden wall of 'Priorwood', James Curle's home, along Abbey Street. It was erected in 2006 (Figure 6.11). The wording, by the late Ian J.H. Brown, reads:

> Priorwood – home to James Curle (1862–1944) and Alexander Ormiston Curle (1866–1955), who, with George Macdonald (1862–1940), were the then 'Big Three' of Roman archaeology in Scotland

The 'Big Three' description was given by Sir Ian Richmond of Oxford (1902–1965),[8] who had hoped to undertake a second *Trimontium* excavation along with James Curle in 1939. He did so in 1947 with the help of German POWs in what had become for him 'the dutiful fulfilment of a pledge'.[9]

Figure 6.11. Plaque commemorating James and Alexander Curle and George Macdonald on the wall of 'Priorwood', the Curle family home. © Donald Gordon.

---

[8] Richmond 1944: 145.
[9] Richmond 1950: 1.

Chapter 7

Glimpses of the *Dramatis Personae*

This cast-list includes short pen-pictures of people who appear as correspondents of Curle in this collection and individuals who appear regularly in the correspondence, with a brief summary of their role and connections to James Curle. Individuals who occur only sparingly are explained in footnotes to the relevant letter.

Oscar Almgren (1869–1945)

Member of the Royal Swedish Academy of Letters, History and Antiquities from 1908 and Professor of Scandinavian and Comparative Archaeology at Uppsala University, 1913–1925, retiring early due to ill health. An authority on brooches, on which he wrote to Curle over some of the latter's finds from Newstead (Letter 4.2).

Joseph Anderson (1832–1916)[1]

Keeper of the National Museum of Antiquities of Scotland for a remarkable 43 years, from 1869 to 1913 (succeeded by A.O. Curle), and a dominant figure in Scottish archaeology over this time, giving four series of published Rhind Lectures which 'had sketched the essential outlines of Scottish prehistory in a comprehensive and scientific survey such as then existed in no other country'.[2] Like Curle he had an international perspective, especially towards Scandinavian scholarship. He also fought the corner of the Scottish national collection strongly, which led him into conflicts with the British Museum reflected in Letter A5. He appears in various guises in the Letters; his work on brochs influenced Curle in his early correspondence with the BM (Letter 1.2), he advised Curle on Newstead finds (Letter 4.1), discussed funding and publication of the site (Letters 4.1, 4.5), and appears in passing acquiring finds and antagonising other scholars (e.g. Letters 1.7, 1.13).

Gerard Baldwin Brown (1849–1932)

First Watson-Gordon Professor of Fine Art, Edinburgh University, with broad interests in ancient and medieval art, especially of the Anglo-Saxon period. His book on *The Care of Ancient Monuments* (1905) was instrumental in leading to the establishment of the Royal Commission on the Ancient and Historical Monuments of Scotland in 1908, on which he served as a Commissioner for many years.[3] Appears here in Letter 4.13, where he was soliciting an article from Curle on Viking finds from Lewis for the *Burlington Magazine*.

---

[1] D.V. Clarke 2002.
[2] Childe 1935, xi. Anderson 1881a; 1881b; 1883; 1886. For the Rhind lectures see pp.33–34 and notes to Letter 1.41.
[3] See Breeze 2001.

J. Graham Callander (1873–1938)

A.O. Curle's successor as Keeper of the National Museum of Antiquities (1919–1938),[4] who appears in passing in Read's correspondence with A.O. Curle (Letter A5). James Curle wrote to him over the sale of the Torrs pony cap (Letter 5.6).

George Gordon Coulton (1858–1947)

Fellow of St John's College, Cambridge, medieval historian and controversialist,[5] who gave the 1931 Rhind lectures on 'Monastic life and its influence on the civilisation of Scotland', published in 1933 as *Scottish abbeys and social life*, with Melrose Abbey's south entrance as frontispiece. Curle wrote to him to clarify a translation in a document connected to the boundaries of Melrose (Letter 4.16).

James Curle (1862–1944)

A local solicitor all his working life, James Curle's antiquarian interests took him into the archaeological world, producing a magisterial excavation Report on his work at Newstead (*Trimontium*). His interests had already led him to build a collection of Scandinavian (predominantly Gotlandic) antiquities, and Scandinavian material culture remained a core interest, though he collected other material spasmodically. He read, travelled and corresponded widely in order to build the networks needed for his research.

Alexander Ormiston Curle (1866–1955)[6]

The youngest brother of James Curle, Alexander was employed from 1908 as the first Secretary of the newly established Royal Commission on the Ancient and Historical Monuments of Scotland, producing the first of the County Inventories of ancient monuments. He then enjoyed a career in and around museums. From 1913 to 1919 he was Director of the National Museum of Antiquities of Scotland (in succession to Joseph Anderson), and from 1916 to his retirement in 1931 Director of the Royal Scottish Museum in Chambers St, Edinburgh, presiding over the modernising of museum practice in both. He is probably best known archaeologically for his excavations on Traprain Law, East Lothian, which led to the discovery of the Traprain Treasure, a late Roman hoard of hacksilver.[7]

Joseph Déchelette (1862–1914)[8]

Author (inter alia) of a key book on samian,[9] the topic on which he and Curle corresponded (more intermittently than Curle would have liked; see Letters 1.25–1.26) and an encyclopaedic multi-volume *Manuel d'archéologie préhistorique, celtique et gallo-romaine*. Curator of the Musée Roanne in Auvergne, close to the central Gaulish potting centre of Lezoux. Killed at the western front in the first year of World War I (Letter 3.25).

---

[4] *Proceedings of the Society of Antiquaries of Scotland* 72 (1937–1938): 232–233; *The Scotsman* 19 March 1938: 17.
[5] Summerson 2018.
[6] Ritchie 2002.
[7] Curle 1923. See now Hunter *et al.* 2022.
[8] Péré-Noguès 2014.
[9] Déchelette 1904.

Hans Dragendorff (1870–1941)[10]

Renowned German archaeologist, best known for his classification of samian ware (*terra sigillata*); his type-numbers are still used today.[11] He was the founding Director of the Römisch-Germanische Kommission of the German Archaeological Institute in Frankfurt from 1902–1911, before he became Secretary of the Germany Archaeological Institute itself in Berlin (1911–1922). He then took up a Professorship at the University of Freiburg. He wrote to Curle as Secretary, inviting him to be a corresponding member of the Institute (Letter 4.8), probably because he was impressed by Curle's publication of Newstead.[12] There is no other surviving indication of direct correspondence, for instance over samian.

Ernst Fabricius (1857–1942)[13]

German archaeologist and ancient historian: excavated in Greece and Asia Minor, and on the German limes. Professor of ancient history at Freiburg (1888–1926) and Director of the Reichslimeskommision, the state organisation overseeing the investigation of the Roman frontier (*limes*) in Germany, from 1902. His links to Curle are quite late, it seems; he met him when invited to visit the British frontier in 1928.[14]

Sir Augustus Wollaston Franks (1826–1897)[15]

British antiquarian described as 'arguably the most important collector in the history of the British Museum', donating much of his private collection to the BM and setting up the Department of British and Mediaeval Antiquities and Ethnography, of which he was Keeper; succeeded on his retiral by his protégé, Charles Hercules Read. He is referred to several times in the Letters 'off-stage',[16] but there is no direct correspondence with him, though he was one of Curle's sponsors for election to the Society of Antiquaries of London.

Leopold Frölich (1860–1933)[17]

Director of Psychiatry at the Königsfelden Health and Care Institute, who started excavations around the legionary fortress of *Vindonissa* (Windisch), Switzerland, mostly on the rubbish heap (*Schutthügel*) from 1903, using patients for his workforce as part of their therapy. Letter 4.10 sees him sending Curle some samian from *Vindonissa*; Curle had clearly visited him in Switzerland.

---

[10] Schröer 2020; Hofmann *et al.* 2020; Freeman 2007: 199–200 n.4; https://sempub.ub.uni-heidelberg.de/propylaeum_vitae/wisski/navigate/2942/view (accessed 31 August 2022).
[11] Dragendorff 1895; 1896.
[12] Dragendorff 1911 for a review.
[13] Stade 1942; Freeman 2007: 134; https://sempub.ub.uni-heidelberg.de/propylaeum_vitae/wisski/navigate/12108/view (accessed 31 August 2022).
[14] Reception Committee's report of Professor Fabricius' visit, *Proceedings of the Society of Antiquaries of Newcastle* (4th series) 3 (1928): 280–286
[15] Wilson 1984; 2004a.
[16] Letters 1.2, 1.5, 1.7, 1.11, A5.
[17] *Gesellschaft Pro Vindonissa. Jahresbericht 1932-33*: 1–2.

Harold St George Gray (1872–1963)

Antiquary based in Somerset and renowned in particular for his work on the lake villages of Glastonbury and Meare.[18] He corresponded with Curle over scale armour as a parallel for a find of his from Ham Hill, Somerset (Letter 5.2). In 1906 he excavated in Aberdeenshire for the Hon. J. Abercromby, so he may have met Curle personally in the course of this work; he would certainly have been aware of Scottish antiquarian circles.[19]

Thomas Hardy (1840–1928)

Curle sent the famous novelist and poet a copy of his Report, inspired by Hardy's evocation of the past in his work, and received a generous reply (Letters 5.4–5.5).

Francis J. Haverfield (1860–1919)

The foremost figure in Romano-British archaeology in the late 19th and early 20th century, based at Christ Church College, Oxford. His contribution and links to Curle are summarised by Freeman (Chapter 5).[20] One of Curle's key correspondents.

Hans Hildebrand (1842–1913)[21]

Researcher at the State Historical Museum in Stockholm from 1871, becoming Riksantikvarie in 1879.[22] He wrote widely across prehistoric and medieval topics on a European scale, with a strong interest in typology. Knew Curle from his Gotland researches and collecting, though he appears only indirectly in this correspondence (Letters 1.2, 1.7, 1.12).

Sir William Henry St John Hope (1854–1919)[23]

Assistant Secretary of the Society of Antiquaries of London (1885–1910), an authority on ecclesiastical architecture but with wide-ranging interests, including a key role in the excavations of the Roman town of Silchester. Knighted in 1914 for his architectural history of Windsor Castle. Curle's correspondence with him (reflected here in secondary references) was in the course of Hope's role as Assistant Secretary, especially in relation to exhibitions of finds (Letters 1.9, 1.10, 1.63).

---

[18] See Minnitt and Coles 2006.
[19] Gray 1907.
[20] See also Freeman 2007.
[21] Hildebrand 1973.
[22] Riksantikvarie means 'National Antiquarian'. The position is the equivalent of a director general, the person in charge of the Swedish National Heritage Board (Riksantikvarieämbetet). This was founded in 1630; there have been 31 'riksantikvarier' since. It is one of the single most important positions in Swedish archaeology. We thank Dominic Ingemark for his comments.
[23] Thompson and Nurse 2004; *Archaeologia Cantiana* 34 (1920): 149–152.

Viktor Hoffiller (1877–1954)[24]

Classical archaeologist, becoming Professor of Classical Archaeology and Director of the Croatian National Museum. He wrote to Curle while he was researching a book on the equipment of Roman soldiers (Letter 4.6).

Peter Hume Brown (1849–1918)

First Professor of Scottish History at Edinburgh University (1901–1918), biographer of George Buchanan and John Knox. Wrote to Curle to garner information for his school textbook on Scottish history.[25]

Thomas Athol Joyce (1878–1942)[26]

Ethnographer in the British and Mediaeval Antiquities and Ethnography Department at the BM from 1902–1921, with a speciality in South America. He served as Deputy Keeper when the Ceramics and Ethnography Department was carved out of the larger entity in 1921, retiring in 1938. Curle sent him a Peruvian gold cup from his collection for comment, which Joyce published (Letters 1.67, 1.68).

Gerard Marius Kam (1836–1922)[27]

Kam was a Rotterdam steel trader who moved to Nijmegen on his retirement in 1897 and began to amass a large collection of artefacts, predominantly purchased in the course of development work around Nijmegen, though he also collected from the Rhineland more widely. He established a private museum in 1903 and in 1922, shortly before his death, gave the collection to the state, to be displayed in a museum in Nijmegen which he had built himself, the Rijksmuseum G.M. Kam. This collection is now amalgamated into the Museum Het Valkhof in Nijmegen. He corresponded with Curle over helmets from the Nijmegen area (Letter 4.12), one of which Curle subsequently published.[28]

Sir George Macdonald (1862–1940)[29]

Classical scholar, teacher, University lecturer, civil servant, George Macdonald was a dominant figure in the world of Romano-British studies and beyond in the early 20th century. After five years of teaching and twelve years as a Lecturer in Greek at Glasgow University, he moved to the civil service in 1904, rising to head the Scottish Education Department. However, he maintained a strong interest in numismatics and Roman archaeology, especially of the Antonine Wall, reflected in his magisterial works on the topic.[30] He was a good friend of Haverfield's,[31] and a close friend of both James and Alexander Curle. He appears regularly in the correspondence as sender, recipient, and subject of repeated comments, especially in the Haverfield Letters.

---

[24] Saria 1960.
[25] Hume Brown 1910; Letter 4.7.
[26] Wilson 2002: 200, 224; Caygill 2002: 387.
[27] Swinkels 2000. Our thanks to Stefanie Hoss for drawing our attention to this source.
[28] Curle 1915.
[29] Curle 1940; A.O. Curle and Keppie 2004.
[30] Notably Macdonald 1911; 1934.
[31] Bringing Haverfield's Ford lectures to posthumous publication; Haverfield and Macdonald 1924.

Alexander Mackie (c.1847–c.1925)[32]

Mackie had begun excavating the Iron Age hillfort of Castle Law, Abernethy, off his own bat in 1896–1898;[33] the work impressed the Society of Antiquaries of Scotland who subsequently employed him as their Clerk of Works, supervising workmen on their excavations from around 1899 on various Iron Age and Roman sites, including Newstead.[34] Valued and retained by Curle despite Haverfield's doubts (see Letter 3.1). After Newstead he worked on the excavations at Cappuck and Balmuildy for S.N. Miller. Letter 4.9, when he wrote to Curle about the Balmuildy excavations, is rare in giving him a voice, as he is otherwise a silent labourer, but was clearly a skilful excavator. He was elected a Corresponding Member of the Society in 1904.

Sir Herbert Maxwell (1845–1937)[35]

MP, author, antiquary and amateur artist among many other interests, who lived at Monreith House in Wigtownshire. He was a Rhind lecturer, like both Curles, in 1893 and in 1911, and held senior positions as President of the Society of Antiquaries of Scotland (1900–1913) and Chair of the Royal Commission for the Ancient and Historical Monuments of Scotland (1908–1934). He would have known James Curle from the Society of Antiquaries of Scotland, as he was President while Newstead was being excavated, (and Curle was also an office-bearer at the time). The surviving correspondence comes from late in their lives, and concerns Galoshins, a form of folk play (Letter 5.7).

Johanna Mestorf (1828–1909)[36]

Prehistoric archaeologist who spent time in Sweden before moving back to northern Germany and taking a job in Kiel Museum, rising to become its director, the first female museum director in Germany in a sphere dominated by men. She had a particular interest in bog finds and bog deposits, the topic on which she wrote to Curle (Letter 4.3), prompted by Curle sending her an offprint.

Oscar Montelius (1843–1921)[37]

Prehistorian at the State Historical Museum in Stockholm and a key proponent of typological change as a method of establishing chronological sequence; rose to become Riksantikvarie, State Antiquary (the key post in Swedish archaeology) from 1907–1913. 'Curle was in constant correspondence' with him,[38] though in the current Roman-focused collection he only appears in passing (Letter 4.2).

---

[32] The 1891 census records Mackie's age as 44; his death was reported on 30 November 1925 as occurring over the previous year (*Proceedings of the Society of Antiquaries of Scotland* 60 [1925–1926]: 5).
[33] Christison 1900: 76.
[34] Stevenson 1981: 177; D.V. Clarke 2012: 24–25. He was certainly working for the Society from 1899 on the Camelon excavations (Christison *et al.* 1901: 338). For a brief obituary, see *Proceedings of the Society of Antiquaries of Scotland* 60 (1925–1926): 5.
[35] Meikle and Matthew 2008; Behan and Hutchinson 2011.
[36] See Koch and Mertens 2002.
[37] Gräslund 1987.
[38] Wilson 2002: 235. Kidd (1994: 91) noted that both Montelius and Salin helped Curle obtain objects and seemingly visited his collection in Melrose.

Alexander Stuart Murray (1841–1904)[39]

Keeper of Greek and Roman Antiquities at the BM (and a native of Arbroath). Curle wrote to him about Roman glass, and he supported Curle's application to join the Society of Antiquaries of London (Letters 2.1–2.2).

Henry Oldland (fl. 1902–1921)

A clerk in Read's department who fulfilled many of the practical aspects key to running the department. He was seconded to Melrose to organise Curle's Gotlandic collection at one stage,[40] and appears regularly in the Letters, 'the industrious Oldland', arranging photographs and packaging finds. The 1881 census records him in Lambeth (London) as a civil servant / attendant, British Museum, suggesting he moved from this role to one within a curatorial department. It records that he was born in 1855; he retired in 1921.

Sir Charles Reed Peers (1868–1952)[41]

Architect and archaeologist, architectural editor of the *Victoria County History*, Secretary of the Society of Antiquaries of London (1908–1921), Inspector of Ancient Monuments from 1910 and Chief Inspector from 1913 to 1933. He appears fleetingly in Letter 1.78 in his role with the Antiquaries, encouraging Curle to write up his Gotland collection.

Sir Charles Hercules Read (1857–1929; Figure 2.4)[42]

Read was the protégé of Sir Augustus Franks, Keeper of the Department of British and Mediaeval Antiquities and Ethnography at the British Museum, whom he succeeded as Keeper in 1896. Like all members of staff at the time he had to range very widely in covering the Department's collections, giving him a great breadth of knowledge but not a great depth. He wrote no major books but contributed many articles to journals and encouraged his staff to publish catalogues. A public man and an impressive speaker, with knowledge of a wide circle of collectors and antiquaries; knighted after his presidency of the Society of Antiquaries in 1912. He was one of Curle's most regular correspondents at the BM.

Emil Ritterling (1861–1928)[43]

Noted scholar of the Roman army and one of the foremost excavators for the Limeskommission in the early 20th century, excavating and publishing the key forts of Hofheim and Wiesbaden[44] (where he was museum director from 1899–1911 and 1915–1923). He succeeded Dragendorff as Director of the Römisch-Germanische Kommission in 1911–1914. We see him indirectly in the Letters, sending Curle a copy of the Wiesbaden report (Letter 3.22).

---

[39] Caygill 2002: 388; Wilson 2002: 182.
[40] Kidd and Thunmark-Nylén 1990: 157–158, 160.
[41] Doggett 2004.
[42] Wilson 2004b.
[43] https://sempub.ub.uni-heidelberg.de/propylaeum_vitae/wisski/navigate/3097/view (accessed 31 August 2022).
[44] Ritterling 1904; 1909.

Bernhard Salin (1861–1931)[45]

An authority on Germanic art of the early Medieval period, he worked at the State Historical Museum in Stockholm from 1889–1902 and then the Nordic Museum from 1905–1913, before becoming Riksantikvarie (national antiquarian, the leading post in Swedish archaeology) from 1913–1923. He came to know Curle from the latter's collecting interests in Gotland and was on friendly terms with him, from the tone of the surviving letters (Letters 1.7, 4.11).

Karl Schumacher (1860–1934)[46]

Director of the Römisch-Germanisches Zentralmuseum in Mainz (1901–1926), who corresponded with Curle over helmets (Letter 1.61) and is thanked in the preface to the Report.

William McDowell Selby (1873–1933)[47]

Doctor in Port William (Wigtownshire) and local antiquary. His collection (now in Stranraer Museum) includes finds from Newstead, suggesting contacts with Curle, and this is supported by Letter 5.7, where Curle refers to Selby's work on the Galoshins play.

Sir Cecil Harcourt Smith (1859–1944)[48]

Corresponded with Curle while he was Keeper of Greek and Roman Antiquities at the British Museum (1904–1909); thereafter Director of the Victoria and Albert Museum (1909–1924).

Reginald Allender Smith (1873–1940; Figure 7.1)[49]

Appointed to the Department of British and Medieval Antiquities at the British Museum under Read in 1898, becoming Keeper in 1928. Worked across the prehistoric and medieval collections, writing a series of guidebooks[50] and innumerable articles. He was Curle's go-to man for points of detail once he started the Newstead excavations. 'Letters to Hercules' may be the title of Chapter 8 but the invaluable assistance of Reginald Smith to James Curle is reflected

Figure 7.1. Reginald Allender Smith (1873-1940), curator in and later Keeper of the Department of British and Mediaeval Antiquities at the British Museum, and a regular correspondent of Curle. © Trustees of the British Museum.

---

[45] Östergren 2002.
[46] https://sempub.ub.uni-heidelberg.de/propylaeum_vitae/wisski/navigate/6410/view (accessed 31 August 2022).
[47] Murray 2005.
[48] Wilson 2002: 199; Caygill 2002: 391.
[49] Wilson 2002: 200, 208,
[50] e.g. Smith 1905; 1923.

in the fact that his is the sole British Museum name accorded thanks in Curle's Preface to his magisterial 1911 Report.

Margerie Venables Taylor (1881–1963)[51]

Researcher on Roman topics on several *Victoria County History* volumes and for the Royal Commission on the Historic Monuments of England; based in Oxford, and served as Haverfield's research assistant for several years. Brought much of his material to publication after his death, as well as bringing other unpublished Roman excavations in the Oxford area to publication. Subsequently Secretary of the Roman Society (1923–1954) and editor of its *Journal of Roman Studies* (1923–1960). The surviving Letter (5.10) shows Curle sending her his Memoir of George Macdonald; its mentions of his family indicate they were well known to one another.

Henry Beauchamp Walters (1867–1944)[52]

Joined the Dept of Greek and Roman Antiquities in 1890, becoming Assistant Keeper in 1913 and Keeper 1925–1932. Wrote catalogues of classical bronzes and of pottery, the latter leading him into contact with Curle; no letters are preserved but they are indicated from references (e.g. Letters 1.34, 3.19).

---

[51] Freeman 2007: 379–381.
[52] Wilson 2002: 199; Caygill 2002: 392.

Chapter 8

Letters to Hercules

Letter 1.1

No home address.

3rd July, 1891

Dear Sir,[1]

I am sending you today a small box containing a couple of Gotlandic 'boars head' Brooches.[2] I must apologise for offering such poor specimens but I have no duplicates among my better ones at present. However, I may be able at some future time to give you more perfect ones. Of the two I send the flat one is, I think, the earlier. I imagine that they are both of the middle period of the iron age; both preserve the tradition of the earlier form.

I also send you a rough sketch of one of my best specimens,[3] it is not very correctly drawn, but it will give you some idea of the pattern.

If it is not giving you too much trouble would you kindly let me have the name of the Book in which your Livonian[4] specimens are described as I should like to get it. I believe there is also a book called NecroLivonia[5], do you know anything of it? If you are ever up in these parts I shall be glad to show you my small collection. I think of going over to Sweden next week and shall have a look at Lund on my way to Stockholm.

I remain,

Yours truly,

James Curle Jr

---

[1] Curle's original, very formal mode of address to Read became 'My dear Sir' and then 'Dear Mr Read' in the course of the month; from 1894 onwards he used 'My Dear Read' (from Letter 1.7, 27 May 1894). The two men clearly met in person at least from 1892; Letter 1.4 (15 November 1892) refers to 'when we last met'.
[2] Curle was a keen collector of bronze brooches and other metalwork from the Swedish island of Gotland. For thorough discussion drawing on this correspondence, see Kidd and Thumark-Nylén 1990: esp. 157–160; Kidd 1994.
[3] Curle's sketches have been redrawn by Alan Braby to allow clearer reproduction..
[4] Gotland lies across the Baltic Sea from the Livonian coast of Latvia.
[5] In fact *Necrolivonica*; Kruse 1842, revised version 1859.

Letter 1.2

No home address

5th November, 1891

My dear Sir,

I hope you will excuse my troubling you but I am anxious to have some information on an archaeological matter which will perhaps interest you. We have recently been clearing out a Broch structure in this neighbourhood at Torwoodlee in Selkirkshire [Figure 8.1].[6] The charcoal which covered the floor to a depth of 2 inches was carefully sifted and in it we found a coin of Vespasian, a number of fragments of pottery and glass, a small portion of a glass armlet, a harness mounting and a round button-like object the upper surface of which has been filled up with red enamel. I send you rough sketches of these three.[7]

As you know Dr Anderson[8] has laid it down that the age of the Brochs did not begin before AD 400 or thereabout and therefore they were <u>post-Roman</u>. Now this particular broch is only the third which has been found south of the Forth and I believe it is the first ever properly cleaned out. None of the pottery found in it is of the class usually found in Brochs and I believe nearly all of it is Roman. There is 'Samian' ware,[9] fragments of a mortarium, pieces of great bulging vessels with narrow necks. We have found the same in the Roman station at Inveresk.[10] There is also a soft yellowish white pottery and a hard black which I find at Inveresk and at Newstead only a mile from here, where was undoubtedly a Roman station.[11] No post Roman structure in Scotland hitherto excavated shows such remains <u>alone</u>. The glass is distinctly Roman of two kinds, dark blue and amber[12] – it has no signs of wearing – one large handle of blue is exactly similar to one found about the end of last century on the banks of the Almond.[13]

---

[6] Brochs were drystone tower-like roundhouses native to Iron Age Scotland, found mostly in northern Scotland, with a few in the lowlands such as Torwoodlee, and Edin's Hall in Berwickshire. See Armit 2003; Macinnes 1984 for lowland brochs. It is striking that Curle uses the first person here, as in the published report (Curle 1892) his personal engagement is not made clear: the work was done 'Under the superintendence of Mr Wilson' of Galashiels, editor of the *Scottish Border Record*, with members of the Gala Ramblers' Club (and, it can be inferred, workmen hired for the task since 'a subscription to defray the cost' was opened; Curle 1892: 71, 72, 75).

[7] These do not survive.

[8] See *Dramatis personae*. For his discussion of broch dating, see Anderson 1874: 146–147, 152–153; for an assessment of Anderson's contribution to broch studies, see MacKie 2002: 33.

[9] This term used in Anglophone scholarship has long caused some controversy. In the Report, Curle preferred the continental terminology of *terra sigillata* and used 'Samian' within quotation marks for this Gaulish red slipped fineware (1911a: 190–242), though he used it unmarked in this way in the Letters in preference to *terra sigillata*. Samian remains the usual form in Britain today: Tyers (1996: 105) noted that both terms are misnomers.

[10] The location of the fort at Inveresk, south of Musselburgh in East Lothian, was known from antiquarian accounts of discoveries, and from finds turned up in building work and grave-digging, but had not seen systematic investigation. See Bishop 2004: 3–6.

[11] This seems to be the earliest evidence of Curle's knowledge of the site at Newstead; the publication makes it clear that this is gleaned from material in NMAS collections (Curle 1892, 75).

[12] The site produced three different types of glass vessels: blue-green cylindrical bottles, a blue-green globular jar, and an amber-coloured tubular-rimmed bowl (Ingemark 2014: 265–266).

[13] Curle is referring to one of the 'portions of glass vessels, found with Roman pottery, &c., in pits near junction of Almond and Tay', given to NMAS in 1781 (Anon. 1892: 221; registration numbers X.FR 204–207). They derive from the Roman fort of Bertha, Perthshire (for which, see Woolliscroft and Hoffmann 2006: 144–148).

The rims are not solid but the glass of the vessel has simply been turned back leaving a hollow so –

Can you tell me if that is a characteristic of Roman glass-making?

The things, however, I want to ask you about are the glass armlet, the harness mounting and the enamel [Figure 8.2]. These, I believe, are late Celtic, the two latter certainly. We know of 10 or twelve armlets found in Scotland, mostly in the South – 1 in a Broch at Edinshall in Berwickshire, 5 in Lake Dwellings, 3 in Borness Cave, 1 in a moss, 1 in a cairn with a jet necklace and 1 at Torwoodlee, also in a Broch.[14] I see they were found at La Tène, and at Berg Hradischt[15] in Bohemia they seem to have been found with late Celtic products, and in Scotland chiefly in the area from which we have our best specimens of these things. Do you think that they belong to the same time? The harness mounting belongs to the same class as one found on Polden Hill, Somerset.[16] It is much corroded and has no trace of enamel. The round button-like object has no trace of any attachment at the back but it is also much decayed. The enamel, where it remains, is bright red. We have nothing of the sort here. Have you any specimens of such an object in the British Museum or do you know of any in England?

I believe Mr Franks[17] puts the period, during which 'late Celtic' arms were produced, between 300BC and 100AD. I presume he also includes this enamel work and these mountings. I should like to know if our find here belongs to that period – I believe that this Broch is Pre-Roman or at least was built before they left the country, though one does not quite like, with a limited knowledge of such things, to theorize. I hope the story won't weary you and shall be obliged for any information you can give me.

---

[14] The letter shows Curle in the course of building his comparanda for the publication. This is the first extended collation of such Romano-British glass armlets, which would not be fully synthesised for another 40 years (Kilbride-Jones 1938).

[15] The publication makes it clear that Curle's source for this was Robert Munro's book on *The lake-dwellings of Europe* (1890: 292–293, 549) and further information provided by Munro, who was one of the secretaries of the Society of Antiquaries of Scotland at the time. La Tène is the type site of the later Iron Age, consisting of a series of votive deposits placed in a former arm of a river running from Lake Neuchâtel (Switzerland), though its character was not understood at the time. 'Berg Hradisch' is the German form of the Czech 'Hradiště', which simply means fortified settlement; the site was an oppidum (Iron Age central fortified place), named today after the nearby settlement of Stradonice (Czech Republic); see Rieckhoff and Fichtl 2011: 41–42.

[16] A hoard of late Iron Age horse and vehicle gear from Somerset; see Brailsford 1975.

[17] Sir Augustus Wollaston Franks (1826–1897), first Keeper of British and Medieval Antiquities and Ethnography at the British Museum; see *Dramatis personae*. Franks offered the first substantive commentary on Celtic art in his comments on the plates in Kemble's *Horae Ferales* (Franks 1863).

I had a pleasant trip to Sweden this summer and saw your friend the Docent Söderberg[18] at Lund and the RiksAntiquary Hildebrand,[19] who were most kind. My most lucky find was a very fine old glass beaker of the middle iron age, about two inches high, found in Gotland.[20] Not so fine as your Taplow beaker[21] once was, but mine has the advantage of being perfect [Figure 8.20].

They are very scarce in any condition, I fancy.

I got some good brooches and one or two bracteats.[22]

Believe me,

Yours sincerely,

James Curle Jr

Figure 8.1. The broch at Torwoodlee, sitting within an older hillfort. Photo by courtesy of the Trimontium Trust, © J. Reid.

[18] We are grateful to Dominic Ingemark for identifying this as Sven (Otto Magnus) Söderberg (1849–1901), who worked at the Historiska Muséet in Lund (the archaeological museum) from 1875, becoming its director in 1888. While originally a philologist specialising in north Germanic languages (in which topic he became a professor in 1901), his strong interest in archaeology arose from working on one of Oscar Montelius' excavations, and later on Hans Hildebrand's excavations in Skåne. These were his mentors in the archaeological field (see *Dramatis personae*), and became close friends. His best-known works are *Forngutnisk ljudlära* (1879), *Om djurornamentiken under folkvandringstiden* (1893) and *Ölands runinskrifter* (1 1900; 2 1906). See *Nordisk Familjebok* (2nd edition), Stockholm 1919, s.v. Sven Otto Magnus Söderberg; Hjelmqvist 1902.

[19] Hans Hildebrand (1842–1913), Swedish archaeologist and State Antiquary. See *Dramatis personae*.

[20] This must be the beaker disputed in Letters 1.80–1.81. It is from Gotland, its precise provenance uncertain; see Kidd and Thunmark-Nylén 1990: 164, fig. 9.

[21] Four Anglo-Saxon olive-green glass claw beakers of the late 6th–7th century were found in a tumulus at Taplow, Buckinghamshire, in 1883; Evison 2008: 57, nos 78–81, figs 15–16, colour pls 4–5.

[22] Gold uniface medallions; Axboe 2007.

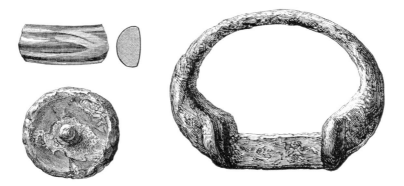

Figure 8.2. The three Torwoodlee fittings, re-scaled to 1:1; glass bangle top left, enamelled disc bottom left, terret on right. Modified from Curle 1892: figs 9–11.

Letter 1.3

No home address.

13th November, 1891

Dear Mr Read,

I have to thank you for your letter of yesterday. I am glad you think that the three articles of which I sent you a drawing may be considered as Late Celtic. It is sufficient for my purpose that they are considered Celtic. I can quite understand that it is very possible that this style of art prevailed in the North long after it had become extinct in the South at the same time.

I fancy you cannot say with certainty that these things are undoubtedly post-Roman. They may have been made during the Roman occupation or even earlier. Now these three things are the <u>only</u> undoubtedly Celtic productions we have unearthed at Torwoodlee. There was not a fragment of the pottery usually found in brochs or underground structures, though the charcoal which formed the relic bed was very carefully sifted. It might be argued then that the inhabitants did not make the pottery usually found in Northern Brochs, but two miles from Torwoodlee on a hill top we have found another broch,[23] and among the debris a piece of the same rude hand-made pottery which was found in the Broch of Burrian,[24] and bearing the same ornament. I believe that all the glass and all the pottery we have found is Roman and I hope to be able to establish that, by comparing it. Of course I use the word 'Roman' as denoting of the age of the Roman occupation.

---

[23] Bow or Bowland 'Castle', excavated in 1890 by the Gala Ramblers' Club; Curle 1892: 68–70.
[24] Broch of Burrian, North Ronaldsay, Orkney. For the site, see MacKie 2002: 255–258. In the publication, it was the broch of Lingrow (Orkney) which Curle referenced (1892: 70).

We have no instance, as far as I can learn, of an undoubtedly post-Roman structure in Scotland containing Roman remains in the proportions in which we have found them here. It is only on undoubted Roman sites that we have found such glass and pottery.

Another curious point about this Broch. If you take the average diameter of the 19 Northern Brochs, of which dimensions are given in the Archaeologica,[25] you find it to be 58 feet. Our diameter here is 75 feet. The only Broch to be compared with it is Edinshall in Berwickshire and secondly this Torwoodlee structure shows a perfect knowledge of the usual plan and harder lines than any known to Dr. Anderson.[26] Its one perfect chamber is rectangular, instead of having the corners rounded off in the usual way. The masonry is very good.

Don't you think these facts are very significant? Dr. Anderson admits at once that it is a very early Broch *from the relics*: they must have been deposited in it, if not during the Roman time at least very shortly after it. But the structure is larger and better than the average. It surely is hardly likely that we should find the largest and best built Brochs at the beginning of the period – and I therefore believe that it must be put at an earlier date than has been believed hitherto. This is a capital problem and can only be solved by some patient 'howking' in this South country.[27]

Please excuse my giving you such a quantity of it. If you can find time will you please tell me if you have anything like the red enamel in the Museum.

I shall look forward to seeing your Saxon things. Mr. Evans[28] told me about the glass. Mine is 9 inches high. I shall send you a photo of it. I have a good copy of Horae Ferales[29] but I should be glad to have Ackerman's Pagan Saxondom[30] if it is still in the market.

I got an importation of things from Gotland a few days ago, among them the contents of a Middle Iron Age grave with a specimen of the very early boarshead fibula showing the open eyeholes, which almost makes my series complete.

I have one beauty with the eyeholes filled up and I also have a pretty complete series of the round box fibula from the small flat brooch to the heavy ornament of the Late Iron Age.

Yours sincerely,

James Curle Jr.

---

[25] 'Archaeologica' is presumably *Archaeologia Scotica*, where Anderson published a major article on brochs (1874), but the data are most likely taken from Petrie's tables of Orkney and Shetland brochs (1874: 92, Appendix I) in the same volume, as Anderson did not provide such data. There are in fact measurements for 23 brochs, averaging 57' 4½" (17.5m) in diameter.

[26] See *Dramatis personae*; Curle had presumably been discussing the matter with Anderson.

[27] It is noteworthy that Curle's comments on dating in the publication (1892: 83–84) are markedly (and unnecessarily) more cautious, suggesting that he was not keen to contradict Anderson: (without further excavation) 'I do not think we are in a position to assign ... a date to the occupation of the broch of Torwoodlee'.

[28] Sir Arthur Evans (1851–1941), excavator of Knossos; 'discoverer' of Minoan civilization. Ashmolean Museum Director, 1884–1908. Oxford Professor of Prehistoric Archaeology from 1909.

[29] Kemble 1863.

[30] Ackerman 1855.

Letter 1.4

No home address

15th November, 1892

Dear Mr Read,

I can let you have one or two Gotland Brooches 'djurhufudfibulaer'.[31] None of them are good ones but you told me when we last met that you would be glad to take even the Common forms. I am going over to Dresden on Thursday so I shall be in town on Wednesday and I will come and see you at the Museum between 11 and 12. I am going to see the Berlin Collection[32] on my way home. Could you give me a note to anyone there who wouldn't mind showing a duffer round?

Believe me,

Yours very truly,

James Curle Jr

Letter 1.5

Priorwood,
Melrose NB

2nd December, 1892

Dear Mr Read,

Thanks for your letter. I expected to be able to come back to the Museum and see you on Wednesday but I could not manage to do so.

I got on very well at Berlin and Dr. Voss[33] was extremely kind in showing me round, though the want of possessing a really satisfactory language in common was a drawback. His collection from Brandenburg and the Northern Provinces is very interesting, and he has some very good Russian things as well as Kruse's[34] collection, which I know from illustrations in *Necrolivonica*.[35] The collections in the Antiquarium[36] are particularly good, but of course in a couple of days one can't do more than glance at them.

---

[31] Swedish term for 'animal-head brooches'.
[32] The Antikensammlung in Berlin (Antiquities Collection) is one of the most important collections of classical art in the world, now held mostly in the Altes Museum and Pergamon Museum on the Museums Island.
[33] Albert Voss (1837–1906), head of prehistoric collections in the Berlin museums.
[34] Friedrich Kruse (1790–1866), ancient and medieval historian, professor at Halle (Germany) and Dorpat (now Tartu, Estonia).
[35] Kruse 1842; 1859. This is the book Curle was seeking the reference to in Letter 1.1.
[36] Antiquarium or Antikensammlung, the collection of classical antiquities in the Berlin Museums; see note 32.

As to the Society of Antiquaries[37] I looked over your list which I shall return. There are very few Scotch members and I can't say that I personally know any of them. There are none from this part of the world and curiously none of the men who take a lead in the Scotch Society[38] are members. I can ask Sir William Crossman,[39] Mr Murray,[40] and perhaps Mr Hartshorne[41] to sign the papers but I don't know any others unless perhaps Mr Franks would be good enough to do so. Now, please tell us whether it would be advisable, knowing as I do so few people, to put my name up as I shouldn't like to do so if that was likely to tell against me.

If you will kindly let me know, I shan't in the meantime write to anyone.

Had your journey to Spain been to come off later I should have rather envied you, but my experience of the last fortnight is that it is not the best time of the year for travelling.

Believe me,

Yours very truly,

James Curle Jr

PS I am a Writer to the Signet[42] by trade.

JCJr

Letter 1.6

14th December, 1892

Dear Mr Read,

I return the papers for the Antiquaries signed by Sir William Crossman, Mr Murray and Mr Hartshorne. I am afraid in the meantime that exhausts the people I can write to. Mr Hartshorne kindly says he will do what he can for me, if in town when the election comes on. I suppose that won't be for some time, perhaps however you would let me know beforehand. If I can

[37] The Society of Antiquaries of London; the context makes it clear that Read had suggested Curle should be proposed for Fellowship, and was looking for suitable sponsors. His Blue Paper (the election form) shows the following sponsors, signed from personal knowledge of Curle: Charles H. Read himself; W. Crossman; A.S. Murray; Albert Hartshorne; Augustus W. Franks of the BM. His grounds for election were noted as 'Attachment to the study of Antiquities, especially those of Northern Europe'. We are grateful to Dunia Garcia-Ontiveros (Society of Antiquaries of London) for this information. Curle was elected FSA on 18 May 1893 and admitted to the Fellowship (by attending a meeting) on 17 January 1895, when he exhibited some Scandinavian gaming pieces and a Byzantine spoon (*Proceedings of the Society of Antiquaries of London* [2nd series] 14 [1891–1893]: 356; 15 [1893–1895]: 273–274). For the finds, see Letters 1.8 and 1.9.
[38] The Society of Antiquaries of Scotland; founded 1780, incorporated by Royal Charter 1783 'to investigate both antiquities and natural and civil history in general...'.
[39] Sir William Crossman (1830–1901), an officer in the Royal Engineers for many years, and MP for Portsmouth on his retirement from 1885–1892. Curle presumably knew him from Border social circles; he inherited the family estate at Cheswick in Northumberland in 1883 (Vetch and Jones 2008).
[40] Listed as A.S. Murray on Curle's Blue Paper; Letter 2.1 makes it clear this is Alexander Stuart Murray (1841–1904), Keeper of Greek and Roman Antiquities at the BM, and a native of Arbroath (Caygill 2002: 388; Wilson 2002: 182).
[41] Albert Hartshorne (1839–1910), a Derbyshire-based antiquary (Dix 2004); it is unclear how Curle knew him.
[42] Writer to the Signet. Scottish solicitors were known as 'Writers', and senior solicitors were entitled to supervise the use of the Signet, the personal seal of the early Kings of Scotland, from the 14th century.

manage to meet Canon Greenwell[43] I shall do so but I don't know if there is much chance of my being in Durham.

I am sending you two copies of my paper about that Brooch as it looks more respectable than the thing I sent you before.[44] Will you please give one to Mr Griffith.[45] The conclusions are probably of no value but I think the facts are curious. Don't trouble to acknowledge receipt.

If you care to join the Scotch Society of Antiquaries[46] I can get you in, there is no difficulty of any kind and you have only to let me know. I hope your journey to Spain will prove more pleasant than you anticipate.

Believe me,

Yours very truly,

James Curle Jr

Letter 1.7

Typewritten.

27th May, 1894

My dear Read,

I promised to get you a set of the Gotlandic fibulae photographs I showed you when I was last in town. On my return home I wrote to Stockholm for them, and I have a letter from my friend Salin[47] to say that the Riks-antiquarian Hildebrand[48] will have much pleasure in presenting the Museum with a set which he will send direct. I merely write in order that you may understand how they come when they reach you. 'Joseph'[49] got a grand bargain a few weeks ago in Edinburgh – a most excellent set of harness rings and bits of Late Celtic work for a mere trifle.[50]

I am glad to see your chief has been promoted.[51] I hope to hear from you one day soon if you have not abandoned the custom of writing letters.

Yours very sincerely,

James Curle Jr

---

[43] Canon William Greenwell, Durham (1820–1918), a renowned antiquarian; see Hodgson 1918; Kinnes and Longworth 1985: 10–14.

[44] We have not been able to establish what this paper is; it is too early for his note on Gotlandic brooches (Curle 1895).

[45] Francis Llewellyn Griffith (1862–1934), assistant in Read's department from 1888–1896 (Caygill 2002: 386; Wilson 2002: 199, 368 n.20); latterly Egyptology Professor, Oxford, 1924-32.

[46] Read was elected to the Society in 1893 but resigned in 1904 owing to a dispute with Joseph Anderson over the Bronze Age burial finds from Melfort, Argyll; see notes to Letter A5.

[47] Dr Bernhard Salin, (1861–1931), Keeper of Antiquities at the National Museum in Stockholm. See Letters 1.9, 4.11 and *Dramatis personae*.

[48] See *Dramatis personae*.

[49] Dr Joseph Anderson, Keeper of NMAS; see *Dramatis personae*.

[50] The surviving components of the hoard of Iron Age horse harness and a sword hilt guard from Middlebie (Dumfriesshire), purchased from the collection formed by Sir John Clerk of Penicuik; *Proceedings of the Society of Antiquaries of Scotland* 28 (1893–1894): 237.

[51] Augustus Wollaston Franks (1826–1897), who was knighted in 1894 (Wilson 2004a). See *Dramatis personae*.

Letter 1.8

No home address.

4th February, 1895

Dear Read,

I return the letter from Mr Cocks,[52] which is interesting. He assumes that the Chessmen are Norwegian and being Norse and being of Walrus ivory are probably from the northern part of the country.[53] Now I have every reason to believe they were found in Gotland [Figure 8.3]. I myself got them in the island and I must say that throughout my dealings with the man from whom they were purchased I have seen nothing to make me suspect that he gathered together antiquities for my benefit from other parts of the country. Assuming then that the set was found in Gotland, I do not think the fact of the Walrus ivory denotes a Lapp origin. Of course the set might have been brought from the north but the pieces are not divided into their varieties and the dies are not like those Mr Cocks describes. There is no doubt that from an early period – the 3rd or 4th century – they played a game resembling chess in Denmark and Scandinavia. I see from one of my notebooks the following sets are in the Copenhagen Museums:-

X Amber 17 pieces Ditto 13.

X Blue Glass 13 White Paste 16 Black 16.

Mixed Paste 14 Black Paste 16.

Four sets of bone 17. 12. 13. 19.

The most of these are Early Iron Age and flat button-like objects.

In Norway Rygh mentions 30 finds of pieces and 15 of dice.[54]

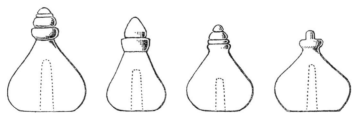

FOUR OF A SERIES OF TABLEMEN FROM BOGE, IN THE ISLAND OF GOTLAND.
(Full size.)

Figure 8.3. Gaming pieces from Gotland, exhibited by Curle to the Society of Antiquaries of London in 1895. From the Proceedings of the Society of Antiquaries of London (second series) 15 (1893–1895): 273.

[52] Alfred Heneage Cocks, FSA (1851–1928), naturalist and antiquary; sometime curator of Buckinghamshire County Museum. He worked extensively in Norway; his collection of Norwegian antiquities was acquired by the British Museum in 1891 (*Records of Buckinghamshire* 12/3 [1929]: 149–150; Wilson 2002: 235; www.britishmuseum.org/collection/term/BIOG67434 [accessed 2 January 2022]; www.whitingsociety.org.uk/old-ringing-books/cocks-bells-of-buckinghamshire.html [accessed 2 January 2022]). His letter was in response to Curle's exhibition of gaming pieces from Gotland; see the following note.
[53] Curle exhibited a group of 14 ivory gaming pieces, three dice and a gilt bronze 'box' from Boge, Gotland, to the Society of Antiquaries of London on 17 January 1895; see *Proceedings of the Society of Antiquaries of London* (2nd series) 15 (1893–1895): 273–274. On the gaming pieces and dice, see Kidd and Thunmark-Nylén 1990: 170, fig. 22.
[54] Rygh 1885: 68.

'Elles portent toujours un trou percé dans la face inferieure et ont en consequence indubitablement été employées avec des damiers ayant de petites chevilles sur lesquelles on fixait les dames.'[55]

The same applies to the pieces of the Ultuna[56] find, 37 in number.

This characteristic connects my set with those generally found in Norway and Sweden and the dice are the same. It is seldom that the pieces show indications of value. Sometimes a single one is marked by a metal mounting.

Thanks for your information about these German books.

The weather here is worse than ever.

Yours very truly,

James Curle Jr

Letter 1.9

No address given

27th March, 1895

My dear Read,

A friend in Stockholm writes to tell me that Dr Bernhard Salin[57] of the Stockholm Museum is in London 'studying our ancient remains.'

I don't know whether he has arrived as yet to study your ancient remains but if he does or if you should know where he is I should be very much obliged if you would give him the enclosed.

I hope you are flourishing. I have had this vile influenza and feel somewhat feeble still. I think I must go off on a travel for the good of my health.

I have heard nothing of my Chessmen or the spoon[58] and am thinking of asking Mr St John Hope[59] to send them back.

I got three brooches from the North[60] a few weeks ago, rather late ones but very well preserved.

Do you still think of going to Namur,[61] or have you been?

Believe me,

Yours very sincerely,

James Curle Jr

---

[55] 'They always have a hole pierced in the bottom and because of that they have undoubtedly been used with draughtboards which had little pegs on which the pieces were fixed.'

[56] From a seventh-century boat grave near Uppsala, Sweden; Ljungkvist 2006: 421.

[57] See Letters 1.7, 4.11, and *Dramatis personae*.

[58] The 'chessmen' are the gaming pieces Curle exhibited to the Society of Antiquaries of London on 17 January 1895, along with a Byzantine inscribed bronze spoon, the latter 'recently purchased in Edinburgh'; see *Proceedings of the Society of Antiquaries of London* (2nd series) 15 (1893–1895): 273–274, and Letter 1.8.

[59] Assistant Secretary of the Society of Antiquaries of London at this time. See *Dramatis personae*.

[60] Sweden.

[61] Museum in Belgium.

Letter 1.10

BRITISH MUSEUM,
LONDON WC

18 March, 1896

My dear Curle

Pardon my delay.[62]

Your locality for the engraved glass is correct LEVNA, Merseburg,[63] Prussia – as is also the rest of your note. The inscription on the smaller cup describes the subject of APTEMIC and AKTAION.[64] Cut glass is comparatively rare in classical times and found hardly ever in Saxon graves. You know the Roman cut tumbler in the B.M. from Colchester covered all over with pointed oval cuttings.[65] It may be just worth referring to.

I have been making Hope's[66] life a burden to him re the Heraldic Cat.[67] He is to get a little money for passing it through the press – I wish to avoid the Greek Kalends coming into it.[68]

Yours very truly,

Charles H Read

---

[62] The earlier correspondence is not preserved, but the context must be research for the notes Curle prepared on vessels with cut-glass decoration to contextualise the find of one from the Birrens excavations (in Christison *et al.* 1896: 190–191). It is an impressively thorough review of such glass, particularly examples from beyond the Roman frontier, and shows Curle's early interest in this topic.

[63] 30 km west of Leipzig. Site of a Germanic burial rich in Roman finds; see Schulz 1953; for the glass, Harden *et al.* 1987: 197.

[64] Well-known Greek myth where the goddess Artemis transformed Actaeon into a stag, and he was pursued and killed by his own hounds. Ovid, *Metamorphoses* III.140.

[65] A search of the British Museum's catalogue has not produced this vessel; it may be that Read intended to refer to the faceted beaker from Barnwell, Cambridgeshire, acquired with the Slade Collection in 1868 (Harden *et al.* 1987: 194).

[66] Assistant Secretary of the Society of Antiquaries; see *Dramatis personae*. 'Hope's relations with the society's secretary, Sir Hercules Read, were notoriously bad' (Thompson and Nurse 2004).

[67] Hope worked on seals and their heraldry, but did not apparently produce a catalogue of them, though Harvey (1980) noted that he was working on a card index of those in the Public Record Office in 1912, which was probably part of the same project. We are grateful to Alice Blackwell for advice on this matter.

[68] The Greeks did not have Kalends on their calendar; the phrase means 'never'.

Letter 1.11

22nd March, 1896

My dear Read,

Very many thanks for your note about the two vases from Leuna. I shall add the Colchester vase to my note. I think the Birrens[69] excavations is [*sic*] rather interesting as there seem to have been two occupations of the place.

I hope to hear of your promotion before long. I suppose Sir Wollaston[70] goes very soon. Any chance of seeing you up in Scotland this summer? I wish you would come.

Yours very truly,

James Curle Jr

Letter 1.12

Black bordered mourning quarto notepaper

PRIORWOOD,
MELROSE, N.B.

18th May, 1897

My dear Read,

There are one or two things to be sold at Christies on Friday 21st we are rather anxious to get for the Scotch National Museum[71] and the Council has deputed Mr Carfrae[72] to attend the sale. The lots are the Glenlyon Brooch[73] and Charmstone,[74] lots 455 and 456, and two Highland Brooches, lots 457 and 458.

If you can do anything to help us we shall feel grateful. Mr Carfrae will call for you at the Museum on Thursday.[75]

I shall be passing through town next week but I am afraid I won't be able to see you as we shall only stay the night. Ever since my father died in January I have had a great deal to do

---

[69] Birrens (*Blatobulgium*), a Roman fort near Ecclefechan in Dumfries and Galloway on the westerly Roman route into Scotland. For these excavations, see Christison *et al.* 1896, with the note by Curle on a glass beaker with facet-cut decoration (Figure 4.4) which prompted these letters.

[70] Franks retired from the BM as Keeper of British and Medieval Antiquities and Ethnography on his 70th birthday (20th March 1896) and was succeeded by Sir Charles Hercules Read. The changeover had taken place just before Curle wrote this letter. See *Dramatis personae*.

[71] Curle was on the Society's Council, as Librarian.

[72] Robert Carfrae, one of the two Honorary Curators of NMAS, whose image, with those of many other officials, was included in the stained glass window unveiled at the Museum's opening in 1892; D.V. Clarke 1990: ill. 24.

[73] The Glenlyon brooch is a 16th-century annular brooch, silver-gilt, set with crystals, amethysts and pearls, inscribed on the rear with the names of the three Magi (Tait 1976: 223, 369c; Robinson 2008: 140).

[74] The Glenlyon charmstone was a rock crystal ball; Black 1893: 437–438. 441.

[75] Robert Stevenson (1981: 180) noted that a 'painful argument on the morning of the sale' between Carfrae and Read led to the two museums bidding against one another, and the BM acquiring the brooch.

and want a change badly, so I am going with my mother to Royat in Auvergne.[76] I believe it is an interesting country and if you can tell me anything about what there is to see, or give me a line to anyone in these parts, I should be grateful.

I haven't got very much since I saw you last. I got one or two good brooches in Stockholm last summer, one especially good:– silver of the 'Teutonic' type.

Not very long ago I got the mountings of an Early Iron Age drinking horn with studs, which have had enamel in them and a pair of belt ends with silver mountings. I have also got – but this is a <u>secret</u> – two gold bracteats,[77] not very fine ones but, as you know, anything of the kind is rather scarce. You needn't mention this as I don't want Hon [*sic*] Hildebrand[78] to drop on the finders.

Yours very sincerely,

James Curle Jr

Letter 1.13

12th May, 1898

My dear Read,

There was a man of the name of Galloway,[79] an architect by trade, who died lately I think in Wigtownshire.

He possessed various antiquities, among them a number of bone harpoons, I understand, of a type resembling those of the Reindeer period. They were about fourteen in number and were found in a mound on the Island of Oronsay. He exhibited them at the Fishery Exhibition in London a number of years ago.[80] Now that he is dead the harpoons cannot be found, only the card upon which they were mounted, and Anderson,[81] who is anxious to trace them, wonders whether you have added them to the 'British' collection under your charge. If it is not bothering you will you tell me if you know anything about them.

I enclose a rough sketch of a circular brooch – bronze-gilt, one of my latest acquisitions, which I think you will rather covet. The original being in high relief is much more effective than the drawing. The setting in the centre is unfortunately awanting.[82]

---

[76] In the Puy-de-Dome département of central France. Since Roman times its thermal springs have made it a spa town and the remains of the Roman baths are still visible.
[77] A flat, thin, single-sided gold medallion worn as jewellery in the Germanic Iron Age (e.g. Axboe 2007).
[78] Hans Hildebrand; see Letter 1.7 and *Dramatis personae*. Curle's use of 'Hon' is slightly tongue-in-cheek in this context. Kidd and Thunmark-Nylén (1990: 167) read this as 'Bror', but Bror Emil Hildebrand (1806–1884), Hans Hildebrand's father and also an archaeologist, was dead by this point.
[79] William B.M. Galloway (1832–1897), architect and antiquary; *inter alia* he surveyed the ruins of Iona, worked on the excavation and restoration of Whithorn Priory, excavated the remarkable Viking burial at Kiloran Bay, Colonsay, and mesolithic shell middens on Oronsay (Ritchie 2012). Fell out with Joseph Anderson, Keeper of NMAS (seemingly not an unknown occurrence), which probably affected the acceptance of his output.
[80] The International Fisheries Exhibition, London, 1883 (Ritchie 2012: 445–446).
[81] Joseph Anderson, Keeper of NMAS; see *Dramatis personae*.
[82] Two 'rubbings' of this brooch accompany the letter – one very rough and the other tidied up. Kidd and Thunmark-Nylén (1990: fig. 8) describe it as a 'Cast gilt copper-alloy disc brooch from the Vendel period, decorated in Style II … D: 3.8cm'.

By the way, who is a really good man to do a Bookplate?[83] I want to get one and I don't know who to apply to. I don't want it unless I can get one well done.

Believe me,

Yours very truly,

James Curle Jr

Figure 8.4. Curle's bookplate by Sir David Young Cameron, showing the south transept of Melrose Abbey. © Yale Center for British Art, The Edwin M. Herr, Yale PhD 1884, Memorial Collection; Gift of Mrs Herr, transfer from the Yale University Art Gallery.

---

[83] Curle's bookplate was a monochrome etching of the south entrance of Melrose Abbey, done by the foremost etcher of the day, Sir David Young Cameron, RA (1865–1945); see Greenshields-Leadbetter 1919: 69; Lee and Campbell 2006.

Letter 1.14

9th February, 1900

My dear Read,

If it is not giving you too much trouble, could you send me a list of recent publications of the BM. There are several books among them we should have in the Edinburgh Library[84] and I want to make an appeal to the Chief Librarian.

I was over in America in Autumn. I was surprised to find the Charvet[85] glass, which I knew from Fröhner's[86] pictures, in the Metropolitan Museum, New York. What a beautiful collection it is!

I wasn't much taken with the American prehistoric collection in Washington.[87] It seemed confused and badly managed.

I hope you have escaped influenza. We have a lot of it round about here. By the way, in the excavations the Scots Antiquaries have been making at Camelon[88] they have got one or two nice enamelled fibulae.

With kind regards,

Yours very truly,

James Curle Jr

Letter 1.15

16th April, 1902

My dear Read,

Very many thanks for your letter. I shall certainly write to Christie's for the catalogue of Carmichael's[89] sale. I saw Lady Carmichael yesterday busy hunting for a small house somewhere in this county. I am sincerely sorry for them.

I should have written before to thank you for your earlier letters but last week was a very anxious one for us all as my mother developed influenza with many complications and is only now struggling back to life again.

It is a big 'trouble', as we say in Scotland.

Yours ever,

James Curle Jr

---

[84] At this point Curle was one of the Society of Antiquaries of Scotland's honorary librarians.
[85] The Charvet collection of ancient glass, containing over 400 pieces, was purchased in 1881 for the Metropolitan Museum of Art, New York.
[86] Froehner 1879. (The publication renders ö as oe).
[87] Now collectively called the Smithsonian Institution, this world-renowned museum and research complex consists of 17 museums, galleries and a zoo. It includes what is now the National Museum of the American Indian.
[88] In the Forth valley, 2.1 km from Falkirk, north of the Antonine Wall; site of Flavian and Antonine forts. For these excavations, see Christison *et al.* 1901.
[89] Sir Thomas David Gibson Carmichael Bt (1859–1926), Castle Craig, Peeblesshire. Sale 12–13 May 1902, following insolvency.

Letter 1.16

On black-bordered paper

PRIORWOOD,
MELROSE N.B.

6th September, 1902

My dear Read,

Mr Henry Oldland[90] has finished his work on my Gotlandic collection and it has been most successful. It really looks as well again and I am much obliged to you for suggesting him and facilitating his coming. It seems a sad way to spend a holiday sitting in a stuffy room sticking pins in tablets but he, poor soul, seems to enjoy himself and thinks the outlook more satisfying than Great Russell Street.[91] I am gathering my belongings together and working hard to get my affairs in some sort of order before leaving home on the 16th. I shan't be sorry to get the wedding[92] over and find myself in Italy where I hope there will be some summer weather in store for us.

With kindest regards,

Believe me,

Yours very sincerely,

James Curle Jr

Letter 1.17

2nd December, 1902

My dear Read,

A young cousin of mine has gone up to London lately and is going into a publishing house. My Uncle asks if I could get him a reader's ticket for the BM Library.[93] I can vouch for his entire respectability. I don't exactly know what is needed but I have given him a card of introduction to you and I would be grateful if you would put him on the right track. I have told him to call and I hope it won't be a bother to you.

We are having very dull weather here, which I don't appreciate after Italian skies. On the other hand one is glad to get back to one's own belongings. I am so glad to have the Slade book, which is most interesting.[94]

With kind regards,

James Curle Jr

---

[90] A clerk in Read's department who was seconded to Melrose to organise James Curle's Gotlandic collection of bronzes (Kidd and Thunmark-Nylén 1990: 157–158, 160). He appears regularly in the Letters, fulfilling various practical needs; he retired in 1921. See *Dramatis personae*.
[91] The site of the British Museum.
[92] Curle's own wedding to Blanchette Nepean and honeymoon in Italy.
[93] Forerunner to the British Library.
[94] Given Curle's interest in ancient glass, this must be the catalogue of Felix Slade's collection of glass, bequeathed to the British Museum in 1868 and published privately in 1871 (Chaffers *et al.* 1871).

My cousin's name is

R.H.P. Curle,[95]
2 Colville Square,
Bayswater.

Letter 1.18

8th October, 1905

My dear Read,

I have been busy superintending the digging out of the Roman station at Newstead, quite near here. We started with a ploughed field and no surface indications, and we are gradually marking out the defences and buildings of a very large place. Our most striking find has been made in digging out a great pit in the Courtyard[96] of the Praetorium[97] some 20 feet in diameter at the surface, narrowing to 6 feet at the bottom, 25 feet down.

In the top levels we found quantities of building stone, in fact more or less all the way down, which must have formed portions of the building above. At 8 feet we found parts of a skeleton and something gold, glass beads and a very nice penannular brooch. At 12 feet an altar to Jupiter[98] and a coin of Hadrian below it, and then, going down in the black mud, heads of oxen and sheep, two horses, a pick of deer horn till we reached 22 feet when we found the skull of a man and parts of his armour, some 350 brass scales of 'lorica squamata'[99] – this sort of thing.

---

[95] Richard Henry Parnell Curle (1883–1968), who worked as a journalist and in publishing before becoming a wide-ranging and far-travelled author and critic (A. Curle 1975).

[96] Pit I in Curle 1911a: 47–49, 116–117; 'Cleaned out 23 September, 1905. 25½ feet deep'. See Letters 3.3–3.9 for his extensive correspondence with Haverfield on this pit in August and September 1905.

[97] Curle used the term *praetorium* for the headquarters building throughout his correspondence but used the correct term, *principia*, in the publication. This reflects a shift in knowledge around this time. Evidence from ancient authors was ambiguous, but articles by von Domaszweski and by Mommsen in 1899 and 1900 established *praetorium* was the term for the commanding officer's residence (summarised in Johnson 1983: 104–105, 310 n.9). This had not yet taken root in British scholarship by the time of Curle's excavations; the 1907 fifth edition of the *Hand-book to the Roman Wall* variously used 'Forum' at Chesters and 'Praetorium' at Housesteads (Collingwood Bruce 1907: 91–93, 141–142). The preceding series of excavations on Roman sites by the Antiquaries were notable for avoiding the problem: in the excavations at Ardoch, Birrens, Camelon and Castlecary, all of which exposed the *principia*, the building was not named. The Lyne report ventured to argue the central building was 'facing down the Via Prætoria, and is therefore presumably the Prætorium' (Christison and Anderson 1901: 179), but the Society's 1902–1903 excavations at Rough Castle found an inscription in the central building naming it as the *principia* (Buchanan *et al.* 1905: 470–472; RIB I: 2145). By the following year, George Macdonald was calling the central building at Bar Hill 'The Praetorium – or, as it might perhaps be more correctly termed, the Principia', quoting the Rough Castle inscription (Macdonald and Park 1906: 33). Curle was a late adopter, and one can track his change in terminology. By the time he lectured to the Royal Philosophical Society of Glasgow in November 1910, he was using the term *principia* (*The Scotsman* 3 November 1910: 6), but all previous references in correspondence are to *praetorium*, and a later instance in a 1913 lecture suggests he found this a hard habit to shake off (Curle 1913d: 54). Strikingly, a review of his book in *The Scotsman* (10 January 1911: 5) includes the following line: '... the ground once covered by the 'Principia' of the fort – 'Praetorium', Jonathan Oldbuck would have called it ...'. Oldbuck, the eponymous *Antiquary* of Sir Walter Scott's novel, was a caricature of the breed; the term that antiquaries had used unhesitatingly until very recently was now being ridiculed!

[98] RIB I: 2123. See Letters 3.4–3.5.

[99] Armour made from small overlapping metal scales; see Curle 1911a: 158–159. When found, they were identified as gold because of their condition; see Letter 3.9. Curle also corresponded with H. St George Gray on the find, in the context of similar items from Ham Hill in Somerset (Gray 1906: 136, footnote); see Letter 5.2.

We also got a lot of leather. On the bottom of this pit we got a small bucket, a couple of knives, a quern and steel yard and a good many pieces of an iron corselet ornamented with strips of what looks like gilt bronze and several of the plates from the ~~shoul[der]~~ arms.[100] We also found part of a second skull and some shoes.

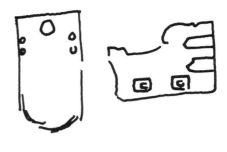

Can you tell me of any finds of Roman armour in England? We are washing out the mud and a number of small fragments turn up, difficult to fix up, among them a small bit of what looks like chain armour. I hope you are flourishing.

Yours very sincerely,

James Curle

Letter 1.19

7th January, 1906

My dear Read,

I am still busy digging away at Newstead and always finding a little. Outside the camp I am trenching a field which I think was their cemetery. It lies on the South side ~~of~~ just beyond the defences and we have discovered already a number of pits and I hope to find more.[101] The first one was met with in searching for a road. It was about 6 feet deep and contained a large decorated Samian bowl, the greater part of a large blue glass vessel with a reeded handle and pieces of two other pots. There were fragments of burnt bone and grain at the bottom.[102]

Our next pit was 32 feet deep.[103] We took out the bones of nine horses. Then the skeleton, almost complete, of a dwarf, 4 feet 6 and a half inches high, below it the skull of a dog, pieces of leather, oyster shells, finally a big iron hammer. The place was evidently a rubbish pit. The earth was very black, full of twigs. I picked up a hazelnut. We then followed along the side of the pits and found one or two more pits not very deep with nothing in them but in what might have been a drain near one of them we got the pieces of a Castor ware pot with a band of decoration, stags and hounds [Figure 8.5]. Among the pieces we got a number of fragments of burnt bones.

A few pieces of another pot were got near it. No doubt it was a burial but there was no sign of any stones protecting the vases or otherwise suggesting a grave.

---

[100] The now-famous Newstead 'lorica segmentata'. See Curle 1911a: 155–158; Bishop 1999.
[101] These are the famous pits which are such a distinctive feature of the site; at this stage their character was not clear. Curle followed the interpretation of John Alexander Smith (1857: 425–426) who saw the pits uncovered in a railway cutting through the South Annexe as burials, due no doubt to the presence of a skeleton in one. See Curle 1911a: 106–107.
[102] Pit XV; Curle 1911a: 119.
[103] Pit XVII; Curle 1911a: 120.

I then began on the other side of the field about 100 yds away and there we have got yet another pit full of black stuff which we are clearing out. So far nothing has come from it except some small bits of red and black pottery and what might be the bottom of a small brass ladle.[104]

Can you tell me where to look for a description of such pits in England? I see Roach Smith[105] mentions them at Richborough[106] and I know that some were found at Ewell[107] in Surrey. I should be grateful for any information. I think our Castor ware[108] pot is the first that has been found in Scotland that can be reconstructed. We also got bits of a straight-sided Samian bowl which upsets a theory that

Figure 8.5. Castor ware pot with hunting scenes, found in 1906.
© National Museums Scotland (X.FRA 1392).

Haverfield propounded a few years ago.[109] I must come and see your Roman pots on the first opportunity as there is nothing to study here. Have you many of these Castor vessels?

Who is the man who examines the seeds from the Silchester[110] pits? I wonder if he would like to see some of the stuff we are getting here.

With all good wishes for the New Year.

Believe me,

Yours very sincerely,

James Curle

---

[104] Pit XXVI, from the description and date, though this is much more than 100 yards from the preceding pit; Curle 1911a: 123.
[105] Charles Roach Smith (1806–1890), English antiquarian. Pharmacist/chemist by trade. Leading authority on Roman London. His 1854 Catalogue of his collection made him well-known, and his finds eventually formed the nucleus of the national collection of Romano-British antiquities at the BM (Wilson 2002: 133–134; Rhodes 2004).
[106] Richborough, north of Sandwich on the eastern coast and marshes of Kent, with fort and amphitheatre; Roach Smith 1850: 55–56.
[107] Settlement astride Stane Street, the Roman road running south-west from London. The discovery was reported in Diamond 1847; Curle quoted it in the Report (1911a:105).
[108] Nene Valley colour-coated ware (or Castor ware) is a type of Romano-British fineware produced in the lower Nene Valley, Cambridgeshire. See Tyers 1996: 173–175. Curle returned to the topic repeatedly.
[109] Probably Haverfield 1899.
[110] Near Reading. Originally a tribal centre of the Iron Age Atrebates, it became the important town of *Calleva Atrebatum* with city walls and amphitheatre. Target of early excavations by the Society of Antiquaries of London (see Fulford 2021); the innovative botanical work was by Clement Reid, assisted by A.H. Lyell (Fulford 2021: 8–9).

Letter 1.20

12th March, 1906

Dear Mr Smith,[111]

Is there such a thing as black 'Samian'?[112] Since I got back I have found the bottom and enough of the rim to show that the whole formed a shallow saucer like vessel of a ware just like undecorated Samian of a good period but <u>black</u> [Figure 8.6]. It bears the stamp [CINT·VGENI]. CINTVGINVS is found on Samian at Neuss.[113]

I have got a big bowl of CINNAMVS, his mark very nearly complete but the best find is a bronze vessel eleven inches high with a beautiful handle in fair preservation.[114] I noticed one of the foundation walls had sunk so we dug for a pit and 14 feet down we found this vase. It contained nothing but a slight trace of charcoal and iron rust. The pit, however, had a number of pieces of burnt bone in it. At the bottom lay part of a mill stone and an iron hammer or some such article rusted beyond recognition. The vase is something of this shape, not so wide at the mouth as I have it.

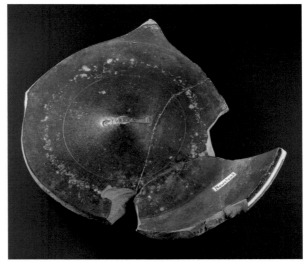

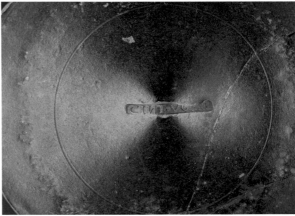

Figure 8.6. Burnt samian (interpreted by Curle as 'black samian') with stamp of Cintuginus. a overall view. b detail of stamp. © National Museums Scotland (X.FRA 1519).

---

[111] This is Curle's first letter in what became a long correspondence with Reginald Smith, who had been appointed to Read's department in 1898 (Wilson 2002: 200). Whether Curle had been directed to Smith by Read or from his correspondence with Haverfield, who also knew Smith, is not clear. The letter ('Since I got back') implies prior acquaintance.

[112] Central Gaulish black-slipped ware, made in the central Gaulish samian production sites in the later second century, is attested (Walsh 2017: 74). However, subsequent scholars have seen this Newstead fragment as a piece of burnt samian of form 31 (Hartley 1972: 21; NOTS 3: 32–33, stamp 3a). Symonds (1992: 10–17) noted that the dark-slipped versions of *sigillata* forms all had a red fabric; Dr. 31 forms are also absent from the types he discussed. Curle returned to the topic repeatedly (Letters 1.21 and 1.23), and published it as 'a platter of Type Drag. 31, but made of a fine black glazed ware. The colour is so uniform that it can hardly be a piece of Terra Sigillata blackened through accidental burning' (Curle 1911a: 230).

[113] Neuss (*Novaesium*), legionary fortress on the Rhine in Nordrhein-Westfalen, opposite Düsseldorf. Neuss is not listed among the examples of CINTVGINVS in Dragendorff's (1896) catalogue of stamps; Curle probably found it in Lehner 1904: 339, where two related stamps are given, one CINTVGNATVS, one CINTVG.

[114] The samian bowl must be the one found in the *praetentura*, as it is the only intact vessel with a stamp of Cinnamus recorded (Curle 1911a: 224, pl. 44; 233–234). The bronze jug came from Pit II (Curle 1911a: 117, 275).

The handle is detached. The arms catching the rim end in birds' heads with long beaks. The whole of the upper part is in perfect preservation. The handle terminates where fixed to the vase with a head, much corroded unfortunately, but it has been very fine, beardless, with large ears and ivy tendrils in the hair. I suppose Bacchus [Figure 8.7].[115] This undoubtedly belongs to the earlier occupation of the camp. Does this help to date it? I shall

be glad of any references. I have got a lot of small things – fibulae, girdle ends etc but the earth here corrodes them badly. A large fibula of the harp-shaped type turned up last week but so rotten I can hardly touch it. I got another of these Late Celtic-looking mountings, something like this.[116] I haven't got the thing before me but you will understand what I mean.

Believe me,

Yours sincerely

James Curle

Figure 8.7. Bronze jug with Bacchic head (detail). © National Museums Scotland (X.FRA 1193).

---

[115] God of wine. See Henig 2012: 162.
[116] Boss-style harness strap junction, from barracks in the *praetentura*. Curle 1911a: 302, pl. 75.3; MacGregor 1976: no. 25.

Letter 1.21

12th April, 1906

My dear Read,

I am sure you will be interested to hear of our Newstead finds. Since I saw you in February we have been very lucky in our exploration of pits.

The first thing we got was a very fine bronze vase. I suppose Italian, end of the first century, eleven inches in height with a beautiful handle.[117]

Then we got a Samian bowl, fairly perfect, with the stamp of CINNAMVS.

Our next find of importance consisted of a man's skull cleft with an axe and beside him two chariot wheels like the one found at Barr Hill[118] but plain and without decoration. The ash felloe[119] made of a single piece, the hubs of elm, the spokes beautifully turned.

However, we have done still better. On Tuesday we took out of a pit a sword, a small Samian bowl, two chisels, an entrenching tool – half pick, half spade – a battered bronze thing which I take to be a helmet. I see graffiti on the crown and can make out the word LVCANI.[120]

Yesterday we got from another pit an iron helmet shaped and modelled like a human head with hair and the face for a visor, much broken, unfortunately [Figure 8.8].[121] A lorica consisting of 2 shoulder pieces, 2 arm pieces, eight circular discs of bronze evidently intended to be fastened to leather as in those figured by Lindenschmidt 'Tracht und bewaffnung' [Figures 8.9, 10.4].[122] A larger disc, perhaps belonging to a shield[123] and a magnificent brass helmet without, so far, the visor.

The helmet is decorated with figures in relief.[124] We also found two horses' bits. The pieces of armour are all the more interesting as I see that most of them have graffiti, probably the owner's name on them.[125] So far I have not managed to make them out, but we shall no doubt do it. I fancy this must be one of the best armour finds ever made in this country and you can appreciate how pleased I am about it.

---

[117] See Letter 1.20 for this and the samian bowl.
[118] Now styled Bar Hill fort, it lies on the Antonine Wall and occupies a superb strategic hilltop location looking north over the Kelvin Valley to the Campsie Fells. For the wheel, see Macdonald and Park 1906: 92–98, fig. 34; Robertson *et al.* 1975: 48–50. The wheel was decorated with an inlaid wavy metal strip around the edge of the hub.
[119] The outer rim of the wheel to which the spokes attached from the central hub. The wheels came from Pit XXIII; see Curle 1911a: 122, 292–293, pl. 69; Manning forthcoming.
[120] Pit XIV. It proved to be a bronze vessel or 'camp kettle', inscribed 'troop of Lucanus'. Curle 1911a: 119, 274, pl. 53.6, fig. 37.2: RIB II, 2: 2415.65. See also Letter 1.24, no. 4.
[121] Pit XXII. This is the famous iron parade helmet. Curle 1911a: 168–170, pl. 26 no. 2, pl. 29; Keppie and Arnold 1984: 19–20, no. 54; Manning 2005.
[122] Here Curle associated two separate elements as components of one set of armour: the inscribed *phalerae* from military medallions (Curle 1911a: pl. 31), and the four 'bronze objects of uncertain use' (as he captions them; Curle 1911a: 177–178, pl. 32). The latter are now recognised as saddle horns (Connolly and van Driel-Murray 1991). See also Letter 1.36 n.197. The reference is to Lindenschmidt 1882: pl. 1, pl. 7.1.
[123] Curle 1911a: 178, pl. 54.5; Henig 2012: 155, fig. 14.3; Bishop 2012a: 171. It is one of two items which are probably *imagines*, discs from a standard bearing the portrait bust of the emperor.
[124] Curle 1911a: 166–168, pls 37–38; Henig 2012: 157–158.
[125] RIB II, 3: 2425.4–5, 2427.4–12, 2427.21–24.

Figure 8.8. The iron helmet and mask from Newstead.
© National Museums Scotland (X.FRA 121).

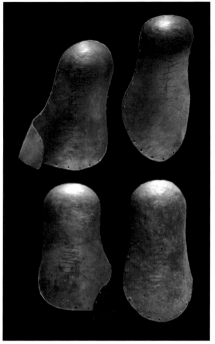

Figure 8.9. The set of saddle horns from Pit
XXII, interpreted by Curle as parts of armour.
© National Museums Scotland (X.FRA 130).

Will you tell Mr Smith[126] about this and tell him that I see from the Corpus that there is a piece of Samian in the BM, mentioned by Roach Smith, Roman London, with the stamp CINTVGENI and I should like very much to know on what sort of vessel it is.[127]

My black piece has never been any other colour. It has not been burnt by chance and it would be interesting to find the same stamp on both black and red ware.[128]

Believe me

Yours very truly

James Curle

---

[126] R.A. Smith of the BM; see *Dramatis personae*.
[127] CIL vii, 1336.314; Roach Smith 1859, 103; Walters 1908: 336, M1951.
[128] See Letter 1.20 n.112.

Letter 1.22

To J. Curle Esq, Jr   *The British Museum,*
Priorwood, Melrose. N.B   *London W C*

April 18th, 1906

Dear Mr Curle,

I must congratulate you on the interesting and important discoveries of Roman armour and hope to see photographs of them in due course.

With regard to the Gaulish pottery, I find that CINTVAGENI occurs more than once at Cirencester;[129] you will find it in the list in Church's Guide to Corinium Museum, 9th edition, 1905[130] but as the vessels were not decorated the name does not occur in Déchelette;[131] but I have no doubt that they are all from Lezoux.[132]

The outline of the Roach-Smith specimen on which the name occurs as CINTVGENI is this [omitted in the BM copy].

I am sure that Dr George Macdonald[133] will be pleased to hear about the find of chariot wheels, and I suppose there will be no objection to regarding them as British, and belonging to the period of Roman invasion. Further, I shall be glad to have an outline of the sword found with the bowl and chisels, as a fine bone hilt has recently been found at Dorchester.[134]

With all good wishes

I am

Yours very truly

Reginald A Smith

Letter 1.23

20th April, 1906

Dear Mr Smith,

Many thanks for your letter. My CINTVGINVS pot is apparently just the same as yours. So we have an example of the same potter making both red and black ware.[135]

I had another great haul yesterday – about 70 pieces of iron from a pit, quite uncorroded:-[136]

---

[129] Cirencester (*Corinium*), *civitas* capital of the *Dobunni* in Gloucestershire.
[130] Church 1905: 27.
[131] Déchelette 1904.
[132] Central Gaulish samian production site.
[133] See *Dramatis personae*. Macdonald published a similar wheel from Bar Hill (see Letter 1.21, with references).
[134] Miks 2007: 566, pl. 160, no. A133.
[135] Curle's sherd has been seen as burnt samian by subsequent scholars; see notes to Letter 1.20.
[136] Pit XVI. Curle 1911a: 119–120.

1 sword 5 spears 4 scythes 2 pairs of smith's tongs 4 picks 1 axe several hammers; 1 small anvil; chisels, gouges, wedges; mountings of wheel hubs; and a quantity of other things I can't quite make out. If we go on at the present rate our collection will be very big.

The sword is about 2 feet long, the tang 5 inches. The mounting of the handle in this, as in the previous find, is quite gone. I shall hope to send you some photographs one of these days.

Believe me,

Yours very truly,

James Curle

I should be grateful if you can give me any references to helmets. I know the Torsberg[137] and Cannstadt[138] finds and the one in Vetusta Monumenta.[139] Also to these Phalerae-like discs and to the shoulder pieces of armour.[140]

JC

Letter 1.24

25th April, 1906

My dear Read,

Many thanks for your letter. We have really been most lucky at Newstead. I hope to add very considerably to our collection before we are done.

I want to ask your opinion about these helmets we have found. No. 1 is a headpiece of brass [Figure 8.10].[141] It resembles closely a specimen found in Roumania and now in Vienna.[142] (There is a small bad picture of it in the Mitteilungen aus Heddernheim.)[143] Most of it is quite bright and I have cleaned the dirt of [*sic*] it with a little lemon juice which I suppose can't do any harm. The back part is covered with a black incrustation which won't wash off and I won't try stronger methods. There are two winged figures embossed on it. One drives a chariot

---

[137] T(h)orsberg (Schleswig-Holstein) on the North German moors, a major bog offering; see Engelhardt 1863; Matešić 2015: 187–207, pls 100–103.

[138] It is not entirely clear what find Curle means here. The face mask from Stuttgart-Bad Cannstatt (Baden-Württemberg) was only found in 1909 and not published until 1962 (Klumbach 1962; Garbsch 1978: 66, O20); it is not in Curle's list of comparanda. Assuming it was a find in the Württemberg region around Stuttgart, from entries in his listing (Curle 1911a: 179–180, I.1, II.7, III.7) he may have meant the bronze helmet and visor mask from Bettenberge, the bronze mask from Gräfenhausen or the iron mask from 'Wurtemberg'. He gave no source for the latter, though it was published by Lindenschmidt (1900: pl. 8.3), a volume Curle referenced; it comes from Ruit (Baden-Württemberg; Garbsch 1978: 69, O34). The Bettenberge provenance has been corrected to Pfrondorf (Garbsch 1978: 71, O48; O46 for Gräfenhausen).

[139] The reference is to the Ribchester (Lancashire) helmet, published by Townley (1815). See Robinson 1975: 110, 112, figs 133–134, pls 310–313; Garbsch 1978: 58.

[140] A *phalera* was a sculpted disc, gold, silver or bronze, worn on the breastplate during parades by Roman soldiers who had been awarded it as a decoration e.g. for distinguished conduct in action. The reference is to the medallion backing plates and saddle horns from Pit XXII; see Letter 1.21, with references.

[141] Curle 1911a: 166–168; Keppie and Arnold 1984: 20, no. 56.

[142] Curle 1911a: 168, 180, II.4. The resemblance is in the inscription, as this is a face-mask more similar to the Newstead bronze mask. Found in the river Olt near Resca, Romania; Garbsch 1978: 69–70, O40, pl. 24.

[143] Donner-von Richter 1894: 41, fig. 42.

with a couple of griffins or tigers; the other seems to float in the air. I can't so far explain them. The art is not very high and the thing has to me a rather oriental feeling.

No. 2 is very frail and badly broken [Figure 8.8].[144] The metal is iron with a collar of bronze round the neck. We have the most of the headpiece which is moulded to represent hairs and has one or two loops on top as if to hold a crest. The mask is broken in two pieces vertically down the side of the nose. A small portion, including one side of the mouth, is awanting. The whole thing is strongly modelled. My own inclination would be to put the whole things [sic] in the hands of a competent restorer and have it put together as far as possible. Do you agree as to this, and, if so, who would you employ? Of course I don't know what line they may take in Edinburgh, but I should much like to have your opinion.

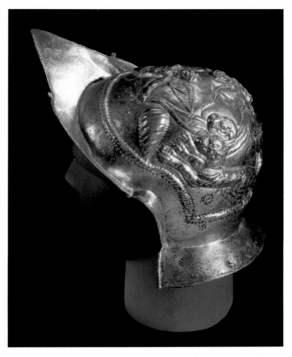

Figure 8.10. The brass parade helmet from Newstead.
© National Museums Scotland (X.FRA 125).

No. 3. is also of iron. It has had some silver mounting on the collar. It is too much broken to do anything.[145]

No. 4. is the battered bronze thing you suggest might be a shield boss. I don't think it is that. It might after all be a cooking pot. It appears to be a round hemispherical or slightly domed object flattened on the top which is fixed to the sides by rivets. On this flat part the owner has twice scratched his name LVCANI.[146] This seems against the pot theory. The edges of the object are turned over to make a rim and there are two loops, also of bronze, projecting from the rim. I suppose the proper course with this thing would be to have it hammered into shape? and then one could arrive at some conclusion about it.

Since we found the helmets we have got a great many iron tools. Many seem to belong to smiths or wheelwrights. Four of the axes[147] are peculiar – something like this – I can't quite make them out.

144 Curle 1911a: 168–170, pl. 29; Keppie and Arnold 1984: 19–20, no. 54; Manning 2005.
145 A battle helmet, with traces of ornate decoration. Curle 1911a: 164, pl. 26 no. 1.
146 Inscribed 'troop of Lucanus'. Curle 1911a: 119, 274, pl. 53.6, fig. 37.2: RIB II, 2: 2415.65. See also Letter 1.21.
147 *Dolabra*, a versatile axe which could serve as a pickaxe for miners and excavators, as an entrenching tool and for the religious slaughtering of animals. Curle 1911a: 278–279, pl. 57.2–5.

Do you know of any examples in England or elsewhere of the shoulder and arm pieces of bronze and of the round discs, which must have formed a sort of breastplate.[148] I know there are phalerae in Berlin[149] but our discs are not in any way decorated. Please excuse my inflicting such a long letter upon you.

Believe me,

Yours sincerely,

James Curle

Letter 1.25

30th April, 1906

Dear Mr Smith

Where can I find particulars of the Chassenard[150] find mentioned in your Iron Age catalogue? You quote Déchelette as your source of information.[151] I tried writing to him on pottery. My first attempt was successful as he answered the letter twice in the same terms in a fortnight. Since then he maintains an obstinate silence.

Nothing very important since I wrote last but we are cleaning out a pit which I hope may have something in it.

Yours sincerely,

James Curle

Letter 1.26

To J. Curle, Esq   *The British Museum, London*
Priorwood, Melrose. N.B.   *May 2nd 1906*

Dear Mr Curle,

In reply to your letter of this morning, Déchelette's paper on Chassenard will be found in the 'Revue Archaeologique' 1903, part 1, p235.

I have had in mind your inquiry as to helmets, and have been waiting for the return from the binders. The most recent article I know of is in the 30th volume of the 'Jahrbuch' of the German Archaeological Institute,[152] but I am not sure how late they come down. Anything else that turns up I will let you know of promptly.

---

[148] See Letters 1.21 and 1.23 for the context.
[149] From Lauersfort, near Krefeld (Nordrhein-Westfalen); Maxfield 1981, 94–95, pl. 15.
[150] Chassenard (Allier, France): rich burial with (*inter alia*) an iron face mask. Déchelette 1903; Smith 1905: 132–134; see now Beck and Chew 1991.
[151] Déchelette 1903. See *Dramatis personae*.
[152] In fact, volume 20; Schröder 1905.

Déchelette's silence is by no means extraordinary: we have all suffered in the same way: but he means well.

Yours sincerely,

Reginald A Smith

Letter 1.27

13th May, 1906

Dear Mr Smith,

Thanks for your letter of the 2nd. I foresee that you will probably find me somewhat of a nuisance before I have done with Newstead.

I got the Jahrbuch[153] which figures a lot of helmets not included in Benndorf[154] or the Heddernheim book.[155] Two of them especially interest me Ant Fr 1022 and L.86 on page 21.[156] The latter, found in the Jordan, appears to me to be very much the same class as our brass helm.

This is a very rough sketch. In the front is a winged figure floating in the air and round the back is a representation of a chariot driven by a winged figure to which is harnessed a pair of griffins?

The art is not of the highest type. The nearest thing I have seen is the Nikopolis[157] helm in Vienna, but this Jordan piece must also resemble it. Who is Bruno Schröder who writes this article and how could I get a photograph of the helmet? I see he dates it at the end of the second century, while Benndorf and the Heddernheim man put the type in the third century. I expect the second century is the proper time.

The pit in which we found it contained a number of pieces of a bowl of Samian, three and a half inches high, six and a half inches in diameter with small medallions with cupids, the alternate panels being this sort of thing.[158]

---

[153] Schröder 1905. W.B. Schröder (1878–1934) was at the time in the Antikenmuseum in Berlin; he subsequently became director of the sculpture collection in Dresden.
[154] Benndorf 1878.
[155] Donner-von Richter 1894.
[156] Ant. Fr. 1022 is a helmet in the Berlin Antiquarium collection catalogued by Carl Friedrich in 1871, hence Fr. 1022 (Pflug 1988: 8; Bottini *et al.* 1988: 537–538); it is from Antinoupolis (Sheik 'Ibada) in Egypt. L.86 is from the Lipperheide collection. It was published more fully in Bottini *et al.* 1988: 534–536, where the provenance is simply given as 'allegedly from Jordan'.
[157] Nikyup (*Nikopolis ad Istrum*), Bulgaria; Garbsch 1978: 65, O16, pl. 19.
[158] Pit XXII; Curle 1911a: 121–122. For this pot, see Curle 1911a: 210 no. 31, pl. 43.1

The paste is fine and hard and I should think early second century. If I thought Déchelette would answer I would try another letter on the subject.[159]

Is Mr Read at home?

Believe me

Yours sincerely

James Curle

Letter 1.28

To J. Curle, Esq,
Priorwood. Melrose. NB

The British Museum, London
June 8th, 1906

My dear Curle,

I am sorry I have not been able to answer your letter before. Your discoveries at Newstead are really quite marvellous, and will open up a new chapter in the Archaeology of Britain.

I really should not try to clean the metal objects too much; if they are left alone, the cleaning can always be done later, but a drastic treatment may destroy some indication that afterwards would have been better preserved; but to whom you should entrust them for putting straight, I am puzzled to say. It is practically useless to send anything to Ready,[160] who seems to have more private work than he can accomplish, and I really know nobody in London, or in this country, who is to be trusted.

---

[159] See Letters 1.25 and 1.26. BM pencil annotations: 'Lezoux about 70 AD / Leadenhall St. 37 bowl.'
[160] One of the sons of Robert Cooper Ready (1811–1901), a modeler and sealmaker, who was hired by the British Museum in 1859 as a specialist restorer. His sons Augustus, Charles, and William Talbot continued after him with the British Museum (Oddy 1993: 11; Wilson 2002: 357 n.128), though the last (1857–1914) left in 1884 when he became a dealer and took over the auction company of Rollin and Feuardent. It seems from Read's comment that the Ready referred to did private work as well as working for the BM. For the original query see Letter 1.21.

The domed object[161] will require very careful treatment if it is hammered out – to do this with safety the metal must be heated, and probably re-heated, many times.

For your iron tools, the best book to consult is that on the Saalburg[162] at Homburg, by Jacobi: there are also some from Silchester,[163] but these are of less importance.

Yours very truly,

C.H. Read

Letter 1.29

9th June, 1906

My dear Read,

Many thanks for your letter.

I send you a few photographs of Newstead things which please show to Mr Smith. I would be grateful if you can give me any indication of parallel finds of armour. I wrote about them some time ago to Lord Dillon[164] but have had no reply. I believe he is learned in such things. Do you know of any set of phalerae except those found at Lauersfort?[165]

Yours very sincerely,

James Curle

Letter 1.30

23rd June, 1906

My dear Read,

I have a message from Dr Macdonald[166] that you might help me with one or two letters of introduction when I go to Germany. I propose to leave here on the 7th and to go to Homburg.[167] I am going to take my Brother[168] with me. He has just had the misfortune to lose his wife and wants a change. We should settle down there for about three weeks and drink waters. I shall study the Saalburg things and we shall be able to visit Mainz and Frankfort [*sic*]. On the way

---

[161] The copper-alloy camp kettle. See Letter 1.24, no. 4, and n. 146.
[162] A Roman fort on the main ridge of the Taunus Mountains near Frankfurt; Jacobi 1897.
[163] Fulford 2021.
[164] Harold Arthur Lee-Dillon, CH FBA (1844–1932), an authority on the history of arms and armour; at this point he was curator of the Royal Armouries (ffoulkes and Blair 2004).
[165] Lauersfort, Moers, Nordrhein-Westfalen; site of discovery in 1858 of an ensemble of silvered relief *phalerae* from Roman military decorations; Maxfield 1981: 94–95, pl. 15.
[166] George Macdonald; see *Dramatis personae*.
[167] Bad Homburg, a spa conveniently close to the Saalburg fort, has a 200-year tradition of healing and healthcare, associated with its mineral springs and medicinal clay treatments.
[168] Alexander Ormiston Curle (1886–1955), youngest of the three brothers. See *Dramatis personae*.

home I should like to see the Museums at Trèves[169] and Namur. I should like to go to Berlin but I fear I can't manage it just now. I fancy the Museums I have mentioned will give one a good idea of Roman German [*sic*] things. What about Bonn?

I should be very glad if you could help me. I am prepared to speak French but I am not strong in German so I should be a nuisance to anyone who only has German. I am particularly anxious to see their pottery and to get any help I can about our armour finds.

I hope you were interested in the photos I sent you. I wish I could find what the circular embossed plate was used for.[170] We are working away but have had no luck for some weeks.

Believe me,

Yours very sincerely,

James Curle

Letter 1.31

29th June, 1906

My dear Read,

I am very much indebted to you for sending me so many letters of introduction. I hope I shall be able to use them. If the cure at Homburg[171] is not too exacting I should manage to pay several visits to Mainz, which, as you say, is the best of them.[172]

I shall hope on the way home to report myself at the BM and perhaps see you if you are not off for a holiday.

I hope you got the photographs all right. We are working away improving our plans but there are no more finds of importance.

The Scottish Historical Review for July has reproduced the brass helmet in a note that I wrote about the finds.[173] I shall send you a copy later. Again thanking you.

Believe me,

Yours very truly,

James Curle

---

[169] Trier.

[170] Curle 1911a: 178, pl. 54.5, from Pit XXII; Henig 2012, 155, fig. 14.3. Probably to hold an *imago* of the emperor on a standard.

[171] See previous letter.

[172] Read has clearly offered advice to Curle on the museums mentioned in his previous letter. The Römisch-Germanisches Zentralmuseum in Mainz had a wide-ranging collection of originals and high-quality copies (e.g. Panke-Schneider 2009); Mainz also hosted a fine Landesmuseum.

[173] Curle 1906.

Letter 1.32

10th November, 1906

Dear Mr Smith,

I have only found one piece that I think must be black Samian.[174] It is the whole of the bottom and part of one side of one of those flat saucer-shaped patterns Type D 31.[175] It bears the stamp CINT.VGINVS. You have a piece of the same form with the same stamp in red ware from London.[176] Of course I know that many of the black fragments one finds have simply been burnt, but in this piece the black is on the whole so uniform not only on the surface but in the break that I think the colour is not the result of any accident. Dr Macdonald,[177] who examined this piece lately, came to the same conclusion. From the depth at which we found it I think the piece must be second century. I doubt if we have any third century remains.

I lately cleared out a part of the early ditch which surrounded the fort, which was filled up by the rampart of the 2nd occupation being put over it and I got fragments of a number of vessels which we can definitely, I think, ascribe to the 1st century. In the ditch we found two fragments of what I take to be pottery covered with a brilliant lavender-blue glaze, very smooth, and even the back of the fragments is of a whitish colour and rather rough.[178] I know 1st century yellow and green glazes in Germany but I have seen nothing like this. Do you know it?

I wish I could get some information about Castor vases.[179] I should like to know whether they occur earlier in Germany than in this country. I suspect they come from Germany to begin with.

Can you refer me to any British excavation where the finds are not earlier than the end of the 2nd or beginning of the third century. On the Rhine, places like Haltern and Hofheim help to break up the period but we have a lot to do here in dating our finds.[180]

We are still digging away at Newstead, always finding small things but of late not much of importance. At present, as far as the wet weather will permit, we are working at the Bath Building. I haven't begun the report, which, I fear, will be a serious matter.

Believe me,

Yours very truly,

James Curle

---

[174] Curle was eager to gather evidence for this pottery type, and returned to the topic repeatedly (Letters 1.20–1.23) In the publication he described it as 'a fine black glazed ware' and reaffirmed he did not consider its colour was due to burning (Curle 1911a: 230), but other scholars have taken it as burnt samian, notably in Hartley's classic study of samian ware from Scotland (Hartley 1972: 21). See notes to Letter 1.20.

[175] Typology following Dragendorff 1895.

[176] See Letter 1.21. Walters 1908: 336 no. M1951, with earlier references.

[177] See *Dramatis personae*.

[178] Curle 1911a: 230. These sherds do not appear to have attracted more recent study.

[179] Decorated coloured-coated ware from the Nene Valley near Peterborough (e.g. Tyers 1996: 173–175). It was a topic Curle devoted attention to in various letters and the final publication (Curle 1911a: 254–256).

[180] Haltern fortress (Nordrhein-Westfalen) was Augustan; Hofheim (Hessen) dated to c. AD 40–60. Curle (1911a: 190–191) discussed both in his overview of dating. The letter illustrates his early concern with clarifying chronology and the value of well-dated assemblages.

Letter 1.33

27 January, 1907

Dear Mr Smith,

I enclose a list of potters' marks from Newstead [not preserved]. It is not complete as there are some I can't so far make out.

You know the early barbotine decorated pots on the Rhine with this sort of thing

The decorative part of the bowl is defined by these rows of dots. Does this occur in England? In Germany this sort of thing goes back to the beginning of the first century and it is, of course, the beginning of the decoration one sees in the vases with hunting scenes which we find at Castor and which I believe originated on the Rhine.[181]

We had another good find on Thursday – a second set of armour pieces all of bronze.[182] They must have been covered with leather and part of it remains on the edges. There were also these circular phalerae?[183] Thin plates of metal, perhaps silver-embossed in a palmette design with a backing of brass, to which are attached studs of bronze. There were also three plates of brass and a number of bronze and brass studs varying in size, which must have been fastened on leather. We found a couple of pits some distance from the fort and I hope there may be more. What a lot of similar pits there must be for someone to find along the walls.[184]

Believe me,

Yours sincerely,

James Curle

How is Ready[185] progressing with my pot?

---

[181] A coda to the discussion of the origins of Castor ware in Letter 1.32.

[182] In fact the horn stiffeners from a saddle, though not identified as such at the time, from Pit XXVII (Curle 1911a: 177–178, pl. 32 lower). See Letter 1.21 for the earlier find.

[183] Described in his report as mountings which 'must have belonged to the belt of some soldier of rank' (Curle 1911a: 162–163, pl. 25). They are in fact cavalry harness fittings (Bishop 2012a: 170).

[184] Curle meant Hadrian's Wall and the Antonine Wall, not the walls of Newstead.

[185] One of a family of restorers who worked for the British Museum, and seemingly also undertook private work; see Letters 1.28, 1.35, 1.39. 1.40.

Letter 1.34

5th February, 1907

Dear Mr Smith,

Many thanks for your letter. I think I am on the right lines about these Castor vases. I must endeavour to see what they have at Peterborough and Northampton.[186] I am not sure that a name enables you to say in every case to what pottery the piece belongs. Avitus is possibly Graufesenque, but if I remember rightly, there are a number of pieces bearing the same name at Rheinzabern.[187] Mr Walters,[188] from the occurrence of the name in Germany, considered PROBVS as belonging to that country but I am pretty sure you will find him at either Graufesenque or Lezoux.[189] I am writing away from my books.

I have come to the conclusion that the circular pieces which I called phalerae in my last letter are really the mountings of a belt.[190] We washed out of the bottom deposit about 100 small studs for leather and we found what appears to have been the clasp of the belt. This piece of brass was fixed by small studs to leather. So were the circular pieces but one of them in addition to the studs has a tang like this fixed on the back near the edge of the circle and I have no doubt it was intended to fix into the plate above. We are having very cold weather and have cleared out three pits without any result, which is disappointing.[191]

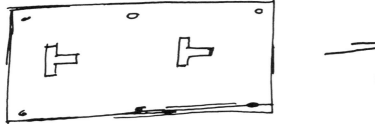 

Believe me,

Yours very sincerely,

James Curle

---

[186] Implying Curle intended to visit museums in the area where this pottery was made. He discussed Castor ware frequently in letters and at some length in the report (Curle 1911a: 254–256). See Letters 1.32 and 1.33 for the origins of this discussion.

[187] Curle (1911a: 226-242) discussed samian stamps in detail in the Report; La Graufesenque was the main production site for southern Gaulish samian, Rheinzabern for east Gaulish. He listed five instances of Avitus and suggested that two different potters were represented (Curle 1911a: 231–232), a point on which later scholars agree (Hartley 1972: 20); eight different potters using variants of such a stamp are recorded (NOTS 1: 372–384).

[188] This is presumably from correspondence with H.B. Walters (1867–1944) of the BM, although no letters survive. The name does not occur in his study of pottery in the British Museum (Walters 1908), which must have been in active preparation at this time.

[189] Three potters (or groups of potters) stamped their wares as Probus, in the mid-first century at Montans and probably La Graufesenque, and in the late Antonine period in eastern Gaul (NOTS 7: 268–271). The Newstead stamp is die 2a.

[190] From Pit XXVII; see Letter 1.33.

[191] Pits XXIX–XXXIII, excavated in late January and February, are recorded as having no finds; Curle 1911a: 123–124.

Letter 1.35

28th February, 1907

Dear Mr Smith,

The small Samian pot arrived safely last week. Mr Ready[192] has done it beautifully. Will you kindly ask him to let me know how much I owe him for it.

We are not finding very much at Newstead – we have drawn eight pits blank – which is rather disappointing.[193] I have got a few more potters' marks and coins but nothing good. Do you think it would be worth going to Vienna to see the Roman things there? I suppose they must have a lot of interesting things. I don't quite know where the Carnuntum[194] finds are preserved.

Do you know of any good monuments of Roman soldiers in England showing dress etc other than those figured by Bruce[195] and the stone to M. Favonius[196] at Colchester?

Believe me,

Yours sincerely,

James Curle

Letter 1.36

11th May, 1907

My dear Read,

Now that the meeting is over I am anxious to know how the Society of Antiquaries in its combined wisdom interprets my Newstead finds.[197] I hope someone was able to throw light on them. You might also send them back as soon as convenient.

---

[192] See notes to Letter 1.33.

[193] Pits XXIX–XXXIII are recorded as having no finds, while pits XXXIV–XXXVI were quite sparse; Curle 1911a: 123–124.

[194] Roman legionary fortress at Bad Deutsch-Altenburg, 32 km east of Vienna, in lower Austria (Bishop 2012b: 51–52). Curle used finds from *Carnuntum* as parallels for his armour discoveries (von Groller 1901).

[195] Rev. John Collingwood Bruce FSA (1805–1892), a schoolmaster in Newcastle, was the early interpreter of Hadrian's Wall on which he led the first 'Pilgrimage' in 1849. His 1851 book became a standard for its study and in 1863 there followed a 'Wallet book' for pilgrims wishing to explore the Wall on foot. A 'Pilgrimage' of renewed study along the Wall every ten years continues to this day (Breeze 2020). Curle was referring to his *Lapidarium Septentrionale* (1885)

[196] Centurion of Legio XX whose tombstone (AD 43–50) was found at Colchester and is in that museum; RIB I: 200; Huskinson 1994: 23, no. 47.

[197] Curle exhibited 'a number of Roman military ornaments' to the Society of Antiquaries of London on 2 May 1907; he had clearly sent them to Read, who introduced them at the meeting and offered comments (*Proceedings of the Society of Antiquaries of London* [2nd series] 21 [1905–1907]: 469–471). The items consisted of four saddle-strengtheners from Pit XXII (Curle 1911a: 177–178, pl. 32) and two large harness discs and some studs from Pit XXVII (Curle 1911a: pl. 25). See Letter 1.21 for the discovery, where Curle referred to the strengtheners as shoulder and arm pieces from armour. This was the interpretation he conveyed at the meeting, but the published proceedings show that Read raised concerns and wondered, perceptively, 'Is it conceivable that these bronze mounts belong rather to the saddle or to the yoke than that they served as defensive armour'. It was to be another 80 years before this was confirmed; see Connolly and van Driel-Murray 1991.

[BM handwritten note by C.H. Read at top of letter '11/5 Curle, Jas. Have written to send things back regd']

I have found a few things since I returned[198] but nothing of real importance. A very good specimen of a Knee fibula[199] which the Germans put down at 200 AD or later – I suppose the same must apply here, and an early (Graufesenque) dish or rather half of one from the old ditch.[200] No more pits in the meantime. I think we shall find some more in the autumn.

Believe me

Yours sincerely,

James Curle

Letter 1.37

The British Museum
London WC

May 17th, 1907

Dear Mr Curle,

At the Antiquaries[201] last night I was presented with the enclosed piece of pottery which, as you see, has on the lower part the lattice pattern commonly found on Early Roman work.[202]

What struck me as curious about it was the formation of the lip; and, as it comes from Newstead, I thought it as well to return it to the rightful owner, as it would be useless down here.

Believe me,

Yours sincerely,

Reginald A Smith

---

[198] It is unclear where Curle had been travelling.
[199] The type was discussed and illustrated in Curle 1911a: 325–326, pl. 87, nos 28–33. This specimen is probably no. 33, as Curle specifies it as 'of the type known as a "knee fibula"'; it was found in the *retentura* 'above the filled-up ditch of the early fort', and the rest of the sentence indicates this was where he was digging at the time of the letter.
[200] The ditch of one of the Flavian forts. La Graufesenque was the main samian production area in south-western Gaul in the later first century.
[201] Society of Antiquaries of London.
[202] Suggesting it was a piece of Black-burnished ware or a copy thereof. All the examples illustrated in the Report are provenanced, suggesting Curle did not find it particularly 'curious'.

Letter 1.38

20th May, 1907

Dear Mr Smith,

You are very honest and I am much obliged for the trouble you have taken in returning this Newstead fragment. I wonder if much of real value has been carried to the South![203]

Oldland[204] sent me a photo of that Lincoln pot which must be first century. It impresses one with the feeling that it is meant to represent a leaf pattern.[205] I feel sure that on the fragments I have here a leaf has been used in some way in doing the decoration. Can this be the beginning of Castor ware, which, in England at least, is, I believe 2nd century?[206]

Newstead is going on capitally. We have for a long time suspected four periods of occupation but could not get satisfactory proof till last week we stumbled on a wall[207] with the foundations of gate towers run right across the fort, cutting the size down to about ten acres. This must have been done at the beginning of the third occupation and explains various changes which puzzled us.

I got a very good specimen of a knee fibula the other day in very good presentation.[208] Does this suggest any thing to you? It is the upper part of a fibula very much corroded – bronze – the pin evidently worked on a hinge. I want to identify it as I found it in a drain belonging to the fourth occupation.[209]

Believe me

Yours sincerely,

James Curle

---

[203] Newstead fragments occur in a number of private collections around this time, for instance that of James Roberts (now in Perth Museum; Hoffmann in prep.) and Drs R. and W. McD. Selby of Port William (now in Stranraer Museum; Murray 2005: 155, 163). Letter 5.7 shows that Curle knew the younger Selby; this letter suggests that he was aware other fragments were leaving the site without his involvement.

[204] Clerk in the BM department who features regularly in the Letters; see *Dramatis personae*.

[205] None of the vessels from Lincoln in the BM published by Walters (1908) are a close match from their published descriptions. The most likely candidate is Walters 1908: 393, M2447. This is a Rhenish ware jar with white painted decoration showing a scroll pattern with berries.

[206] Castor ware occurs frequently in the correspondence (e.g. Letters 1.32–1.34), and was clearly a topic of considerable interest to Curle: see Curle 1911a: 254–256.

[207] The Reducing Wall (Curle 1911a: 82–84) 'erected in order to reduce the size of the fort' by about one third during the Antonine period.

[208] Probably the same brooch referred to in Letter 1.36.

[209] NMS X.FRA 798, a plain headstud brooch fragment with crest on the bow. See Elliot and Hunter 2012: 204.

Letter 1.39

14th June, 1907

Dear Mr Smith,

I told you of my digging in the early ditch in Newstead. I think the pottery from it is all or almost all Graufesenque.[210] I am now digging out a later ditch. The quantity of pottery is not large but it is perfectly distinct from the early ditch. This ditch cuts in two the large bath (?) building of the West Annexe [Figure 10.5].[211] The reduction in size of the building probably corresponds with the reduction in size of the fort which we have found was effected at the third occupation. I want to arrive at some idea as to the period at which this reduction took place. It ought, I think, to be of the Antonine period. From the ditch have come some four pieces of decorated bowls; all belong to the period of large medallions.[212] One piece has a figure of Venus which is used by Cinnamus – an Antonine potter. Another has a design – probably erotic, which is to be found on a bowl from Camelon illustrated in Proc. Soc. Antiq. Vol XXXV p384 fig.13.[213] This bowl has the stamp DIVIX.F. In addition to the erotic design there is a sea monster which also occurs on my piece from the ditch. The piece I have found is probably by the same potter.

In another part of the fort I found, not very far down, a bowl with medallions bearing the same erotic design.[214] About the same level was found a bowl by CINNAMVS (mid 2nd century). At Birrens,[215] where, by the way, there is no early pottery, I find a fragment of a bowl bearing three of the designs associated with the erotic one and which probably came from the same potter as the bowl we found here. I believe Birrens is not earlier than the Antonine D (pottery) period,[216] but here I have a difficulty with Déchelette. He states that in his second period of Lezoux – 75 to 110 AD – DIVIXTVS (late 1st century) is one of the principal potters.[217] He cites the Camelon bowl as one of his products, notwithstanding that the medallions belong, not to the second but the third period of Lezoux. Of the seven pieces by Divixtus cited by Déchelette, most are in England – one of them is in the BM. Will you oblige me by having a look at it and tell me how it strikes you as to date. If Déchelette is right in putting such medallion bowls as early as 110 AD then the great bulk of our pottery belongs to that period, which I don't believe. It is not typically early.[218]

---

[210] Southern Gaul; late first century.

[211] Curle 1911a: 92–102.

[212] See Curle 1911a: 218–219, nos 67–70.

[213] Fort just north of the Antonine Wall, north of Falkirk, dug by the Society of Antiquaries of Scotland in 1900; Christison *et al.* 1901, 384, fig. 13.

[214] Not illustrated in Curle 1911. The Cinnamus bowl is likely to be Curle 1911a: 224, no. 87, pl. XLIV, found in the *praetentura*.

[215] Fort near Ecclefechan in Dumfriesshire, dug by the Society of Antiquaries of Scotland in 1895; see Christison *et al.* 1896.

[216] Meaning obscure.

[217] Déchelette 1904: vol. I, 165, 182, 269.

[218] The stamps at both Camelon and Newstead are those of Divixtus i, die 9d, AD 145–175 (NOTS 3: 284–287).

Mr Ready still has my saucer.[219] Will you be so kind as to hurry him up with it.

I should like to have it back.

Believe me

Yours sincerely,

James Curle

PS I see you have a bowl 30.4 a fragment

I wonder if the 30 is a very coarse specimen I suggested as being late.[220] JC

Letter 1.40

22nd June, 1907

Dear Mr Smith,

Many thanks for your letter. Ready has returned my saucer, very nicely done.[221]

I think there must have been two DIVIXTI. The man at Camelon is of the same period as CINNAMVS and is certainly not of the second period of Lezoux, ending 110 AD.[222] If you come across Déchelette[223] in France I wish you would put this to him. The point is very important for me.

If Cinnamus belongs to the end of the figured vases at Lezoux we ought to find some later types of Samian at Newstead. Cinnamus made medallion vases, décor libre, décor à grand niveau.[224] At Newstead we have four distinct occupations. I believe one is Antonine; one must, I think, be post-Antonine; but as far as I can see, we have no period in which decorated Samian is not found. I expect it goes on well towards the end of the second century. As regards other pottery, I feel sure that these black flat cooking vessels are second century.[225] They may also have existed in the first century – it is quite possible – but they are common here in association with other types.

---

[219] Restorer who worked for the British Museum as well as undertaking private work. He had previously restored another vessel for Curle; see Letter 1.33.
[220] This addendum suggests Curle initially overlooked that Déchelette (1904: vol. I, 269, nos 2–3) noted two fragments with a DIVIXTUS stamp in the BM, one a form 37 like Curle's, one a form 30 which he refers to here. In fact there were three in the collection at this time, one omitted by Déchelette; two such stamps on form 37s from London (Walters 1908: 220, nos 1153–1154) and one on a form 30 from Castor, Northamptonshire (Walters 1908: 199, M1038).
[221] See previous Letter.
[222] Continuing a discussion from Letter 1.39; see notes there.
[223] See *Dramatis personae*.
[224] Freestyle decoration, large-scale decoration.
[225] Black-burnished ware, which is indeed an overwhelmingly Antonine phenomenon in Scotland.

We found a nice intaglio this week,[226] but there isn't much turning up. I have set down my theories on the number of occupations for the Scot. Hist. Review,[227] which I shall send you when it is printed. I hope you will enjoy your time in France.

Yours sincerely,

James Curle

Letter 1.41

9th August, 1907

Dear Mr Smith,

I enclose a sketch of a bit of Samian ware[228] which I think belongs to a vase by CINNAMVS which I have seen somewhere. Can you identify it? Have you any date points about this potter beyond the fact that he is Antonine? It is important in the dating of some of the Newstead alterations to know where he comes. I wrote to you when you were in France about DIVIXTVS.[229] Did you find that Déchelette is certain that the medallion fragments from Camelon[230] are by the same man as the maker of your bowl 30?[231]

I am going to give the Rhind lectures[232] in Edinburgh in Spring and one of them must be devoted to pots. Newstead continues to supply material. Here are the contents of the Bath waterhole cleaned out this week:-[233]

---

[226] Curle found two intaglios (1911a: 333, pl. 87 nos 35–36; Henig 2007: 95 no. 30, 152 no. 473). Both are referred to in his correspondence (see Letter 3.11 for the other, from 1905); his publication gives no findspots, but a report in *The Scotsman* (28 October 1905: 9) reveals the Ganymede intaglio was found in 1905, so Curle is referring here to the Sol intaglio. This is confirmed by Letter 2.4, to Cecil Smith in the Department of Greek and Roman Antiquities, where he asks him to identify this gem and includes an impression of it.

[227] Curle 1907a.

[228] Not surviving.

[229] Letter 1.40.

[230] See Letters 1.39–1.40.

[231] Dragendorff form 30. Subsequently published as Walters 1908: 199, M1038.

[232] A prestigious annual series of lectures given by a respected scholar on their chosen topic at the invitation of the Society of Antiquaries of Scotland, funded by the estate of Alexander Henry Rhind of Sibster, Caithness, and initiated in 1874. The structure of Curle's lectures shaped the content of his book (Curle 1911a: viii); see pp 33–34.

[233] Pit LVII; Curle 1911a: 128–129, with references to individual items therein.

A human skull

A rusted sword doubled up, but with its bone handle preserved

Fragment of another sword, with bronze mounting at upper end of blade

Blade of a 'gladius' 19 inches long, in good preservation

A die of bone – a strigil of iron – an iron lamp

Several iron rings – three bronze cooking vessels

A very fine bronze oenochoe[234] complete, with a decorated handle and a band of lotus pattern round the body

A magnificent bronze or copper mask for a helmet like our iron one[235] but almost complete. It is somewhat doubled up but I have no doubt we can get it straight [Figure 8.11].

Figure 8.11. Bronze face mask from a parade helmet. © National Museums Scotland (X.FRA 123).

Among other things we picked up lately is one of those zoomorphic fibulae[236] almost identical with one figured by Romilly Allen[237] and now in the BM.

Believe me,

Yours sincerely

James Curle

Letter 1.42

20th November, 1907

Dear Mr Smith,

Have you got your Pudding Pan[238] papers in print yet? I should very much like to see your list of names.

I feel quite certain that DIVIXTVS is not a very early potter, not earlier than the Antonines.[239] He is probably a contemporary of CINNAMVS. We have him here at Newstead in the 3rd

---

234   Wine jar with maenad head on handle.
235   Curle 1911a: 168–170; Keppie and Arnold 1984: 20, no. 55.
236   A dragonesque brooch; Curle 1911a: 320, pl. 85 no. 7, pl. 89 fig. 8.
237   Allen 1904: plate opposite p.100, bottom left.
238   A Roman shipwreck near Herne Bay, Kent, its cargo including plentiful amounts of samian. Published by Smith in 1907, with an addendum in 1909a; see now Walsh 2017. Curle was interested in the potters' stamps for comparative purposes.
239   Continuing the discussion from Letters 1.39–1.41.

occupation ditch. We find him at Camelon with medallions. I have just found his stamp at Birrens where there is no early pottery and I am pretty sure his wares were at Castle Cary.[240] I always thought your 30 bowl looked late and I am inclined to think that possibly Déchelette puts the transition from the 2nd to the third period rather early.[241] His evidence for the date at which his second period ends is not his strongest point and no doubt the early forms were not eliminated all at once.

I have dug out a lot of the 1st occupation ditches here and I find that bowls 29 and 30[242] went on all through the period. I think the red pottery is all Graufesenque, Montans or Banassac[243] but I can't be quite certain of some of the designs. The pottery of the pits where we found so much last year belongs to the same period so our helmets etc are undoubtedly 1st century. I am very anxious to know if there are any potters' names which can be identified as belonging to the early second century. Can you help me in this? I have got one distinct piece of Rheinzabern, probably of Reginus,[244] who is said to be of the time of Marcus Aurelius. I am quite sure there is also German pottery at Birrens.

Can you tell me if the BM possesses Die Provincia Arabia[245] by Petersen and Domascewski? I am anxious to see it but it is rather too big to buy.

Believe me,

Yours sincerely,

James Curle

Letter 1.43

The British Museum
London WC

21st November, 1907

Dear Mr Curle,

The book you mention is in the library (apparently in process) the pressmark being 7709s. With regard to the pottery I have interviewed Mr Walters[246] this morning, who thinks that

---

[240] All sites which had been dug by the Society of Antiquaries of Scotland in recent years. For Camelon and Birrens see Letter 1.39. Castlecary lies on the Antonine Wall; Christison *et al.* 1903.
[241] Déchelette's production periods.
[242] Types in the classification of Dragendorff 1895.
[243] Three production centres for samian in southern Gaul in the later first century AD (Oswald and Pryce 1920: pl. 1; Webster 1996: fig. 1).
[244] Rheinzabern was the centre of east Gaulish samian production. Curle (1911a: 239, no. 80) recorded two stamps of Reginus, from Pits XLIX and XCVIII, and this was confirmed by Hartley (1972: 21, nos 102–103). This is probably the one from Pit XLIX, recorded as being 'Cleared out January, 1908', but the lack of a specific date in contrast to most other pits suggests Curle was relying on imprecise notes, and it was being excavated or had been emptied by the time of this letter. He records the stamp variously as being on a Dr. 31 platter and a Dr. 33 cup (Curle 1911a: 126–127, 239), but Hartley (ibid) confirms it was a Dr. 33.
[245] Curle has the authors' names wrong. Issued in three volumes between 1904 and 1909: Brünnow and von Domaszewski 1904; 1905; 1909 (the latter published after this letter).
[246] Author of the British Museum Roman pottery catalogue (Walters 1908); see *Dramatis personae*.

Déchelette[247] has put CINNAMVS too late, and himself thinks that potter belongs to the early period of the second century, so that your DIVIXTVS pieces may be of that date. Déchelette's leading men for the second period are LIBERTVS, BVTRIO and PVTRIV, the two last possibly being one and the same. Walters also thinks that the large scrolls belong rather to the second century than to the third period.

My paper on the Pan Rock is expected every day,[248] but the Proceedings themselves will be out about the same time. It is only being kept back by the index. I hope you will be able to throw fresh light on the Gaulish Red Ware in your Report on Newstead.

With kind regards,

I am,

Yours very truly,

Reginald A Smith

Letter 1.44

21st February, 1908

Dear Smith,

If I am not giving you too much trouble, will you allow Oldland[249] to photograph for me a typical blue glass bottle with a reeded handle, the square type, I think, and a pillar moulded glass bowl. You will know the things I mean.

The glass at Newstead is so fragmentary that I can't make a slide of anything, though these particular vessels can be easily recognised. I only want him to make me a slide of them.

I have found very little since I saw you,[250] as most of the time we have been filling in. We began digging out again a few days ago and a few small things have turned up – a boss with a head of Mithraic type;[251] a ring with enamelled spotts [*sic*];[252] a late Celtic terret;[253] and the chape of a sword sheath[254] – so there is still something to be found.

---

[247] Déchelette 1904. For the discussion, see Letters 1.39–1.42.
[248] Smith 1907.
[249] An assistant in Read and Smith's department at the British Museum, who appears in other Letters resolving practical issues; see *Dramatis personae*. The images were presumably needed for Curle's Rhind lectures, delivered in late March and early April that year.
[250] Curle's mode of address changed to the less formal 'Dear Smith' after they had met (for the first time?), and indeed was habitually 'My Dear Smith' from October 1908; Smith resolutely used 'Dear Mr Curle' throughout the correspondence until the final extant Letter (1.85), from 1931, when he was Keeper and could afford a 'Dear Curle'.
[251] Curle 1911a: pl. 77 no. 11. The mount is not Mithraic, although the eastern-style hat is found on Mithraic figures and in representations of Attis. The plump, youthful face suggested to Martin Henig (2012: 159) that this represents a cupid. It is a harness mount.
[252] Perhaps Curle 1911a: pl. 89 no. 18, from the *praetentura*.
[253] This is probably the lipped terret (Curle 1911a: 302, pl. 75 no 2; MacGregor 1976, no 63); he recorded 'at least two other specimens ... both much corroded', but it seems unlikely he would have mentioned these to Smith.
[254] Curle illustrated four, without details of findspot (1911a: 187, pl. 35 nos 15–18).

By the way, we have identified an antler found some time ago as Elk.[255] This is the first time, I fancy, we have definitely got him with Roman remains.

Believe me,

Yours sincerely,

James Curle

Letter 1.45

28th March, 1908

Dear Smith,

I am sorry to say I have not yet been able to send you the photograph of our S-shaped brooch.[256] I found the one I had done was too small but I have a drawing which I shall send next week. In the meantime will you be so kind as to ask Oldland[257] to make me a slide of the Samian bowl with the wide flat rim with lotus bud decoration. You remember we discussed the period. It is on the ground level in the case on the right side of the North entrance to your room.

I begin my lectures[258] on Monday but the pottery is not till the following week, so if he will let me have it by the 4th April it will do. Please excuse this bother.

Believe me

Yours sincerely,

James Curle

---

255 Curle 1911a: 110; Ewart 1911: 376. In fact, the antler is of red deer; we are grateful to Dr A. Kitchener, Principal Curator of Vertebrates at National Museums Scotland, for checking this point.
256 Probably Curle 1911a: 319–320, pl. 85 no 6.
257 A British Museum assistant whose services were called upon regularly by Curle; see *Dramatis personae*.
258 The Rhind Lectures. See notes to Letter 1.41 for background, and pp 33–34 for details.

Letter 1.46

SOCIETY OF ANTIQUARIES OF SCOTLAND
NATIONAL MUSEUM OF ANTIQUITIES
QUEEN STREET, EDINBURGH

6th March [sic] 1908[259]

Dear Smith,

I am sorry I have been so long in answering your letter. Enclosed is a full-sized drawing of an S shaped fibula.[260] You might let me have it back when you are done with it.

I cannot answer the last problem you put to me.[261] It is a very curious fact which Dr Anderson confirms that we have no Anglo Saxon finds from the South of Scotland. There is always the possibility that they exist but that we have not found them. Early Iron Age things were also supposed to be awanting till a few years ago.

Many thanks for telling Oldland about the slide which he has sent me.[262] I cannot bring myself to believe that that bowl is the end of the 2nd century. The rim is exactly what I have in the Newstead first period – I have not enough of it to show the Spout.

I give my fourth Rhind lecture this afternoon so I soon shall have the job over, which I shall be glad of. Coming into Edinburgh three times a week with a top hat on is a nuisance.[263]

Believe me,

Yours sincerely,

James Curle

---

[259] Curle was writing while in Edinburgh for his Rhind lectures, delivered to the Society of Antiquaries of Scotland; hence the headed paper, rather than his own writing paper. The date is in error; he delivered his fourth lecture on 6 April.
[260] See Letter 1.45. The drawing must indeed have been returned as it does not survive in the archive.
[261] This is the first instance of Smith asking Curle for advice. He may have begun gathering information to inform his catalogue of the BM's Anglo-Saxon collection, although this was not published till many years later (Smith 1923). Anglo-Saxon finds are now well attested from southern Scotland (Blackwell 2018).
[262] Letter 1.45.
[263] The six lectures were delivered on alternate weekdays over two consecutive weeks (Monday 30 March, Wednesday 1, Friday 3, Monday 6, Wednesday 8 and Friday 10 April) on the topic of 'The excavation of the Roman military station at Newstead, Melrose'. They are discussed on pp 33–34.

Letter 1.47

8th May, 1908

My dear Read,

I was very sorry that business matters here made it impossible for me to go to London to vote for you and for the same reason I have not been able to write to you earlier to congratulate you on your election to so dignified a post as that of President.[264] I am sure no one could fill it better. Now that I have got lots of slides of the Newstead things[265] I must try and give a lecture under your presidency.[266]

I am still finding a few things, though we are working on a small scale. Last week I got a boat hook[267] (?) and a charming pin in bone with a little bust carved on the top [Figure 8.12].[268] I see a number of incomplete specimens in Roach Smith's Roman London.[269]

This week the sludge from an early pit produced a very interesting set of mountings for a coat or belt in brass, some over laid with silver.[270] A large circular plate with three loops at the back, with a central boss plated with silver. Two rectangular plates with raised bosses, eight brass mountings with loops at the end, and two strap-end mountings. I think these loops must have been fastened on leather coats to serve in place of buttons. Circular leather patches with leather loops served the same purpose.[271]

Believe me,

Yours very sincerely,

James Curle

Figure 8.12. Detail of bone pin with female bust. © National Museums Scotland (X.FRA 688).

---

[264] Of the Society of Antiquaries of London.
[265] For his recently-delivered Rhind Lectures.
[266] His hope was unfulfilled; see Letter 3.22.
[267] Curle 1911a: 288, pl. 66 no. 8, from the inner ditch on the west front.
[268] Curle 1911a: 337, pl. 93 no 16, from Pit LVI.
[269] Roach Smith 1859: pl. 34 nos 16–17, 19–20.
[270] From Pit LV (Curle 1911a: 298, 301, pl. 72). By the time of writing the report he recognised them as harness fittings rather than coat or belt elements, drawing on parallels from Roman sculpture and Danish bog finds.
[271] Curle 1911a: 149, pl. 19 nos 1, 6, 7, 10. In fact, they are strengthening patches from tents (C. van Driel-Murray, pers. comm.).

Letter 1.48

18th May, 1908

Dear Smith,

You spoke of coming down here to see the Newstead collection. I wonder if there is any chance of your doing so in the near future. I shall be at home, off and on, till about the 17th June, when I think we shall go off to Germany, Homburg v d H to begin with.[272] If you could come in the first fortnight of June I would be very glad to see you. You could study what I have here and we could spend a day in Edinburgh, or more if you like, as I believe there are some good things in the Loan Collection at the Edinburgh Exhibition.[273]

I think it would be a good thing, now that I know a little more of Newstead, to revisit some of the German Collections – Wiesbaden and perhaps Bonn. Are there any good things to be seen South of Frankfurt in the German towns?

I was very glad that 'Dr' Read was elected President of the Antiquaries.[274]

Believe me

Yours sincerely,

James Curle

Letter 1.49

10th September, 1908

Dear Smith,

I told you that I thought that the flat pans of black ware were of the 2nd century[275] but I now believe this is incorrect. We did not find any trace of them in our 1st period ditch. I have however lately been digging out the Second period ditch and where we have tracked it – it is far too heavy a job to dig it out entirely – the Samian seems indistinguishable from that of the first period. Bowl 29[276] occurs in both. In this 2nd period ditch, which I believe dates from the end of the 1st century and below the fragments of Bowl 29 we have found one of these black pans. The rim seems a little flatter and wider than the pieces of the same dishes from the 3rd (Antonine?) ditch.[277]

---

[272] Bad Homburg vor der Höhe, the spa town in Hessen close to the Saalburg fort. Curle had stayed there in 1906; see Letter 1.30.

[273] The Scottish National Exhibition in Saughton Park, Edinburgh was opened on 1 May by Arthur, Prince of Connaught, son of Queen Victoria. It was attended by 3.5 million people over six months of 'glorious weather'.

[274] See Letter 1.47. Read was awarded an honorary doctorate by St Andrews University around this time (Wilson 2004b).

[275] See Letter 1.40.

[276] Referring to the Dragendorff type-series (1895).

[277] Curle reaffirmed this dating in the Report (1911a: 258), arguing some Black-burnished ware (as it is now termed) was reaching the area in the early second century.

It is rather an important point that we seem to have established viz the enlargement of the fort in the 2nd century.

Can you refer me to an article on bridle bits of the Roman time?[278]

Believe me,

Yours sincerely

James Curle

Letter 1.50

15th September, 1908

Dear Smith,

Please forgive my troubling you so much. My only excuse is that it is a public object. In your designation of the Grimthorpe Burial Cat. p104[279] you mention two semi-circular rods, part of the framework of the shield and you indicate the length about 27 inches, the Thames shield being 30 and a quarter inches.[280]

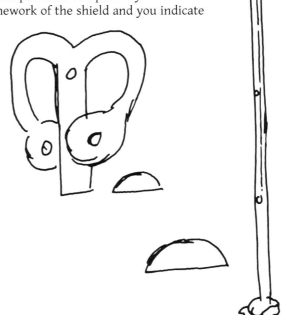

I have found four portions of such rods.

Can they belong to Celtic shields?[281]

I have always put them down as shield frames of some sort. My best piece is almost complete – 28 inches long, expanding at the ends. One end is damaged. The other is beaten out into a flat plate one and five eighth inches in diameter. In the centre is a single round flat-headed rivet, five eighths of an inch in diameter. I have drawn

---

278 This suggests Curle had uncovered the curb bit from the inner ditch on the west front, an unfamiliar type to contemporary eyes (Curle 1911a: 297, pl. 71 no. 3).
279 Smith 1905: 104. This Iron Age burial was found in a hillfort in East Yorkshire. Red coral 'eyes' once decorated the fish-shaped chape of a sword in a bronze scabbard. Grave goods also contained remains of a shield with copper-alloy decorative plates (Mortimer 1905: 150–152, frontis; Stead 1968: 166–170).
280 The Battersea shield; Stead 1985.
281 Curle 1911a: 181–182, pl 34 nos 1, 2, 4, 5, 12. The suggestion that they came from Iron Age shields presumably arose because their curved ends suggested an oval form common in the Iron Age but (as Curle noted in the Report) regularly found in Roman hands on sculpture. They are dissimilar to the Grimthorpe ones, which are sheet bronze spine covers from the front of the shield, whereas the Newstead ones are a sturdy iron frame.

this also – another form of terminal ending. Will you kindly let me know if your dated Celtic Shields can help me?

I suppose you would put the Grimthorpe Sword[282] a little earlier than the Hod Hill specimen.[283] Its guard is more closely related to Central European types.[284]

Another question is about the hub bands for wheels. The type is quite common here. It is also peculiar. If our wheels are Celtic wheels there should be some trace of similar mountings elsewhere.[285]

The depth of the band is 2 inches. The diameter 4 inches. These loops, which ought to be equal, are sharp on the inner edge and so hammered into the wood of the hub. In most specimens we find them broken. Will you let me know if you have any specimens – and where they come from.

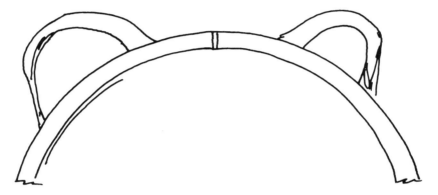

I am having a photo done of the Late Celtic piece of brass[286] and shall send you one later. Again asking you to excuse this trouble.

I remain,

Yours sincerely

James Curle

---

[282] See now Stead 2006: 187, fig. 93 no. 177.

[283] Romano-British, 1st century AD, found at Hod Hill (Dorset), where a Roman fort lay within an Iron Age hillfort. Iron sword with Iron Age style of hilt guard; Stead 2006: 199, fig. 107 no. 234.

[284] The reference is to the curved (campanulate) form typical of middle La Tène swords on the continent; the Hod Hill hilt guard is straight.

[285] Curle uncovered considerable quantities of both nave bands, which encircled the hub to prevent it from splitting, and hub-linings which fitted inside the hub to reduce wear (Curle 1911a: 292–293, pl. 69 no. 2, pl. 70 nos 5, 9, 10). The latter had loops which were driven into the wood to stop it from moving. Their use is clearly seen on the complete wheels from the site. While nave bands were a regular feature of Iron Age chariots in Britain, hub-linings were a Roman phenomenon (Schönfelder 2002: 155–158).

[286] The reference must be to the piece of casket ornament from Pit LVIII, recorded as being emptied on this date; Curle 1911a: 303–304, pl. 75 no. 5. He refers to it again in the following Letter.

Letter 1.51

30th October, 1908

My dear Smith,

This is a bronze mounting of a sword found recently doubled up in an early pit at Newstead.[287]

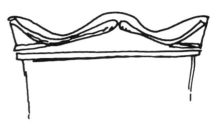

Yesterday I went to look at the late Celtic things in Edinburgh and among the find of horse trappings from Middlebie[288] in Annandale I found the mounting of a sword hilt decorated with late Celtic ornament. When I got home I set to work to examine our sword and found that the mounting, though less well executed, was the same thing. I send you a rough drawing of it. So I think we have got a specimen of the native Sword. The pit had Graufesenque 'pottery' rustic ware and a frilled tazza[289] – the position showed it to be early.

Among the things in it was a bit of brass embossed with Late Celtic decoration.[290]

Will you be kind enough to tell me if you have in your collection any examples of these sword mountings at Stanwix[291] or any other distinctively British site.

Believe me,

Yours sincerely,

James Curle

PS I have, before this, found a broken sword with the same mounting, but without ornament.[292]
JC

---

[287] From Pit LVIII. Curle 1911a: 185, pl. 34 no. 8, fig. 19.1 (wrongly attributed there to Pit LVII); MacGregor 1976: no. 151.

[288] Hamlet 3 km east of Ecclefechan in Dumfriesshire, close to Birrens Roman fort and the Iron Age hillfort of Burnswark; the precise findspot is not known. 28 copper-alloy items of horse trappings and one guard from a sword hilt, mostly in the typical Scottish lowland 'boss' style metalwork found at sites such as Traprain Law and Newstead. Its acquisition is mentioned in Letter 1.7. Wilson 1851: 458–459; MacGregor 1976: nos 5, 6, 11–13, 22, 23, 33–35, 72, 88–93, 149.

[289] A wide, shallow bowl with broad stem and crimped rim; Curle 1911a: 252.

[290] So-called 'casket ornament': copper-alloy sheet with repoussé decoration, often stamped. Curle 1911a: 303–304, pl. 75 no. 5; MacGregor 1976: no. 338.

[291] A mis-spelling of the Stanwick hoard of Iron Age horse gear (MacGregor 1962).

[292] From Pit LVII. Curle 1911a: 185, pl. 34 no. 10; MacGregor 1976, no. 152.

Letter 1.52

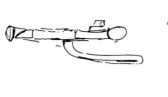

Priorwood

1-XI-08

My dear Smith,

I am delighted to have your prompt
reply to my enquiry and to find you
agree with my view about the Celtic
Sword. I have two more of these mountings but both undecorated. I think
the object I have drawn above is also Late Celtic.[293] The five large circles and
depressions each makes a hole in the centre as though for fixing in coral.
They are not keyed for enamel. The type of object one has in simpler forms
with Late Celtic things – this for example.[294]

It was found in a pit close to the one with Sword, with a long handled weaving
comb.[295] It is also 1st century. Several bits of D 29[296] were in the pit. Can you
tell me of any similar finds?

The same terminal knob seems to occur in the guard of the Sadberge sword[297]
to which you referred me. Among the things in the pit with the Sword are
some pieces of bone which look like parts of the pommel,[298] also a very heavy
bronze pommel-like object with an iron tang.[299]

The most characteristic thing was a piece of thin brass with
embossed ornament.[300]

Believe me

Yours sincerely

James Curle

---

[293] Curle 1911a: 303–304, pl. 75 no 11. It is a variant button-and-loop strap fastener; the form suggests a bunch of
grapes, and is more classical than Iron Age. It is a rare type with parallels from Perthshire (perhaps from the fort at
Bertha) and Castleford, West Yorkshire (Wild 1970: 144; MacGregor 1976: nos 254, 256; Bishop 1998: 72, fig. 24 no. 280).
[294] A button-and-loop strap fastener of Wild (1970) class III.
[295] Pit LIX. Curle 1911a: 290, pl. 68 no. 4.
[296] A Dragendorff type 27 bowl (Dragendorff 1895).
[297] Found at Barmpton, Sadberge, Darlington, Co. Durham; a late Iron Age sword and decorated scabbard. MacGregor
1976: no. 156; Stead 2006: 194–195, figs 102–103, no. 207.
[298] Pit LVIII. Curle 1911a: 129, pl. 84 nos 4 (hilt guard), 10 (pommel).
[299] Curle 1911a: pl. 84 no. 13; perhaps a vehicle fitting.
[300] Curle had already mentioned this to Smith in Letters 1.50–1.51. A note on the sketch reads 'This does not quite do
justice to Late Celtic art'; one of the editors can attest from bitter experience the difficulties of accurately sketching
such complex art.

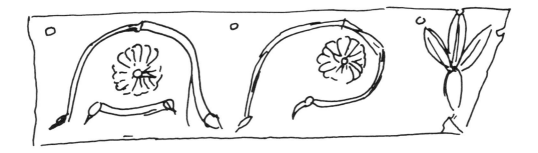

Letter 1.53

The British Museum,
London

4th November, 1908

Dear Mr Curle,

You have hit upon some very interesting late Celtic objects upon which I congratulate you, but we suggest that the sunk circular spaces with rivet holes in the triangular piece may have been filled with enamel, made in buttons and treated as the coral was at an earlier period, not as in the later champlévé enamel. I do not understand the use of that particular specimen, but expect you will clear it all up presently.[301]

The three pieces are of much interest and besides the cabossed[302] strips here I have lately seen some in a hoard of the 1st century in the Cambridge Museum from Santon Downham,[303] Suffolk. There is a designation without illustration in the forthcoming Victorian History of Suffolk, but I am enlarging that account and providing illustrations in a paper for the Cambridge Archaeological Society next February.[304] I shall be glad to mention this example of embossed scroll work. If you have a successful photo of it I should be extremely pleased to have a copy of it.

I will bear your questions in mind and let you know as soon as I see anything similar.

Believe me,

Yours sincerely,

Reginald A Smith

---

[301] See notes to Letter 1.52.
[302] We read this as 'cabossed', a heraldic term where the head of a beast is cut off behind the ears by a section parallel to the face, but suspect it should be 'embossed'.
[303] Located in Thetford Forest on a meander of the river Little Ouse on the Norfolk-Suffolk border. The finds are in the University Museum of Archaeology and Anthropology.
[304] Published as Smith 1909b (where the Newstead parallel is not mentioned).

Letter 1.54

18th December, 1908

My Dear Smith,

I see the Catalogue of Roman Pottery is published.[305] I should like to have a copy. As I don't quite know to whom I should write I send you a cheque for £2 – if I should have added 'carriage' will you kindly let me know.

What do you make of the objects from the Dowker bottom Cave[306] – like spoons with holes in the bowls. I should call them hairpins but the one I have here[307] is not pointed nor is the one figured by Munro from (I think) Lochlee crannog.[308]

Are any of your specimens pointed? Not very much turning up at Newstead but we are still digging out pits, all Early. In none have I seen the flat black pan with lattice work.[309]

We got a good dolabra a few weeks ago a very fine long whetstone an Andernach quern two primitive-looking picks and a gridiron.[310]

Lately we found a very good hanging lamp of iron a surgeon's probe a button of horn a silver penannular brooch with phallic terminals and an oar of oak, five and a half feet long.[311]

Believe me,

Yours very truly,

James Curle

---

[305] Walters 1908.

[306] Dowkerbottom cave, Wharfesdale, North Yorkshire. Prehistoric remains found as well as Romano-British material. See assessment by Branigan and Dearne 1991: 81–86. The bone 'spoon brooches' are described by them (ibid: 70–71, 85) and discussed as a type by Greep and Marshall 2014. Curle would have known it most likely from Boyd Dawkins 1874: 102, although these are not illustrated, but one from the Victoria Cave was (Boyd Dawkins 1874: 90, fig. 22); this material was in the British Museum.

[307] Curle 1911a: 338, pl. 92 no. 21, from the ditch of the early fort. His broad discussion of the topic identifies them as a regional Roman Iron Age rather than Roman phenomenon, with examples in northern England and these two Scottish examples from Newstead and Lochlee.

[308] Lochlee Crannog, near Tarbolton, Ayrshire, was excavated in 1878–1879 under the aegis of Dr Robert Munro, a medical doctor who was able to devote most of his time to antiquarian pursuits. For the perforated bone spoon, see Munro 1882: 112, fig. 76.

[309] Despite some doubts expressed in Letter 1.49, Curle was by this stage using what is today termed Black-burnished ware as a chronological indicator; subsequent work confirmed its origins in Roman Scotland were Antonine (Gillam 1976).

[310] The contents of Pit LXI (Curle 1911a: 130–131), completed on 18th November. The quern was from the well-known Andernach quarries in the Rhine. Recent work identified the whetstone as an import from the Weald in south-east England (Allen 2016).

[311] All from Pit LXV to the north of the fort except the penannular brooch, which was a stray find from the same field (Curle 1911a: 131, with further references for the pit; 1911a: 326, pl. 88 no. 13 for the brooch). The oar or side rudder suggests that the Tweed was navigable by barges from Berwick. See also Letter 3.19.

Letter 1.55

The British Museum
London WC

29th December, 1908

Dear Mr Curle,

I return the cheque you sent for the Pottery Catalogue, and hope you have received a copy safely. With regard to the bone specimens[312] I can offer no brilliant suggestion, but can assure you that several of those in this Collection from the caves at Settle[313] in Yorkshire cannot conveniently have been used as hairpins, and look much more like spoons, though the bowl is almost flat and many are pierced. The enclosed sketches [not archived] will give you some idea of our series.

We have nine or ten, probably dating from the second century AD but only from the Settle caves, as far as I can see at present.

There are, as you know, some mysterious bronze spoons of the Early Iron Age,[314] which resemble those in old-fashioned tea-caddies, but were probably used in some ceremonial way.

Wishing you all success and a Happy New Year.

I am,

Yours sincerely,

Reginald A Smith

Letter 1.56

30th XII.08

My Dear Smith,

Very many thanks for returning my cheque, also for your information about the Dowkerbottom Spoons or whatever they may be. It is quite clear they are not hairpins. I am very busy scheming out plates for the Newstead volume. I hope to be able to illustrate a number of specimens of the designs on decorated vases. It will be a somewhat costly business, I fear.[315]

With all good wishes for the New Year.

Believe me

Yours sincerely

James Curle

---

[312] Responding to Curle's query in Letter 1.54 over parallels for the perforated bone 'spoon'.
[313] The Settle caves have been described as 'an archaeologist's dream' since they reveal a range of material from the bones of mammoths to Roman coins. Their record is confused as most excavations were rather early; see Branigan and Dearne 1991: 70–71 for a summary.
[314] Smith 1905: 137, fig. 125. A pair was subsequently found in an Iron Age burial at Burnmouth, Berwickshire, in 1924 (Craw 1924). For a recent review, see Fitzpatrick 2007.
[315] Curle himself paid £100 for the rag paper on which the 450-page book was printed; D.V. Clarke 2012: 31.

Letter 1.57

6th September, 1909

A postcard bearing a reconstruction of chariot races at *Trimontium* by George Hope Tait,[316] sent by James Curle to Reginald A. Smith without any recorded comment [Figure 8.13].

The verse on it reads:

Mercury urged the charioteers
That tore up the sacred ground,
And the Eildons echoed the merry cheers
Of a Roman victor crowned!

The Romans fought and the Romans played,
And the Tweed went singing by,
And oft in the glade a Pictish maid
Would watch their chariots fly.[317]

THE ROMANS AT NEWSTEAD, MELROSE.
A CHARIOT RACE (2nd Century).

GEO. HOPE TAIT

Mercury urged the charioteers
 That tore up the sacred ground,
And the Eildons echoed the merry cheers
 Of a Roman victor crowned !

TRIMONTIUM.

SPQR

The Romans fought and the Romans played,
 And the Tweed went singing by,
And oft in the glade a Pictish maid
 Would watch their chariots fly.

Figure 8.13. Postcard showing a chariot race at Newstead, by George Hope Tait. Image © Donald Gordon.

---

[316] George Hope Tait (1861–1943) worked as a painter and decorator in Galashiels, and had a flair as a watercolourist and poet. He served on Galashiels Town Council from 1913 until his death, becoming a Bailie of the town, and was instrumental in organising a number of memorials in the Borders, including one at the fort of Trimontium; see https://www.pastinnerleithen.com/people/george-hope-tait (accessed 16 June 2022) and Elliot 1929.

[317] The printed lines are extracted from a longer poem, 'The Roman charioteer! (To a pair of Roman chariot wheels, found at Trimontium camp, Melrose, 1906)'. The first stanza is the second half of verse three; the second stanza is the first half of the ninth and final verse. See Tait 1941: 73–75.

Letter 1.58

18th October, 1909

Dear Smith,

I want a name to distinguish the pottery we talked of as 'rustic' ware [Figure 8.14]. You remember the material – like the pottery you have in the BM from Lincoln.

I want to call it 'Early Barbotine' ware,[318] to distinguish it from Castor ware, which at Newstead is 2nd century. I want to know if this is really a correct term.[319]

I believe the vessel is made and to some extent hardened, and decoration is then applied in slip, but I am very ignorant of such technical processes and I should be grateful for the opinion of yourself and any other experts in the Museum.

I hope pretty soon to get the book into print.[320] We are getting well on with the illustrations, but they tend to grow in numbers as one proceeds.[321]

Believe me,

Yours very truly,

James Curle

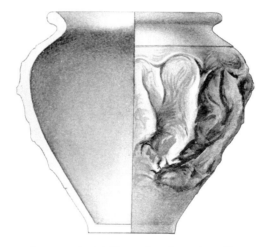

Figure 8.14. Curle's illustration of a rusticated jar
(Curle 1911a: pl. 46 no. 29).

---

[318] Barbotine is French for 'ceramic slip', a clay and water mixture used for moulding or decorating pottery.
[319] In fact, Curle went with 'rustic ware' in the Report, where he illustrated several specimens and discussed the likely production technique (Curle 1911a: 247). This term was used in the standard work on northern British Roman coarse wares (Gillam 1957: 191–192, Types 95–99; 1970: 12–13, Types 95–99), but 'rustication' or 'rusticated decoration' is the preferred term in modern scholarship, for instance in the Elginhaugh report (Dore 2007: 288–289).
[320] The Report is dated 1911, but an advance copy was tabled at the Anniversary Meeting of the Society of Antiquaries of Scotland on 30 November 1910 (*Proceedings of the Society of Antiquaries of Scotland* 45 [1910–1911]: 9). Some copies bear inscriptions from December 1910, and the *Scotsman* reviewed it on 10 January 1911 (p.5).
[321] The expanding content caused considerable inflation to the costs of the volume; D.V. Clarke 2012: 31–32.

Letter 1.59

25th October, 1909

My dear Smith,

Thank you very much for your letter. The term 'rustic ware' does not quite carry conviction[322] but I shall have to put a definition in the Interpretation Clause, which is often a useful thing in Acts of Parliament.[323]

I am getting some very nice illustrations done[324] for the book and I think it is going to look all right.

Have you sent in your name for the Roman Society?[325] I think it would be quite a promising venture, though it would have been better to have started earlier. They seem to have done some quite interesting digging this year in Wales.[326]

Believe me

Yours sincerely,

James Curle

Letter 1.60

18th February, 1910

Dear Smith,

I have been digging again at Newstead, without much success so far, but the other day we cleaned out a pit which was evidently of the later period.[327] It had a number of decorated fragments, either Lezoux or German. There were the stamps of three potters CRACVNA, SVOBNI.M and RVFFI.M and there was a black bowl, practically in shape a copy of Drag. 30 [Figure 8.15].[328]

The outside has almost a polish on it and, in place of the raised figures, it has a crude attempt at decoration in a band of figures like the letter Z impressed in the soft clay. I have noted this sort of thing in other imitations of Samian shapes. Inside, the potter's fingers, as the bowl

---

[322] It was the term he ended up using; Curle 1911a: 247.
[323] Curle's training as a lawyer is clear here: a clause inserted in a statute or contract stipulating the meaning of words.
[324] By Messrs D. and J. Frater of Edinburgh, according to the final page of the report (Curle 1911a: 432). They are recorded in Slater's *Royal National Commercial Directory of Scotland* (1903: 745) as lithographic draughtsmen, based at 13 St James Square (https://digital.nls.uk/directories/browse/archive/90699222?mode=transcription [accessed 16 June 2022]). The same firm was used by A.O. Curle for the illustrations of the Traprain Treasure (Curle 1923: viii).
[325] The Roman Society, more properly the Society for the Promotion of Roman Studies, was founded in 1910 to advance the understanding of ancient Rome and the Roman Empire. A similar Society promotes Hellenic Studies. Curle was a prominent early member; see p. 26.
[326] Between 1909 and 1910 the Liverpool Committee for Research in Wales and the Marches excavated at the amphitheatre at Caerleon, where there was no stonework then showing above ground. See Bosanquet and King 1963.
[327] Pit LXXII; Curle 1911a: 133, with further references.
[328] Curle 1911a: 257, pl. 48 no. 43, pl. 49B no. 8

turned on the wheel, have left their mark and there are tiny specks of mica in the clay. There was a coin of Trajan in the pit. Have you any bowls like this in the BM?

It looks like Upchurch pottery.[329] I don't remember the type on the Continent.

Another question. Is there in the Library a copy of the book on the Lipperheide Collection[330] of Roman helmets? I fancy it is typewritten and that copies are not very plentiful. There are a number of helmets illustrated in it which are not in Benndorf[331] and I am anxious to get one or two references to it checked. Please excuse my troubling you. I have got half the book in print so I should get it finished before the summer is over. I hope you are flourishing!

With kind regards,

Believe me

Yours sincerely,

James Curle

Figure 8.15. Decorated coarse ware pot imitating a Dr. 30 bowl. © National Museums Scotland.

Letter 1.61

26th February,1910

My dear Smith,

Many thanks for your letter. I want to put at the end of my chapter on armour a list of the visor helmets and masks resembling our finds here, known throughout Europe. I send you my list and shall be grateful if you will look over it.[332] I sent it to Director Schumacher at Mainz[333] who kindly drew my attention to the Lipperheide helmets which I had overlooked.

---

[329] A term in common and somewhat uncritical use at the time for decorated wares in reduced fabrics (e.g. Walters 1908: 415–421), named after Upchurch in northern Kent where extensive remains of pottery production had been found in the 19th century (Monaghan 1987: 173). The term remains in use more specifically for particular fineware products of the area (Monaghan 1987: 173; Tomber and Dore 1998: 168), but this vessel has not been identified as such (cf. Monaghan 1987: 213).

[330] Franz von Lipperheide (1838–1906), German financier and art collector, donated his collection of 92 classical helmets to the Antikenmuseum in Berlin. Published as Lipperheide 1896; see also Bottini *et al.* 1988. Copies are inordinately rare; see Letter 1.62 n.349.

[331] Benndorf 1878.

[332] For the final version, see Curle 1911a: 179–180.

[333] The Roman-Germanic Central Museum (RGZM), founded in 1852 by Ludwig Lindenschmidt the Elder. Karl Schumacher was the Director from 1900 to 1926 and greatly increased its size and scope as a research collection; see *Dramatis personae*. He is thanked in Curle's Preface for assistance with the list of helmets (1911a: viii).

He writes of the book as 'das Buch von F v Lipperheide antike Helmen, München 1896' and I thought that was the title.[334] You will note that I have referred to it in this way and also as simply 'Lipperheide'. What I want is the proper title of the book and references. Under Brauch II Luxemburg[335] I cannot quite decipher what Schumacher has written – please explain this. You will see that they include as a helmet (which at one time was a mask) your specimen from Guisborough, Yorks.[336] Are there any traces of attachment? Then, under what country should the helmet found in the Danube at Orsova[337] be classed? Please excuse all this bother. If you can add any helmets to my list I shall be grateful.[338]

Since I wrote to you I had rather a nice pottery find.[339] Four dishes practically undamaged:-

D 18 Stamp OF IXVSCVLI[340]

Hofheim V 1.2 Stamp SABINVS F[341]

D 36[342]

and a large black jar, to which I shall return; a fragment, with stamp OFIRNION[343] an amphora handle, stamp OMRISILVV[344] an amphora neck, with the name APRILIS written on it,[345] and parts of a big jar: - all from one rubbish pit. The black pot is rather interesting and uncommon.

This is by no means the speaking likeness I intended to send you but you will understand what I mean.

It stands nine and three eighths inches high. It has two small handles, one on each side, and two projecting things, like the neck of a small bottle, one on each side.[346] [BM note in pencil 'cf PSA Scot.43.257'][347]

---

[334] The title is correct but the book is rare in Britain; see Letter 1.62. For a modern appraisal of the collection, see Bottini *et al.* 1988.

[335] 'Need 2nd Luxemburg'? But only one such helmet is recorded from Luxemburg, a bronze face mask from Heilingen, found in 1853 (Garbsch 1978: 65, pl. 19.2, O13, where he noted a replica in RGZM; Krier and Reinert 1993).

[336] A 3rd-century Roman bronze cavalry helmet found in 1864 near Guisborough in the North Riding of Yorkshire and donated to the British Museum in 1878 (Garbsch 1978: 73, pl. 31, O59). The phrase (as transcribed) is slightly opaque, but it is clear Curle wanted to know if it had fixings for a mask.

[337] Orşova is a port city on the Danube in south-west Romania, situated just above the Iron Gates where the Cerna river meets the Danube. The helmet was found in 1892 and entered the Delhaes collection in Vienna, but today is in the National Museum in Budapest (Garbsch 1978: 72, O55). Curle's final attribution to country was redolent of a different time: 'Austria-Hungary'.

[338] Curle was leaning quite heavily on Smith for advice here.

[339] Pit LXXVI; Curle 1911a: 134, with further references.

[340] He corrected this reading in the publication to OF.MASCVLI (Curle 1911a: 238, no. 62); the ligaturing of MA made the reading tricky. D is an abbreviation for the types in Dragendorff (1895).

[341] Curle 1911a: 240 no. 86. Hartley (1972: 8) classed it as a Dragendorff 15/17.

[342] Dragendorff type 36, with barbotine decoration on the overhanging rim.

[343] Corrected to O.FIRMON, on a Dragendorff 18; Curle 1911a: 236, no. 44.

[344] With the ligatures fully expanded, he corrected this in publication to C.MARI.SILVANI (Curle 1911a: 269, pl. 52 no. 5)

[345] RIB II, 6: no. 2492.6, APRILIS[...] / HEL...[...], on a southern Spanish amphora.

[346] Curle 1911a: 244–245, pl. 47 type 35, pl. 49B no. 5. The 'projecting things' are small conical sockets attached to the rim, equidistant between the handles.

[347] The reference is to Roman pottery found in caves at Archerfield, Dirleton, East Lothian (Cree 1909: fig. 8). Three of the sherds illustrated here are samian; the comparison is presumably to no. 3, but this is the neck of a flagon with the stump of a handle attachment, and is a poor parallel.

This piece, a surface find, must have come from another urn of the same kind.

I see the same sort of things, much more developed, rising from the sides of a decorated jar at Vindonissa[348] said to be Mithraic. They may have been used to fix a lid with, but I have seen no trace of such lids anywhere.

Can you help me? It is an interesting type and its association dates it with some certainty.

Believe me,

Yours sincerely,

James Curle

Letter 1.62

4th March, 1910

My dear Smith,

Many thanks for your trouble in hunting for the Lipperheide book. I see Schumacher says that it is in many libraries but I suppose they are all German.[349]

Undoubtedly you are right – his references are to pages, not figures. I didn't know there was a helmet at Lewes Museum.[350] I was under the impression that your four and the one at Colchester were the only finds of the kind in England.[351]

If the Lewes type in any way resembles our undecorated helmet I should very much like to know when it has been published.

My pot[352] isn't mediaeval – that is quite certain. I think the little Spouts may have been a dodge for fastening a lid.

This jar from Vindonissa has something in common with it.[353] It is said to be Mithraic.

---

[348] Heuberger 1909: 9–10 and accompanying plate; it was found in the 1908–1909 excavations and restored in the Römisch-Germanishes Zentralmuseum in Mainz. Curle may have known it from correspondence with Frölich, who excavated at Vindonissa (the surviving letter is later [Letter 4.10] but implies earlier contact) or via Schumacher at Mainz, who had sent Curle other information, noted in the current Letter. Curle's published discussion omits the Vindonissa parallel, drawing instead on examples from the German *limes*, and has no suggestion that the find has Mithraic connotations: 'the actual purpose for which such vessels were employed appears to be uncertain' (Curle 1911a: 245).

[349] The book is rare in the UK; the national hub for academic libraries records only two copies, in the Universities of Oxford and Cambridge (https://discover.libraryhub.jisc.ac.uk; accessed 23 December 2021).

[350] The museum houses an early Roman bronze helmet found in the harbour at Bosham, near Chichester, in the 19th century. It is unsurprising Curle had found no reference to it – it remains poorly published today, though it is a little better known. See Dudley and Webster 1965: 103, 201 n.22; Bishop 2011: 116, pl. 19.

[351] This may be an error: Curle references only three from the British Museum (from Witcham Gravel, Ribchester and Guisborough), as well as the one from St Albans which was in Colchester Museum (Curle 1911a: 165, 179–180).

[352] Which he had discussed in the previous Letter, with curious hollowed cones on the rim.

[353] For references see previous Letter.

My pot is not the only specimen of the kind at Newstead as I found, a long time ago, a single spout which rather puzzled me.[354]

I am figuring out the dishes, 1st as types in wash drawings, showing sections, and then in groups, German fashion, but I think it gives the clearest idea of the things.[355]

Believe me,

Yours sincerely,

James Curle

Letter 1.63

7th April, 1910

My dear Smith,

I should have written before to thank you for your postcard of 17th March. I haven't yet had time to look at the fragment you refer me to. I expect it is later.[356]

I want to ask your help in another matter. I want for my book to get the use of the plan of the bath in Lipari[357] – Archaeologia Vol XXIII Plate XV. My last correspondence with Mr Hope[358] does not encourage me to write to him. When should I address my petition with the best chance of success. I also want, in the interest of my publisher, who is doing a great deal which cannot be profitable, to get the last published list of the subscribers to Silchester. It should contain a number of people who might be interested in the Newstead book. When can I get it?

I have had a find of an altar, quite a good one, to Apollo by L. MAXIMIUS GAETULICUS > (CENTURION) LEG.[359] He is somewhat reticent. Luckily, Haverfield knows him and that he belonged to the XXth Legion.[360]

---

[354] This does not seem to feature in his publication.

[355] In a history of Roman pottery studies, Paul Tyers (1996: 11) noted the strong influence from German publications such as Hofheim, Wiesbaden and Haltern, all of which Curle quoted in the Report (Ritterling 1904; 1909; Loeschke 1909).

[356] This may have been Smith's response to Letter 1.62, with a parallel for Curle's curious pot.

[357] One of the Aeolian islands, north of Sicily; the publication is Smyth 1831. He must have obtained permission, as it was reproduced as Curle 1911a: 90, fig. 5.

[358] Assistant Secretary of the Society of Antiquaries of London. See *Dramatis personae*.

[359] From Pit LXXXIII; Curle 1911a: 143, pl. 16; RIB I: 2120. The inscription, to Apollo, is brief, but remarkably two other inscriptions outline his life. Born in Vienne in southern France, he was recruited into the 20th legion, rising to the rank of centurion, the role he held at Newstead (probably commanding a legionary detachment or in acting charge of an auxiliary unit) and on the altar dedicated to Jupiter at *Aesica* (Great Chesters) on Hadrian's Wall (RIB I: 1725). In 184, as senior centurion in legio I Italica at *Novae* in Bulgaria, he erected a dedication for the welfare of the emperor and August Victory at the end of his extraordinarily long career after 57 years' service (Birley 2012: 137–139; Tomlin 2018: 150–153).

[360] No correspondence with Haverfield on the topic is preserved.

Figure 8.16. Leather chamfron for a horse's head. © National Museums Scotland.

My leather find[361] is really very interesting [Figure 8.16]. I think I told you of it. The bits, put together, make a thing like a conventional eagle, 20 inches by 20 inches. I have never seen anything like it.

Believe me,

Yours sincerely

James Curle

---

[361] The chamfron (horse's parade face mask) recovered from Pit LXXVIII. The interpretation escaped him at this point (Curle 1911a: 153–155, pl. 21), but he identified it correctly when a second, fragmentary example appeared (Curle 1913a: 400–405).

Letter 1.64

(a postcard)

18th April, 1910

Very many thanks for your card. I have also a letter from Mr Clinch[362] about the plate.

Yours sinc.

James Curle

Letter 1.65

(typewritten)

6th January, 1912

My dear Read,

We are at present looking out for an Assistant Keeper for the National Museum of Antiquities in Edinburgh.[363] The ordinary staff of the place consists of the Keeper, Dr Anderson, an Assistant Keeper, a Library Assistant and a number of pensioner attendants. Hitherto, our Assistant Keeper has been a man without any special training for the job but one having some interest in archaeology generally, and neither of the Assistant Keepers of whom I have had experience have had any Museum knowledge when they came to us, or technical training. Their duties have been to keep up, under the supervision of the Keeper, the Catalogue (not a very arduous business), to arrange the objects in the Museum, and generally to look after the exhibition of the Collection. In the Museum, I am sorry to say, there is not much skill displayed in mounting the objects, and when a large collection was brought in from Newstead, I found it difficult to get iron or frail objects handled in any satisfactory way.[364] In fact, I had to end by sending a good many things to Young[365] of the Ashmolean Museum. The Committee who have been considering the terms of the appointment have come to the conclusion that it would be desirable that the Assistant Keeper should be a man possessing some skill in handicraft, so that he would be able to undertake repairs and the general treatment of antiquities and also be able to do the mounting which the Collection very much needs. The Keeper would continue as at present to be a man having a knowledge of archaeology, and could be trusted to

---

[362] Not traced. Given similar enquiries in previous correspondence (e.g. Letters 1.28, 1.35, 1.40), this may be a British Museum staff member in charge of a restoration or repair.

[363] This was filled by Arthur J.H. Edwards in the summer of 1912. He had previously worked as a technician in the natural history section of the Royal Scottish Museum on Chambers St, Edinburgh (Stevenson 1981: 182). He subsequently became Director of NMAS from 1938 until his death in 1944 (Childe 1944).

[364] Curle was instrumental in seeking advice from European museums, and encouraged the setting up of the necessary laboratory in Edinburgh; A.J.H. Edwards, when appointed Assistant Keeper, had existing technical skills which he was able to develop thanks to a visit to Berlin in 1913, funded by the Society of Antiquaries of Scotland's Gunning Fellowship. As a result, the condition of the collections was much improved (Childe 1944; Stevenson 1981: 184).

[365] Haverfield had put Curle in touch with Young (see Letter 3.18) to undertake some conservation work. This is most probably William Young, appointed as plaster art restorer at the Ashmolean in 1900, later becoming its Conservator (1905–1937).

supervise his work.[366] The salary which we would be prepared to give would be from £180 to £200 per annum. We hope to obtain a pension for this official.

I have been asked to write to you to ask you whether you know of anyone employed in the British Museum or elsewhere who would be suitable for the post, and who might be likely to come for such a salary. The Assistant Keeper would require to undertake the technical work, the preparation of labels, mounting, and in addition to that he would require to be of sufficient standing to be trusted with the keys during the absence of the Keeper. If you can help us I shall be grateful. The scheme is not perhaps the best possible that could be devised, but with only two officials it seems difficult to put it on a more satisfactory basis.

With all good wishes for the New Year.

Believe me,

Yours very truly,

James Curle

Letter 1.66

15th August, 1912

Dear Smith,

I must apologise for not writing earlier to thank you for the print of your paper on the Wellyn [*sic*] find[367] for which I am grateful. It is a most interesting study. I went to Glasgow early last week to 'inaugurate' the digging of a Roman fort at Balmuildy.[368] Old Mackie[369] has been engaged as chief digger under Mr S.N. Miller of Glasgow University. The place looks to me rather promising and I hope they will get some results.

Perhaps by this time you are off to Zurich. If you should happen to meet my friend Dr Frölich[370] of Anstaldt Königsfelden bei Brugg give him my greetings.

His Vindonissa collection is well worth seeing.

Believe me,

Yours sincerely,

James Curle

---

[366] The implication here of a new Keeper anticipates the retirement of Joseph Anderson, which was delayed as his post was not pensionable; he finally retired in March 1913, aged 81 (Stevenson 1981: 182–183).

[367] Smith's 1912 article described material found in rich late Iron Age burial chambers at Welwyn, Hertfordshire in 1906 'in a lamentable condition', presented to the BM in January 1911. See also Letter 1.70.

[368] On the Antonine Wall. Published as Miller 1922, where Curle is thanked for his assistance (1922: vi), and reviewed favourably by Curle (1923).

[369] Alexander Mackie, who worked as the Society of Antiquaries of Scotland's Clerk of Works on various sites, including the Newstead excavation (Stevenson 1981: 177). See *Dramatis personae*. Valued and retained by Curle despite Haverfield's doubts; see Letter 3.1. He corresponded with Curle over the excavations (Letter 4.9).

[370] See *Dramatis personae* and Letter 4.10.

Letter 1.67

14th January, 1913

Dear Mr Joyce,[371]

What about my South American gold cup [Figure 8.17].[372] Have you published anything about it? If you have done with it I should be glad to have it back. You might get Oldland[373] to pack it up carefully and return it by registered post. I shall be glad to pay any charges. If you write will you let me have your view of the period of the cup and the name of the god upon it. Dr Capitan,[374] I think, put it about the XIV century.

Yours sincerely,

James Curle

PS. I am writing a note to Oldland to ask him to get me a block to stand the cup on.

JC

Figure 8.17. Gold beaker from Lambayeque, Peru, showing three repeated images of a high-status male (deity?) wearing a head-dress and ear-spools, carrying a ceremonial sceptre and either a banner or a trophy head on a staff. © National Museums Scotland (A.1947.140)

Letter 1.68[375]

BRITISH MUSEUM, LONDON WC

18.1.13

Dear Mr Curle,

I have not been able to produce a note on your cup, as there has been such a press of matter for Man.[376] But I will get it written at once[377] and then return the cup to you as soon as the stand has been fitted. The carpenter is engaged on the job now.

---

[371] T.A. Joyce (1878–1942) was an ethnographer at the British Museum with a speciality in South America. See *Dramatis personae*.
[372] A 15th-century gold beaker from Lambayeque in Peru which Joyce published shortly afterwards (Joyce 1913); see also Aldred 1947, who states it was found in a grave. There is no trace of how Curle acquired this. He did not travel in the area, but his cousin James Herbert Curle did (J.H. Curle 1922: 207–211); he may have been the source. It was bought by the Royal Museum of Scotland (now NMS) in 1947, after Curle's death, from one of his daughters (reg. no. A.1947.170). Our thanks to Dan Potter and Tori Adams (NMS) for assistance with this item.
[373] Clerk in the Dept of British and Mediaeval Antiquities and Ethnography, who appears regularly in the Letters. See *Dramatis personae*.
[374] Joseph Louis Capitan (1854–1929), a Paris-based anthropologist and prehistorian who studied and collected widely in South America; see Vaufrey and Maurer 1929.
[375] This answer to Letter 1.67 was found in the 'Home and Abroad' letter bundle.
[376] The journal of the Royal Anthropological Institute.
[377] Joyce 1913.

It is difficult to talk about date; Dr Capitan's suggestion is quite reasonable, though, I think, incapable of proof.

The god (if it is a god) represented must, I fear, remain anonymous, as we know the names of not more than two or three of the coastal deities, and very little about their attributes.

I remain

Yours sincerely

T.A. Joyce

Letter 1.69

13th March, 1913

My dear Smith,

Please forgive my bothering you. I have been worried to do something for this historical congress[378] – and I have very little time. I propose to write a paper on the native things on Roman sites in Scotland and to show that at the time of the Roman occupation here people were living in caves, crannogs, brochs and eirdehouses.[379] I don't know whether I can add hillforts. There isn't perhaps much in it but I think we can show that all these were inhabited in the 2nd century. I hope you don't think the subject too trivial.[380]

I am writing to ask your help about some slides. Will you please look at Newstead Plate LXXV. The most of these are native things not imported from abroad and I want one or two slides showing parallels from <u>native</u> sites in England. Would you be so good as to allow Oldland[381] to make me a slide or slides with parallels of 1 2 3 6 7 8 9.[382]

For 1 2 and 6 the things I have noted below would do.[383]

I want 113 to be set up as I have it.[384] If you can add parallels to the others so much the better. Then I also want a slide giving some of these bone spoons such as you have from the Dowkerbottom cave,[385] which are typically native things. I may have to trouble you again over this job but the period of irritation can't last long.

---

[378] The Third International Congress of Historical Studies was held in London from 3 to 9 April 1913 with 1500 attendees. In the multiplicity of papers heard at the nine simultaneous Congress sections there is understandably no record of the paper read by James Curle. He subsequently published it in the *Journal of Roman Studies* (Curle 1913b).
[379] Underground 'earthhouses' or souterrains.
[380] This returns to a point Curle raised with Read in 1892 over the evidence of Roman finds for the dating of brochs (Letter 1.2).
[381] The Department's assistant, whom Curle regularly sought to co-opt. See *Dramatis personae*.
[382] Curle 1911a: pl. 75. All these items are of central British boss-style metalwork apart from no. 2, which is a lipped terret more typical of southern Britain.
[383] Curle annotated the drawing as follows (left to right): Fig. 113; Fig. 115; Plate V Fig. 4.
[384] Smith 1905: fig. 113. The references in Curle's sketch are also to Smith 1905: figs 113 and 115 are a cruciform strap junction and lipped terret from Stanwick (Melsonby), Yorkshire; pl. V fig. 4 is the Rise (Yorkshire) bridle bit.
[385] Cave system in Yorkshire which had produced rich Romano-British finds including these curious 'spoons'. See Letters 1.54 and 1.56 for references.

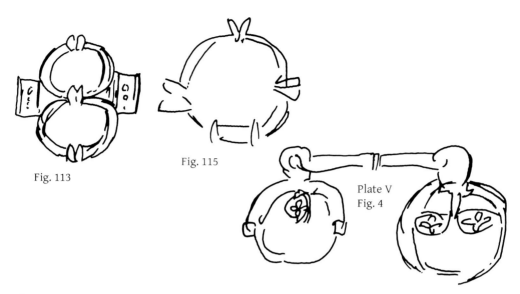

Fig. 113

Fig. 115

Plate V
Fig. 4

Believe me,

Yours sincerely,

James Curle

Letter 1.70

13th April, 1913

My dear Smith,

I am sending you the photograph I promised you of the things from the Middlebie find[386] which I had photographed for my paper to the Hist. Congress.

I have it on my conscience that I did not thank you properly for arranging the things for the slides Oldland made for me.[387]

I enclose a print of a lecture on Romans I gave recently to the Scotch Classical Association,[388] not that there is anything new in it. I went with the trip to Bath, Glastonbury *v.s.*[389] I was much interested with the Lake Dwelling things but the collection was much smaller than I expected.[390]

---

[386] Late Iron Age horse harness hoard in Dumfriesshire. For earlier discussion on this between the two, and references, see Letter 1.51.
[387] See Letter 1.69.
[388] Curle 1913c. The Association is the oldest of the British branches of the Classical Assocation, and was founded in 1902 to promote Classics and Ancient History.
[389] *Vide supra*, 'see above' (in the letter), presumably referring to a trip organised by the Third International Congress of Historical Studies which Curle attended; see Letter 1.69.
[390] The finds from the Glastonbury and Meare lake villages. For a summary see Minnitt and Coles 2006.

By the way, when I was lunching one day in town I sat next a Mrs Wynne French, whose husband possesses a very fine pair of these late Celtic fire dogs[391] like your Welyn[392] [*sic*] find. I advised her to go and see yours. If she calls you will find her pleasant.

Believe me

Yours sincerely,

James Curle

Letter 1.71

20th October, 1913

My dear Smith,

For the second time this year I am going to bother you. I have promised to lecture to some students at Glasgow and I am going to talk about the so-called Samian.[393] I am anxious in connection with this to get one or two slides of silver cups, especially two from the treasure of Bosco Reale.[394] The things are all illustrated in 'Fondation Eugène Piot Monuments et Mémoires' by Perrot et Lasteyrie Tome V Paris Leroux 1899.[395] I don't possess the book and I don't think it is to be found in Edinburgh. I expect it is in the BM Library. If so, could you do me the kindness to get it into your department and let Oldland[396] make me slides of the Cups Plate XVII (2) and Plate XVIII (1) [Figure 8.18].[397]

(By the way, the two figured cups with Augustus seated *v s* are now said to be forgeries).[398]

---

[391] Curle seems to have met Mrs Maud Wynne Finch (1860–1945), widow of Lt-Col. Charles Arthur Wynne Finch (1841–1903), in London and discussed the Capel Garmon fire dog, which was found (alone) in a bog in 1852. It was kept in Voelas Hall, a home of the Wynne Finches near the findspot, after its discovery; in 1913 their son John Charles Wynne Finch (1891–1982), who inherited Voelas on his father's death, was unmarried, so it must be his mother that Curle met. Smith was familiar with the find and its whereabouts (Smith 1912: 7). It was placed on loan in the National Museum of Wales by Colonel J.C. Wynne Finch in 1939 (Fox 1939: 446), and finally acquired by the Museum in 2011 after being accepted by H.M. Government in lieu of tax (Arts Council England 2012: 45). Fire-dogs were iron stands, often with zoomorphic decoration, used singly in front of a fire or in pairs flanking it, containing it and supporting items such as spits (Piggott 1948; 1971).
[392] Smith 1912.
[393] Curle's qualification to the term is interesting, as it does not appear in earlier Letters. See Letter 1.2 n.9. In Anglophone scholarship it is usual to term this pottery samian, but on the continent *terra sigillata* is preferred. Neither is the ancient term. In the Report, Curle preferred the continental terminology.
[394] A large collection of exquisite silver tableware and gold jewellery hidden by its owner prior to the eruption of Vesuvius in AD 79, in the Villa della Pisanella at Boscoreale, near Pompeii. Found in 1895, it is now mostly at the Louvre.
[395] Perrot and de Lasteyrie were editors of the series; the volume is by A. Héron de Villefosse (1899).
[396] The Department's technician; see *Dramatis personae*.
[397] In a later lecture on samian to the Roman Society, reported in *Journal of Roman Studies* 5 (1915): 251, Curle is noted as commenting on Arretine vessels as 'cheap substitutes for the beautiful silver cups', quoting Boscoreale as examples, and in particular 'the wreaths and garlands frequently employed in their decorations'. Plate XVII features a bowl with an olive garland, plate XVIII intertwined plane tree branches and leaves. He drew again on this parallel in a 1917 lecture to the Society of Antiquaries of Scotland (Curle 1917a: 136, fig. 6).
[398] Augustus and Tiberius, enthroned, figure on two of the cups (Héron de Villefosse 1899: 134–148, pls XXI–XXXVI). The cups are not now considered to be forgeries: see Kuttner 1995 for an extended treatment.

Figure 8.18. The two silver cups from the Boscoreale Treasure used by Curle as parallels for samian (Héron de Villefosse 1899: pls XVIII (1), XVII (2)).

I shall be very grateful if you could do this for me and forgive me for the trouble I am causing you. I am sending you a paper which I read at the Historical Congress, about which you also helped me.[399]

With kind regards,

Yours sincerely,

James Curle

---

[399] Curle 1913b; see Letter 1.69.

Letter 1.72

26th October, 1913

(postcard)

Thank you very much for your postcard. There is no hurry about the Slides.[400] Any time within the next 6 weeks will do admirably. Yrs J.C.

Letter 1.73

18th November, 1913

My dear Smith

If I am not giving you a great deal of trouble, could you give me some indication of the date of the enclosed pottery and where it comes from.[401] A lady correspondent has sent it to me with suggestions about amphorae and, arising out of the 'oak' leaves on one piece – of druids. I suppose that it is really quite modern but I found one or two bits at Newstead, no doubt from the surface, and I should like, for my own information, to know what it is. It is more like Wedgwood[402] than any ware I know.

I expect you are very busy, so please forgive my troubling you.

Believe me,

Yours sincerely,

James Curle

Letter 1.74

20th November, 1913

(postcard)

Very many thanks for your note with the pottery, which reached me safely this morning.

Yours sinc.

James Curle

---

[400] See Letter 1.71.
[401] Without illustration of the piece, or a copy of Smith's reply, this must remain elusive, though the description strongly suggests it was modern.
[402] A fine china, porcelain and luxury accessories manufacturer founded on 1 May 1759 by the English potter and entrepreneur Josiah Wedgwood.

Letter 1.75

(postcard, postmarked 11.45 am, 10 Feb. 1914)

Dear Smith,

I am writing a paper on two pairs of Viking brooches recently discovered in the North and I want incidentally to deal with the chronology of the finds we have here of the oval type.[403] The keeper of your department has promised my brother[404] photos of the pair from Ardvouray, Barra Island, Hebrides which you have (Proc. Soc. Antiq. Lond. 2nd series II p229)[405] and I hope he will manage to send them in time for my paper at the beginning of next month.[406]

As Oldland[407] is making the photos he might at the same time make me a slide of one of the brooches and will you kindly tell me what sort of pins they have and how hinged, and whether you have any more specimens found in Scotland. By the way, Oldland's red bowls[408] – the earlier slides – wouldn't come out at all. Please excuse my bothering you.

JC 10.2.14

Letter 1.76

(postcard)

15 Feb, 1914.

Thanks for your Postcard and for arranging about the slide.

I shall certainly send my paper when it is printed. Yours,

J Curle

Letter 1.77

20th February, 1916

My dear Smith,

I am sending you a photograph of a very interesting find from Valtos, Lewis [Figure 8.19].[409] I am sorry to say the things have been given to some Institute in Stornoway, where I suppose

---

[403] Curle 1914. The brooches were from Carn a'Bharraich (Oronsay) and Reay (Caithness).
[404] See Letter A1 to Hercules Read from A.O. Curle.
[405] Note of exhibition: *Proceedings of the Society of Antiquaries of London* (2nd series) 2 (1861–1864): 229–231. For discussion of the burial's location, see McLeod 2015.
[406] A photo of one of the pair was published as Curle 1914: fig. 19.
[407] The departmental assistant; see *Dramatis personae*.
[408] The context of this is unclear.
[409] Valtos is the anglicised form of Bhaltos. In 1915, in a potato patch to the west of Bhaltos school, buried under a sand mound, schoolchildren found a female burial accompanied by: a pair of 9th-century oval brooches, a disc mount with interlace decoration, a penannular brooch, a buckle with interlace decoration, an amber bead, and a

Figure 8.19. The finds from the Viking burial at Valtos/Bhaltos, Lewis, as published by Curle (Macleod et al. 1916: FIG. 1).

copper-alloy chain. Found later in the area were some iron finds, originally seen as a possible knife and parts of a spearhead, suggesting of a second, disturbed male burial. More recently it has been suggested this was a weaving batten, consistent with a female grave (J. Graham-Campbell, pers. comm.). The find was published by Macleod *et al.* 1916; see also Grieg 1940: 75–78.

they will eventually go to bits.[410] I haven't had a chance of seeing them but I have promised to write a few notes on them for the Scotch Antiquaries for a meeting early in March and I should be grateful if you would let me know whether you have in the Museum any parallel to the circular brooch or ornament which forms the centre of the group. It does not appear to have had a pin, but to have been fastened on a band which passed between the disc and the flat metal band, now detached, which is photographed below.[411] The whole group is unusually interesting because of its mixed character. The two oval brooches are purely Scandinavian. The pin and buckle are Celtic, and the circular ornament, I think, belongs to the same category, though I suppose you might find in Norway something of the kind. I am much more familiar with Swedish types than Norwegian and you would not find it in Sweden. I doubt whether you would get any Norwegian work of this character, though circular brooches do seem to occur.

My brother has sent me a copy of Lindenschmidt[412] Alterthumer II Heft XI. Taf 6, with a picture of a disc fibula with a good deal of the same chevron-like decoration as you see round the central boss, but this German thing should be earlier and I don't think there is any real relation between the two. It is practically the same ornament on the terminals of the Croy brooches.[413] I date the find from the oval brooches as belonging to the ninth century, say first half or middle. That would do also for the circular ornament. Does the buckle, with its incised ribbon knotwork, suggest any later date?

I have been looking at Coffey's little guide to the Dublin Museum.[414] He figures an oval brooch of the same type as those from Valtos found at 'Island Bridge' near Kilmainham.[415] Is there any good illustrated description of this find? If so, will you be kind enough to give me a reference to it.

Please excuse my giving you this trouble. Probably you are very busy, possibly you are a Colonel engaged in military duties. The world is full of change and one never knows what has become of one's friends. If you are still a civilian and at the Museum I should feel grateful if you could write me a line before long as I have not left myself much time – in fact I find it very difficult to settle down to anything archaeological.

Yours sincerely,

James Curle

---

[410] The Nicolson Institute, which was the local secondary school. From there they passed to Lewis Museum Trust. The assemblage was subsequently split, with the circular mount, penannular brooch and buckle being given to NMAS and the oval brooches and chain passing to Museum nan Eilean in Stornoway. The amber bead and iron objects are now lost. We are grateful to James Graham-Campbell for information on the find.

[411] Illustrated in Macleod et al. 1916: fig. 1.5.

[412] Lindenschmidt 1870: part 11, pl. 6.1, from a grave at Bopfingen, Baden-Württemberg.

[413] The Croy brooches were part of a scattered hoard found on two separate occasions to the east of Inverness. For a summary, see Grieg 1940: 193-194; for a modern treatment, see Maldonado 2021: 92–97. In fact, the Croy brooches are dissimilar in detail to Valtos; the ribbon interlace around a central cell is more similar to one of the Rogart (Sutherland) brooches, from a hoard discovered in 1868 (Wilson 1973: 81–82, pl. 37d; Youngs 1989: 116, no. 112).

[414] Coffey 1910: fig. 101.

[415] The terminology of these findspots of pagan Norse graves has long been confusing. Kilmainham and Islandbridge were villages just west of Dublin prior to its expansion, and no more than a kilometre apart. A series of Viking burials was found in the area on numerous occasions. The key early publication was Coffey and Armstrong 1910; the discoveries have been authoritatively reviewed by Harrison and Ó Floinn 2014: 242–266.

Letter 1.78

3rd April, 1916

Dear Smith,

I return with many thanks your paper on the Scandinavian things from Island Bridge, which I have kept longer than I intended.[416] They are a very interesting lot. I wish the record of association was more perfect. The buckle, Fig 22, specially interested me as a parallel in some ways to the buckle in the Valtos find.[417] Both seem purely Celtic in character. I confess I am very uncertain what to say as to the disc-like ornament from Valtos, and more than ever impressed with the difficulty of dealing with things one only knows from a photograph.

Peers[418] has been urging me to write a paper on my Gotland things for the London Antiquaries. Is it worth doing? I have always felt that I could hardly add anything to the papers done by better men in Sweden.[419]

Believe me,

Yours sincerely,

James Curle

Letter 1.79

31st December, 1919

My dear Read,

I must apologise for my delay in answering your letter about my Viking Collection. Of course I should like it eventually to go into a Museum and there is nowhere it could fit so well as in your department.[420] For the moment I cannot quite make up my mind whether I should part with it and, if so, what I should ask for it. I am sorry to say there are few people here who take any interest in such things, but I have a somewhat sentimental feeling towards it, recalling as it does a good deal of trafficking and hunting. When I spoke to you early in the war I felt seriously that it would probably be necessary for me to realise any superfluities of the kind, as I could not afford to hold such things, but after it is all over I find myself in a better position than I expected. I shall think over the subject and when I am next in town I shall come and see you. I did call in October but you were from home and I was sorry to hear from Hill[421] that you had been unwell.

---

[416] Reference is to Coffey and Armstrong 1910.

[417] See Harrison and Ó Floinn 2014: 160–161, 448–450, ill. 267. The incised key pattern on the rear of the buckle paralleled the use of insular motifs on the Bhaltos buckle (Macleod *et al.* 1916: 188, fig. 2).

[418] Sir Charles Reed Peers (1868–1952), secretary of the Society of Antiquaries of London at this point. See *Dramatis personae.*

[419] See Kidd and Thunmark-Nylén 1990: 164 for discussion. Curle published almost nothing on his collection beyond his 1895 paper to the Society of Antiquaries of Scotland.

[420] The full context of the sale of Curle's Gotland collection is discussed by Kidd and Thunmark-Nylén 1990: 157–160, and details are not duplicated here.

[421] This must be Sir George Francis Hill (1867–1948), Keeper of Coins and Medals from 1912–1931, and Director from

I am so very much interested to hear that the Greek and Roman department have got a helmet mask from Palestine [Figure 9.1].[422] I wish the industrious Oldland[423] could get me a photograph or a slide of it but I suppose that at present that is impossible.

With all good wishes for 1920

Believe me,

Yours very sincerely,

James Curle

Letter 1.80

9th March, 1921

My dear Read,

I am afraid I have been very rude in not replying earlier to a letter you wrote to me about my Gotland Collection. I find it very difficult to make up my mind and I rather hate the idea of parting. I would in any case like to retain the glass beaker [Figure 8.20].[424]

As regards the rest of the articles in bronze, silver and gold of which you have a list, my position is that if you thought fit to offer the Twelve hundred Pounds[425] I should not feel justified in refusing. If you want to see the collection we can easily arrange that. I may be in London within the next week or ten days. I meant to have gone up on Monday but my eldest girl has come home from school owing to an outbreak of whooping cough and until we know whether she is in for it we can't make our plans.

With kind regards,

Believe me,

Yours very sincerely,

James Curle

1931–1936 (Wilson 2002: 202–203, 238–239); he was the only 'Hill' on BM staff at this time.

[422] From what was then Aintab (Syria) and is now Gazientep (Turkey); Robertson 1975: pls 324–325; Garbsch 1978: 68, pl. 23.2, O30. It is a close parallel for the Newstead bronze mask.

[423] The department's assistant, whose time Curle regularly co-opted; see *Dramatis personae*. Curle was indeed able to get a photograph; see Letter 2.6.

[424] See Letter 1.2, and Kidd and Thunmark-Nylén 1990: 159–160, 164, fig. 9.

[425] The use of the definite article suggests there had been discussions around this topic; it was not freshly introduced at this point.

Figure 8.20. *Glass beaker from Gotland of the Germanic Iron Age, cherished by Curle and purchased from him with the rest of his Gotlandic collection by the British Museum. © Trustees of the British Museum (1921,1101.381).*

Letter 1.81

The British Museum
London WC

March 16, 1921

Dear Curle,

I have been thinking over your letter of 9th March with regard to your Gotland Collection. It needed some thought, as the price is no negligible sum, and a good deal higher than I had anticipated, remembering the various estimates we had discussed before, all of them being on a more modest scale.

I cannot, however, begin to bargain with you. I do not think it decent.[426]

Further, if these things are to come here in my time, this is my last opportunity as I am retiring in a few months, and I confess I should like to 'clear up' before I leave. But I must say that I do not think you ought to withdraw the glass in the circumstances.[427]

If you look back to our earliest talks on this matter and your recollection is as clear as mine, I am sure you will at any rate be able to appreciate my feelings about it.

I hope I may see you here and that young woman will be spared whooping cough.

Yours very truly,

C.H. Read

Letter 1.82

Typewritten

PRIORWOOD   *Sir Hercules Reid* [sic]
MELROSE N.B   *The British Museum*
                                                         London
25th April, 1921

My dear Read,

I have your letter. I quite understand that Reginald Smith won't come here this week, and the matter can quite well lie over till things are more settled.

I don't myself see any prospect of my coming south in the meantime, and, of course, as I said before, I would very much prefer that you should take the risks of packing and handling the Collection.

With kind regards

Believe me,

Yours sincerely,

James Curle

---

[426] The purchase was authorised by the Trustees of the British Museum in July 1921, with a substantial grant from the National Arts Collection Fund (Kidd and Thunmark-Nylén 1990: 153). By the following year it was 'for the most part exhibited in the Iron Age Gallery, Cases 55 and 56' (*Antiquaries Journal* 2 [1922]: 382–383).
[427] The glass beaker was not retained by the seller.

Letter 1.83

16th June, 1921

My dear Read,

Would it be possible for some one, preferably Reginald Smith, to take over these Swedish things during this month?

Just at present there is no prospect of my getting away and I could fix a day next week. So far I am only engaged on Monday and Friday when I have some County meetings. The London trains are running regularly and present no difficulty.

I hope we are within sight of the end of this wretched strike,[428] though the figures in the morning papers are less hopeful than one could have wished.

With kind regards,

Believe me,

Yours very sincerely,

James Curle

Letter 1.84

15th July, 1921

My dear Read,

I hope my collection arrived in good condition and that you are pleased with it. I am a little anxious about my luggage, especially the suit case, which I lent Mr Tonnochie [*sic*],[429] as I expect to be going abroad within the next ten days and I shall require it.

I got the keys which he returned safely but, as yet, I have heard nothing of the bag or suit case. I suppose that you will now send me a cheque for the £1,200.

I should like to get that before I leave home.

---

[428] The miners' strike of April–June 1921, following the return of the industry to private ownership after World War One and corresponding reduction in wages.
[429] The Medievalist Alec Bain Tonnochy (1889–1963), appointed to Read's department in 1914 (Wilson 2002: 201, 235; Caygill 2002: 392).

I am afraid when next I come to the Museum I shall not find you in office[430] and I shall regret it, as you have always been so helpful when I have come to you for assistance.

With kind regards,

Believe me,

Yours sincerely,

James Curle

Perhaps Mr Tonnochie will be kind enough to make enquiries about the suit case and let me know when it was sent off and how.

Letter 1.85

The British Museum
London WC

14th December, 1931

Dear Curle

I cannot trace any Roman things from Scotland in this Museum, but will bear the matter in mind. The gold brooch is a mystery [Figure 8.21]. The Corpus[431] speaks of TATINSHOLM and you write TALMSHOLM.[432] Which is correct? Your reference to Archaeology Journal I leads me nowhere, as not even vol I of the new series of A J contains anything by Haverfield.[433]

The Porth Dafarch (Holyhead) tankard handle here is figured in A J XXXIII opp. p140[434] and has no obvious Celtic features. The Hod Hill specimen is in our IRON AGE GUIDE[435] fig.146, quite unlike that from Aylesford, fig 140, but both Celtic. One still attached to its tankard is in Brentford museum (this and others are referred to in ARCHAEOLOGIA LXIX 23)[436] and one has recently been found at Colchester.[437]

Yours sincerely,

Reginald A Smith

Keeper

---

[430] Owing to Read's imminent retiral.
[431] CIL vii, 1283.
[432] Gold crossbow brooch from Erickstanebrae, Dumfriesshire, found in 1787; see Curle 1932a: 370–371; RIB II.3: 2421.43. The context must be James Curle's preparations for this paper, read before the Society on 14 March 1932; he was clearly trying to locate the brooch, which was still in private hands at the time, and was subsequently sold to the Los Angeles County Museum (https://collections.lacma.org/node/230173; accessed 11 July 2022). A silver-gilt replica was donated to NMAS in 1951 (*Proceedings of the Society of Antiquaries of Scotland* 85 [1950–1951]: 185). Curle's paper provides the wider context: 'Tatiusholm' is the form given in the *Old Statistical Account* for the parish of Kirkpatrick-Juxta, as a pseudo-Latin version of 'Tassiesholm'. The CIL entry corrupted Tatiusholm to Tatinsholm. The correct findspot is Erickstanebrae.
[433] It was in fact published by Haverfield (1893: 305–306).
[434] Stanley 1876.
[435] Smith 1925.
[436] Smith 1918: 22–23.
[437] Curle was pursuing parallels for the tankard handle in the hoard from Carlingwark, Kirkcudbrightshire: see Curle 1932a: 322–323, where the Brentford reference is used.

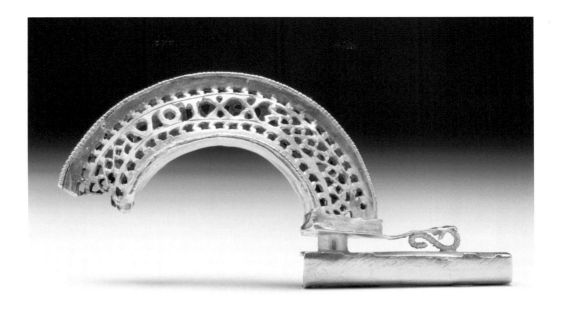

Figure 8.21. The Erickstanebrae late Roman crossbow brooch. (Los Angeles County Museum of Art, 50.22.14).

Chapter 9

From Greece and Rome[1]

Letter 2.1

Priorwood
Melrose N.B.

7th December 1892.

Dear Mr Murray,[2]

I should like to join the Society of Antiquaries if they will have me, and Mr Read has kindly put down my name.[3] As you are one of the few members I know I take the liberty of asking you to sign the enclosed certificate for me and I shall feel very much obliged if you will do so. I find on looking over the list that Fellows of the Society are very rare in these parts.

I spent a couple of days in Berlin a fortnight ago and saw their collections for the first time.[4] They have some beautiful things and I found the Antiquarium of the new museum a most interesting place. With kind regards,

Believe me,

Yours very sincerely,

James Curle Jr

Letter 2.2

Priorwood
Melrose N.B.

20: VII: 94

Dear Mr Murray,

I have been trying to work up some information about the finds of glass vessels in Northern Europe.[5] I daresay you know the series of bowls found in Denmark decorated with painted

---

[1] Letters from Curle to the Department of Greece and Rome in the British Museum. We thank Francesca Hillier and Thomas Kiely for dogged pursuit of our hunch that such letters must exist, and the latter for confirming that none of Curle's letters to H.B. Walters survive, though it is clear the two men were in correspondence (Letter 3.19).

[2] Alexander Stuart Murray (1841–1904), Keeper of Greek and Roman Antiquities at the BM, and a native of Arbroath (Caygill 2002: 388; Wilson 2002: 182). See *Dramatis personae*.

[3] See Letters 1.5 and 1.6.

[4] Mentioned also in Letters 1.4 and 1.5.

[5] This is interesting as it predates the discovery of a facetted glass cup from Birrens which prompted Curle to publish a note on comparanda from Scandinavia and Germany; see Christison *et al.* 1896: 190–191. It shows Curle's pre-existing interest in the topic, perhaps because stimulated by glass (though not of this type, as far as we know) in his Scandinavian collection.

representations of gladiatorial combats or animals.[6] Though undoubtedly Roman, I have read that vessels decorated in this way are unknown further south. I can find in the Rhine Countries nearly all the forms one meets with in the north but as yet I do not find this painted glass.

I wonder if you could give me any hint of the occurrence of this method of decoration in southern finds.

I hope you will excuse my troubling you about this.

Believe me

Yours very sincerely

James Curle Jr

Letter 2.3

Priorwood,
Melrose N.B.

24th April 1907,

Dear Mr Smith,[7]

On my return home this evening I found your letter and am very much obliged to you for kindly sending me the reference I wanted.[8]

Believe me

Yours very truly

James Curle

Letter 2.4

Priorwood
Melrose N.B.

27th June 1907

Dear Mr Smith,

I enclose an impression of a gem we found at Newstead last week.[9] I don't possess a copy of Salomon Reinach's Pierres gravées[10] and I should be grateful if you can tell me who is

---

[6] Ingemark 2014: 60–70.
[7] Sir Cecil Harcourt Smith (1859–1944), Keeper of Greek and Roman Antiquities at the British Museum from 1904 to 1909, thereafter Director of the Victoria and Albert Museum from 1909 to 1924 (Wilson 2002: 199; Caygill 2002: 391).
[8] See Letter 4.4; Curle was seeking a reference for a shoe-shaped vessel with inscription.
[9] See Letter 1.40.
[10] Reinach 1895.

represented. The figure seems to carry a whip over its left arm. I imagine it is Mithraic but you will probably be able to explain it.[11] This is our second gem. The earlier has a Ganymede.[12]

Believe me

Yours sincerely,

James Curle

[A wax impression of the gem formed on a piece of card is attached to the letter.]

Letter 2.5

Priorwood,
Melrose N.B.

29th June 1907.

Dear Mr Smith,

Vey many thanks for your note and identification of the gem. I hope to send you in a few days a short article on the occupation of the Newstead fort.[13]

Yours sincerely,

James Curle

Letter 2.6

Priorwood,
Melrose N.B.

11th January 1920

Dear Sir,[14]

I have to thank you very much for so kindly sending me a photograph of your new helmet mask from Palestine [Figure 9.1].[15] It is really very fine and I congratulate you on your acquisition. It gives me the impression that in the course of time it has been flattened out somewhat but this may be only an effect in the photograph. The brass mask at Newstead was practically

---

[11] Curle was thinking on the right lines; the gem shows Sol (Curle 1911a: 333, pl. 87 no. 35; Henig 2007: 95 no. 30).
[12] Curle 1911a: 333, pl. 87 no. 36; Henig 2007: 152 no. 473.
[13] Curle 1907a.
[14] The formality of this address is at odds with that for previous ones in this series, suggesting this was a new correspondent. It is most likely Arthur H. Smith, Keeper of the Department from 1909–1925 (another letter in BM files indicates that A.O. Curle wrote to him on 28 May 1920).
[15] Robertson 1975: pls 324–325; Garbsch 1978: 68, pl. 23.2, O30. It came from what was then Aintab (Syria) and is now Gazientep (Turkey). Curle first wrote to Read seeking information; see Letter 1.79.

quite flattened out when we found it and was afterwards pulled into shape. If the sides of the mask especially the left ear and the portion below it are in their original position one hardly sees how they would fit into the headpiece. In case it may be of interest to you I send you a note containing an illustration of Mr Kam's helmet which I published in the Journal of Roman Studies.[16] I shall look forward to your publishing your find. I hope you will be able to give us some information as to the source from which these helmets spread across the provinces and the models which inspired the men who made them. Newstead certainly gives a reliable dating.[17]

Believe me,

Yours very truly,

James Curle

Figure 9.1. The helmet face-mask from Gazientep, Turkey. © Trustees of the British Museum (1919, 1220.1).

[16] Curle 1915.
[17] Curle had long recognised the wider dating value of the sequence he had revealed.

Chapter 10
My Dear Haverfield

Letter 3.1

From Haverfield to John Abercromby.[1]

Budleigh Salterton[2]

Easter eve 1905[3]

Dear Mr. Abercromby

Thank you very much for your letter. I heard at Crawford Priory,[4] where I was the other day, that you were in Athens and was hoping that my letter would not have been sent on to bother you. I am very sorry to hear that you have resigned the Secretaryship to the Soc. of Antiquaries.[5]

Mr Curle took me to Newsteads. It promises to prove an interesting site – a fort considerably larger than the average, and just possibly some traces of two periods. But the job is not very easy, and I ventured to suggest to both Dr. Christison[6] and Mr Curle that it was rather too hard for Mackie[7] by himself – one might put it stronger, but is perhaps enough.

Dr Christison, whom I saw for a moment in Edinburgh, told me that he thought March (more exactly perhaps the end of March or early April) would do well for my Rhind lectures in 1906.[8]

I hope you will have an interesting – and not too interesting – tour in Crete.

Yours sincerely

F. Haverfield

---

[1] Found by Donald Gordon among Curle notebooks in the National Record of the Historic Environment, Edinburgh. John Abercromby (1841–1924), 5th Baron Abercromby of Aboukir and Tullibody, was an active member of the Society of Antiquaries of Scotland, and published a major work on Bronze Age pottery (Abercromby 1912).
[2] In Devon; a popular holidaying area for the Haverfields, and in close proximity to their friends the Coleridges (see Letter 3.25 n.167).
[3] 23 April.
[4] Country house 3 km south-west of Cupar (Fife), at this time in the family of the Earls of Glasgow.
[5] The tangential reference is to a major controversy in the history of the Society, when Abercromby resigned as Secretary and withdrew his considerable financial backing as he felt the Society's excavation standards were seriously deficient. For more background to this see Piggott and Robertson 1977: 89–91; Stevenson 1981: 177–179; D.V. Clarke 2012: 26.
[6] David Christison (1831–1912) was involved in the excavation of many Roman forts for the Society, and also led the excavations on the early medieval fort at Dunadd, Argyll which were the particular target of Abercromby's ire; see Piggott and Robertson 1977: 85. Author of the seminal work on Scottish hillforts (Christison 1898), and Secretary of the Society of Antiquaries of Scotland at this point.
[7] Alexander Mackie, who had acted as Clerk of Works on several Society excavations (Stevenson 1981: 177; D.V. Clarke 2012: 25). See *Dramatis personae*.
[8] A prestigious annual lecture series given by a respected scholar on their chosen topic at the invitation of the Society of Antiquaries of Scotland, funded by the estate of Alexander Henry Rhind of Sibster, Caithness. Haverfield delivered the Rhind lectures on 'Roman Britain' in 1906.

Letter 3.2

PRIORWOOD
MELROSE N.B.

10th August, 1905

Dear Mr Haverfield,

Is there any chance of your coming to Scotland this month?[9]

I should like you to see what is being done at Newstead and to have your views about it.

At present we have traced out four large buildings. 1st in the angle of the via principalis and South Rampart a large block corresponding to the so-called Commandant's Quarters at Housesteads; immediately N of that a large buttressed building, further N the Praetorium[10] and N of that a long rectangular building, possibly a granary, and probably a secondary construction as it is built of different stonework and we found a large Andernach[11] mill stone or rather part of one in the foundation. I have no reason to suppose the Station smaller than the extent we thought probable when you were here, about 14 acres.

The soil shows considerable disturbance and suggests more than one occupation but as yet we have found no outline of a smaller, earlier camp. I am hopeful that we may do so as, under the great rampart we found an older ditch and on the inside of the ditch a post which may have formed part of a wooden facing of the rampart, replaced at a later time with stone. I think the stone wall in front does not admit of any doubt. We have it clearly in a cut now open and I see it as still better preserved in a new section further E which we began yesterday. We are also trying to investigate the S gate. The buildings are in a very ruined condition but they seem quite above the average size and there are many points about them you would find interesting.

I am sorry to say that we have only picked up three small fragments of inscribed stones but I hope we may yet get something of importance. We have got quite an interesting collection of small objects and one or two good enamelled fibulae among them. So far we have not cleaned out any of the buildings and I doubt whether funds and time will permit of our doing much more than trace out the walls, which is unsatisfactory. We shall try to have the Praetorium at least cleaned out.

By the way we found so much of the black deposit you noted at various points in the Well Meadow[12] that I feel sure it was not caused by an old ditch but simply by swampy ground.

---

[9] Haverfield's location at this point is not certain, but it is likely it was Bellingham in Northumberland, a favoured base; other correspondence confirms he was there by 27th August.

[10] Curle's use of *praetorium* rather than the more correct *principia* for the headquarters building was typical for the period, but had changed by the time of publication; for background, see Letter 1.18 n.97.

[11] Quern and mill stones from the Eifel area of Germany, variously termed Andernach, Mayen or Niedermendig, were shipped in quantity all over Europe and were widely used in the army.

[12] The main field marking the centre of the fort that the walker encounters going east from Newstead village. The excavation was begun by cutting a trench from west to east across the south half of the Well Meadow field (Curle 1911a: 6). The other fields covering the remains are Red Abbeystead, Fore Ends (south of the road from Newstead to Leaderfoot) and Gutterflat, lying west of and lower than the Well Meadow (Figure 3.3).

We have been up in Sweden for a holiday but do not expect to be much away this Autumn, so if you will come and stay I shall be very glad to see you.

Believe me,

Yours sincerely,

James Curle

Letter 3.3

PRIORWOOD
MELROSE N.B.

14th August 1905

Dear Mr Haverfield,

Certainly let me know whenever it will suit you to come. I don't think there will be any difficulty about putting you up. It is very good of you to suggest that I might see a bit of the Wall. I have never done so as yet and if we could arrange it I would like very much to have the opportunity of seeing it with you. Perhaps when you have been here we may manage to plan a visit.

I wonder if we are going to make a discovery at Newstead. We have blocked out a square. It appears to be a wall of well-dressed freestone. I am hoping when we clean out the earth that it may prove to be a well. In the pit on the N side we found a fragment of an inscription connected with the XX legion.[13]

In our new cut through the S Rampart the old ditch is still running below the mound. The 8' wall is quite distinct in front of the Rampart and comes almost to the surface. I am afraid the gate will be rather a puzzle.

No, I am sorry to say we did not get to Oxford. That must be for another time.

Yours sincerely,

James Curle

Please excuse a hurried note JC

---

[13] RIB I: 2127.

This is a Praetorium

perhaps had roofing tile use

These cross walls are all different and [...]

None of this is cleaned out

These are cobble bases

Some ... shed ...

pit filled in
with debris

fully dressed
stone bases

cobbled masonry
pillars

Letter 3.4

PRIORWOOD
MELROSE N.B.

14th September, 1905

Dear Mr Haverfield,

At last we have got our Altar [Figure 10.1].[14]

Mackie sent for me this morning and I found it uncovered in the pit and saw it turned over.[15] It is still down in the mud but the inscription seems quite clear:–

I O M

G ARRIUS

DOMITIANUS

S LEG XX VV

VSLLM

This is evidently the same man who dedicated the altar found in 1830 to the DIIS CAMPESTRIBUS, only the accounts style him as 'CARRIUS'.[16] Does 'S' stand for 'Signifer'?

Near this altar we got a corroded 1st Brass of, I think, Trajan and lower still a head of Bos Longifrons.[17] We are not at the bottom and so I hope for more.

Yours sincerely,

James Curle

Figure 10.1. Altar erected by Gaius Arrius Domitianus, found in the well in the principia. © National Museums Scotland (X.FV 46).

---

[14] RIB I: 2123.

[15] The pit referred to here and in Letters 3.5–3.8 is Pit I in the *principia*; Curle 1911a: 47–49, 116–117.

[16] Curle has confused the two earlier altar finds from the site. RIB I: 2121, found in 1783, was to the *Campestres* but was not donated by the same man; he erected RIB I: 2124, to Silvanus, which was found in 1830.

[17] An ox.

Letter 3.5

PRIORWOOD
MELROSE N.B.

19th September, 1905

Dear Mr Haverfield,

Thanks for your note. The letter I mistook for a 'S' is, as you say, the sign for a centurion ❯. It is quite distinct.

So also is the G before Arrius. Later on you shall have a photograph. The whole inscription is as clear as the day it was cut. We have had no further finds of importance since the altar, but as we had to rig up a crane to get it out, a good deal of time has been given to other work than cleaning out the pit. Just beneath the altar was a 1st brass of Hadrian, at least as far as I can make it out. Lower down we have had some big stones, roughly squared, a small fragment of a good moulding from an altar, the rest of which may be lower down, some leather and skulls of Bos Longifrons. We have got the turn of the old ditch at the SW corner, and today Mackie[18] will try to locate its crossing to the N.

I saw the plan of Rough Castle the other day, as reduced for the Proceedings.[19] I am afraid, as far as the buildings go, the reduction has rendered it perfectly useless.

With kind regards,

Believe me,

Yours sincerely,

James Curle

Letter 3.6

PRIORWOOD
MELROSE N.B.

22nd September, 1905

Dear Mr Haverfield,

Our well promises to make an interesting chapter. We are now down 22 feet! Since the altar was found we have been going down in wet mud, finding daily heads of Bos Longifrons and other bones, a few building stones and a lot of leather in sheets, with bits of large amphorae and occasional fragments of Samian ware. On Wednesday, at about 20 feet, we picked up an implement made from 2 portions of deer horn.

---

[18] Clerk of Works on the site, who was in charge of the practicalities of the excavations; see *Dramatis personae*.
[19] Fort west of Falkirk on the Antonine Wall. The Society's excavations were published in Buchanan *et al.* 1905. The overall plan (fig. 1) is indeed rather small, though enlargements of the buildings were given in the text.

This sort of thing.

Yesterday we had the usual bones and leather. In the latter I saw some stitched edges for the first time. The necks and handles of two amphorae, a human skull, and within a foot of it a number of small laminae of gold,[20] each with a hole at one end and two smaller holes on each side by which they were fastened together by gold wire. We picked up yesterday 286 and there may be some more in the mud [Figure 10.2].

The largest number still connected with each other is 15 and we have a number of eights, fives, fours etc but I don't know that we can make anything from that. The things were not lying flat but came up in lumps rolled together. They may have been attached to a soft material which has disappeared. At the same level we found a Samian bottom with the stamp 'Probus f'.[21]

Can you tell me of any similar find of gold? The laminae are very thin, so it is not armour. I know examples of small gold stamped ornaments for dresses in Scandinavia.[22]

The hole is narrowing and is now 9 feet 6 inches in diameter. Yesterday a large boulder appeared, projecting into it, but we have no building and not much water.

Yours sincerely,

James Curle

Letter 3.7

From George Macdonald to Haverfield.[23]

17 Learmonth Gardens,
Edinburgh 23:9:05

Dear Haverfield,

I have been down to Melrose today. The bottom of the pit has been reached. No more inscriptions were found but the mystery has grown more exciting. The full depth was 26 feet 6 inches, and the breadth at the lowest part over 6 feet. Beneath the altar (which was at 12 feet) were stones, bases of columns and a broken altar among them – and beneath these again a find that reminds me of the story of Curtius.[24] Near the bottom, about 22 feet down

---

[20] See Letter 3.9 for the denouement of this identification; the waterlogged conditions left brass in an untarnished condition, looking like gold. The material was scale armour, *lorica squamata*; see Curle 1911a: 158–159.
[21] Bottom of a samian (*terra sigillata*) dish stamped by the potter Probus, the f a contraction for *fecit*, 'made it'.
[22] So-called 'guldgubbar' of early medieval date: Watt 2009.
[23] See *Dramatis personae*.
[24] M.' Curtius; Roman myth of an armed horseman hero who saved the state by plunging with his charger into an

Figure 10.2. Brass scale armour found in the well in the principia, and originally identified as gold.
© National Museums Scotland (X.FRA 118).

– animal bones,

– a mass of leather,

– necks of two large amphorae

– Samian one piece, with Probus f

– a human skull

– 286 gold laminae (a sort of apron?) very thin, the small holes for attaching them to each other – many still fastened with wire (also gold)

abyss that had opened in the Forum (Livy, *Ab urbe condita* VII: 6).

– considerable fragments of a lorica segmentata (?) ornamented at certain parts with gold (largest fragment 10" × 5" or 6")[25]

– Two excellent knives – one still in horn handle – and sundry other implements.

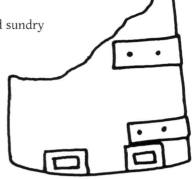

The animal bones and the leather worth sorting and examination. They may be the horse and the dress of the owner of the skull. No other human bones have been recognised, but I suspect they are there. The whole contents were quite unlike those of a rubbish pit, and besides, what on earth would they have a rubbish pit in the praetorium court for?

And it was not a well: there is no water at the bottom.

The men have now started cuttings on the lines you suggested but there is nothing fresh to report yet there. By the way, what of the chamber in the praetorium at the Saalburg, which Jacobi calls the 'sacellum'?[26] There is (apparently) a thing of this sort at Newstead.

Yours ever,

Geo Macdonald

I am going to Bar Hill on Wednesday with Curle[27]

Letter 3.8

PRIORWOOD
MELROSE

28th September, 1905

N.B. Did you see a stupid paragraph in the Times of yesterday about the altar?[28] I don't know where they get such things. JC

Dear Mr Haverfield,

Very many thanks for your letter and for sending me the enclosed which I should have answered earlier, but I have been from home. I feel that the letter would appeal to the public with far more weight over your signature than it could do over mine.[29] If you would be kind

---

[25] Legionary plate armour of iron strips; this is one of the type-specimens. Curle 1911a: 155–158; Bishop 1999.

[26] Louis Jacobi excavated the frontier fort of the Saalburg on the German *limes* in the Taunus, north-east of Frankfurt, and led its reconstruction; see Jacobi 1897. *Sacellum*: small shrine.

[27] Fort on the Antonine Wall excavated by Alexander Park, factor for the landowner, with George Macdonald. Park also corresponded with Haverfield, who visited several times. The 1905 visit came at the conclusion of the excavations. The Bar Hill excavators in turn visited Newstead in October 1905 (Keppie 2002: 33).

[28] *The Times* 27 September 1905: 12, at base of column 4, titled 'Antiquarian discoveries at Melrose', giving a garbled version of the excavation of the altar, with major errors in the dedicant: 'To the great and mighty Jupiter, Carolus, centurion of the 20th legion, valiant and victorious, cheerfully, willingly, and deservedly paid his vow'.

[29] Note JC 'authorising' FJH to circulate information to where the latter thought appropriate (and repeated in Letter

enough to send it to the Times and the Athenaeum or any papers you think should have [it], I should feel obliged.[30]

I can send a letter to the Scotch papers, making use of your facts. By the way, I am not quite sure if your last paragraph quite brings out the full significance of our discovery. The pit is not a well.[31] We touched bottom at 25 feet 6 inches and there is no water. Neither is it an ordinary rubbish pit because there is so little rubbish. Neither is it quite like a grave because they did not repeat the great quantity of clay they took out but filled it up with stones. At the same time the very significant fact remains that there was one and probably two men in the bottom of the pit. About 22 feet down we found a complete skull underneath and surrounded by heads of oxen, horses and other animal bones, a lot of leather and pieces of five or six amphorae. Near the ~~skeleton~~ skull we picked up the gold scales of which I have taken 300 to the Museum and also portions of his iron cuirass ornamented with gold. The largest is like this.[32]

We have also found parts of the armplates with gold rivets.

At the very bottom of the pit we got two good knives, a small pail of wood and what may have been a balance. You see it is not merely a deposit of precious things, for a man went with them.

Please let me know what you do write to the papers. Till I hear from you

Yours sincerely,

James Curle

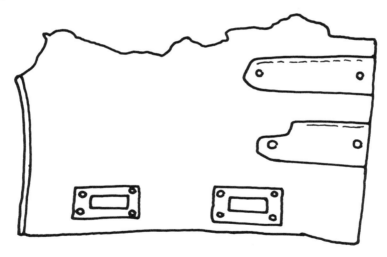

3.10) – a role FJH assumed, sometimes with authorisation, sometimes not, sometimes anonymised, sometimes not, for others. George Macdonald also occasionally played the same part.

[30] The *Times* had previously published a report sent by A Correspondent – 'Roman Remains in Scotland' (*The Times* 25 August 1905: 10), which noted a visit to the excavations by members of the Berwickshire Naturalists' Club on 23 June. Parts of the description from the *Proceedings of the Berwickshire Naturalists Club* (1905: 264–267, 268) are reported in large measure in *The Times* summary along with a postscript update of progress after their visit. Some of this detail is also included in Macdonald's letter to FJH on 23 September (Letter 3.7), where the former says he had been to Newstead that day. The *Times* report notes that the excavations at Newstead were '... at the instance of the Society of Antiquaries of Scotland', a subtle alteration to the *Proceedings* version, emphasising whose excavations they were. Was MacDonald the unnamed *Times* correspondent?

[31] Letters 3.3–3.8 all concern Pit I in the *principia*; Curle 1911a: 47–49, 116–117.

[32] The original image is annotated with dimensions; the brass fittings are labelled 'gold'.

Letter 3.9

PRIORWOOD
MELROSE N.B.

29th September, 1905

Dear Mr Haverfield,

I hesitated to use the words 'pure gold' about the Newstead things[33] till I submitted them to Dr Anderson.[34] He too was misled by the colour and pliability of the metal but I have a letter from him this morning in which he tells me that on analysis they turn out to be brass.[35] I wired this to you in case you might be writing to the papers. It rather takes the glamour off the find but it is still, I fancy, unique in Scotland.

Yours very sincerely,

James Curle

Letter 3.10

From Curle to George Macdonald.

PRIORWOOD
MELROSE N.B.

13th Oct, 1905

Dear Dr Macdonald,

I wrote to Haverfield after our Barhill [*sic*] excursion[36] suggesting that the letter he was good enough to draft would come with far more weight over his signature than mine and suggesting that he should send it to the English papers. Before he had time to get it I discovered that our armour was, after all, not of gold so I wired to him and wrote a note in explanation.

Since then I have heard nothing from him. I hope he has not misunderstood my suggestion about writing to the papers. Of course I should willingly write if he does not care to do so. It was disappointing that our gold was only brass and I dread to meet Mr Mackintosh [*sic*] of Barhill.[37] Otherwise the find is none the less important. They are busy at work over the ~~West~~ East gateway.

We have not found the turn of the old ditch but we find its line running from the N side overlapping the gate somewhat in this form.

---

[33] The brass *lorica squamata* referred to in Letters 3.7–3.8.
[34] Keeper of NMAS; see *Dramatis personae*.
[35] In discussion of the armour finds at Ham Hill, Somerset at the Society of Antiquaries of London on 29 March 1906 (Gray 1906: 139), Professor Gowland commented on the Melrose parallels being 'not bronze but Roman brass', suggesting he either conducted the analysis or knew the analyst.
[36] See Letters 3.7 (mentioning the excursion) and 3.8.
[37] John McIntosh, forester on Gartshore estate who led the digging at Bar Hill (Keppie 2002: 26). Presumably Curle had told him about their 'gold' when they visited the site.

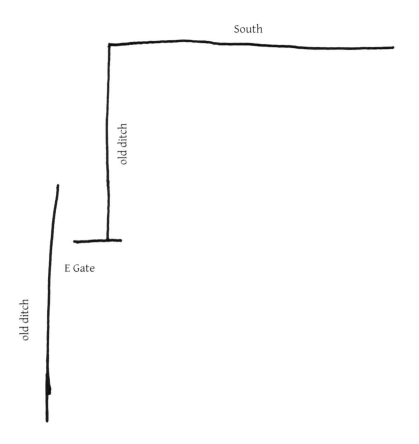

We have still to puzzle it out. Close by this gate we have found another pit which we are cleaning out, but nothing important as yet. In searching for the road on the S side of the camp we have found what I have little doubt is one of the burial pits of the cemetery.[38] It is a considerable distance from the railway cutting so between the two points we may have a number of burials. This may prove far more important than anything we have yet found. I hope you were none the worse of our day at Barhill which I enjoyed very much.

Believe me,

Yours sincerely,

James Curle

---

[38] In fact this proved to be one of the famous pits. Curle's mention of the railway cutting suggests that at this stage he considered the pits uncovered in railway construction across the site in 1846 to be burials, probably due to the discovery of a skeleton of a man with a spear in one of them (Smith 1857: 425; see also Curle 1911a: 4–6).

Letter 3.11

PRIORWOOD
MELROSE N.B.

20th November, 1905

Dear Mr Haverfield,

I send you a photograph of the Newstead altar[39] taken by Mackie. We have not found anything further in the way of inscriptions. I enclose a plan taken from the appeal we are about to issue to the public, which will give you a rough idea of what we are about [Figure 10.3].[40] The old ditch has been traced along part of the N side. Evidently the arm coming from the W has been deflected outward and the most of it is therefore under the modern road. We have however found the point turning inwards as on the E side. At the E gate the old ditch runs right under the guard chambers. The S gate has not been touched since you were here. Evidently the early camp was not so very much smaller than the later one. Is it possible that there may have been a third? We have as yet no trace of it.

I also send you a woodcut of an intaglio[41] found lately and an unfixed print of a Samian Bowl. We found the pieces in what appears to have been a burial pit just beyond the ramparts near the S Gate.[42]

Among the designs I find four in Déchelette:-[43]

S 37 Graufesenque, 63 Lezoux or Graufesenque,

481 Graufesenque or Bouassac 563 Bouassac very slightly round

The evidence seems to favour Graufesenque as the pottery. I found lately a small piece of this black ~~figured~~ pottery, white on the edges and white when the surface is rubbed off, with a portion of an animal figure in relief. Would this be British manufacture?[44]

I have also a bit of a vase of rich ware decorated like Samian with embossed figures of a reddish black. The edges are of a gray colour, close in texture. Is all the imported ware of Samian type red in colour? I would be grateful if you could give me a copy of your paper printed by the Cumberland and Westmorland Soc. on pottery.[45] I am being much harassed in dealing with the farm tenants who, as usual, make absurd demands.

Believe me,

Yours sincerely,

James Curle

---

[39] See Letters 3.4–3.5.

[40] Curle 1907b.

[41] The samian bowl came from the pit, not the intaglio; a report in *The Scotsman* from the previous month (28 October 1905: 9) recorded the discovery of 'a small intaglio ... with a well-cut figure of Ganymede feeding an eagle' in trenches near the east gate. This is a useful insight; Curle found two intaglios, but their findspots are not given in the report (Curle 1911a: 333, pl. 87 nos 35–36).

[42] This is Pit XV, excavated in October 1905, which produced a fine Drag. 37 bowl (Curle 1911a: 119, 210, pl. 43 lower).

[43] Déchelette 1904; the names are production centres for samian (*terra sigillata*).

[44] Curle's first mention of Castor ware, a topic he discussed extensively in other letters; see Letters 1.19, 1.32–1.34, 1.38, and Curle 1911a: 254–257.

[45] Probably Haverfield 1899.

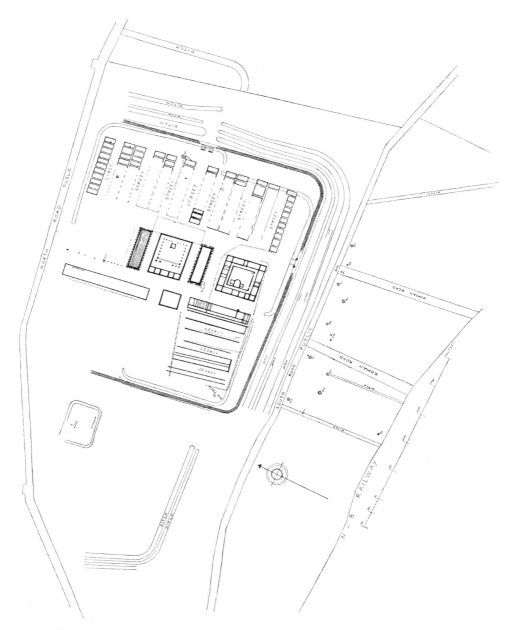

Plan of the Roman Military Station at Newstead. By Mr Thomas Ross, Architect, *December* 1906.

Figure 10.3. Plan of Newstead as known in December 1906 (from Curle 1907b). It is fascinating in revealing progress at that date. Much of the fort plan had been reconstructed apart from the north-west quadrant, but the reducing wall had not yet been found, and detail in the annexes was still sparse, with only partial outlines of the east and west annexes and very sketchy outlines of ditches and roads in the south annexe. © National Library of Scotland.

Letter 3.12

PRIORWOOD
MELROSE N.B.

10th May, 1906

Dear Haverfield,

I wonder if you can help me about this inscription.

I discovered it on the rim of the brass helm at the back.[46] I haven't been able so far to make anything of it. I see a punctured inscription of the same sort on the mask figured by Benndorf found in Roumania and our helm itself belongs to the same time and art as the one found at Nikopolis in Bulgaria, at least so it seems to me.[47]

You were right in doubting my reading of the graffiti as SINOVENIUS. I am now convinced I read it the wrong way and I think we are pretty well agreed that, as Macdonald has suggested, it is SENECIONIS and SENECIO.[48]

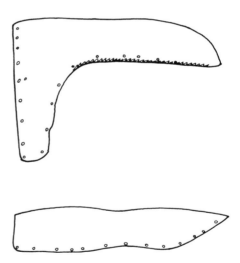

Can you give me any references to finds of pieces of bronze armour like the pieces overleaf? [shown here to right] We have two of each. I take it two are shoulder pieces and two perhaps for the elbow. They don't seem to fit together.[49]

I know of Benndorf and the book or rather paper on the Heddernheim helm[50] and Smith[51] has referred me to a paper in the 20th volume of the German Archaeological Institute, but if you can give me any more references I shall feel obliged.

---

[46] Curle 1911a: 167, where he struggled with the full transcription but understood the meaning; RIB II.3: 2425.5, VFFI.T GES, '(property of) Uffus in the troop of Ges(...)'.

[47] Benndorf 1878: pl. 10, pl. 12 fig. 3. See Garbsch 1978: 65, pl. 19, O16 (Nikopolis); 69–70, pl. 24, O40 (Resca, Romania)

[48] Curle 1911a: 177, pl. 32, fig. 17; RIB II.3: 2427.21–24; inscriptions on the inside of saddle horn mounts (see following note).

[49] Curle 1911a: 177–178, pl. 32, captioned 'Bronze objects of unknown use'. Identified by Peter Connolly and Carol van Driel-Murray as the four horns from the corners of a Roman saddle; see Connolly and van Driel-Murray 1991.

[50] See Letter 1.26 and Curle 1911a: 179–180 for his ultimate listing. The references are to Benndorf 1878 and Donner-von Richter 1894.

[51] R.A. Smith of the British Museum; see *Dramatis personae* and Letter 1.26.

We have found nothing since the ICON find[52] of which I wrote to you except a fine Andernach quern, with all its mountings complete.[53]

Please let me know what you think about the inscription.

Believe me,

Yours sincerely,

James Curle

We have found some references to Dere Street to the N and S of Newstead JC[54]

Letter 3.13

PRIORWOOD
MELROSE N.B.

11th Oct, 1906

Dear Haverfield,

You will be interested to know that we have fully proved the existence of the surrounding wall at Newstead.[55]

Here is the sketch of the inner face of a piece uncovered yesterday. The wall was 7' 7" thick, the scarcement[56] below projects 9" on either side, there is a cobble foundation 9" or so deep, then two courses 18" high of rough quarried sandstone. Then a narrow course 4½" high on which the big stones 11" high are set.

The long stones forming the course above the scarcement are 3' 10" and 3' 7" long. The stones above 1' 6", 1' 3" and 1' long.

---

52 Reference is obscure.
53 From Pit XIX. Curle 1911a: 121, pl. 17 lower right.
54 The line was discussed in Curle 1911a: 7-15, drawing on field data and charter evidence.
55 The stone wall around the Antonine fort.
56 An offset where a wall is set back, leaving a shelf or footing at the base.

I had not time to sketch the front last night. It is not quite so good. The whole fragment uncovered is 8' 6" long. It is striking how thoroughly the stone quarriers have done their work[57] but when one sees the masonry one can better understand it.

We are making sections through the defences on the W where the above piece of the wall lies. I think we shall find some alteration in the line of the old ditch. I begin to lean towards the four occupations theory.[58] I wish I could feel certain who built the wall. I think what we have found proves that it was an independent feature of the defences, not merely the facing of a clay mound.

Believe me,

Yours sincerely,

James Curle

Letter 3.14

PRIORWOOD
MELROSE N.B.

20th November, 1906

Dear Haverfield,

It is rather difficult to get a rubbing of these graffiti. I shall show them to Macdonald tomorrow.

I arrived at them by drawing each stroke and as they seem to agree the reading should be correct, but of course I know nothing of cursive. Here are specimens [Figure 10.4].

I found the Germans read II as E so I put DOMETI.

As we have this name repeated on nine pieces we can be quite certain about it. Once he spells it DMIITI and once the ATTICI has only one T.[59]

We had another good day yesterday. Pit number VIII[60] gave about seventy pieces of iron, five spears, one sword broken, five things like small ornamental nails, a golf club (?), four picks, an axe, smith's tongs (two pairs), chisels, gouges, rims of the naves of wheels, hammers, a small anvil, and a number of objects I can't quite make out.

By the way, I found a mason in Newstead whose father remembered seeing part of the piers of the Bridge.

He says that it crossed the river immediately to the N of the Fort – and can point out the place. I think this will be a better clue to follow than the Galashiels authority.[61]

---

[57] The site had been heavily robbed for stone in later periods (Curle 1911a: 3–4).
[58] See Letters 3.15–3.17.
[59] Backing plates for *phalerae* which formed a military decoration for valour; see Curle 1911a: 174–176, pl. XXXI; Maxfield 1981: 91–95; RIB II.3: 2427.4–12, '(property of) Dometius Atticus'.
[60] Curle renumbered the pits for publication; this is Pit XVI (Curle 1911a: 119–120).
[61] We suspect this was Bailie George Hope Tait, a councillor on the Galashiels Town Council, some 8 km west of Melrose; a local painter, watercolourist and historian. See Letter 1.57.

Figure 10.4. Graffiti of Dometius Atticus on the backing plates of military decorations. Photo by Neil McLean, © National Museums Scotland (X.FRA 129).

Lord Bute[62] has sent me £50 this morning, so the article has brought in something.[63] I rather wish I had full control over some of these objects. The battered bronze cap-looking helmet[64] ought to be hammered out and the broken iron one, with its visor, like a human face,[65] should be restored but I don't think there is anyone fit to do it in Edinburgh. What would you do?[66]

Yours sincerely,

James Curle

---

[62] John Crichton-Stuart, 4th Marquess of Bute (1881–1947).
[63] This may be the short, unsigned article in *Scottish Historical Review* 3 (1906): 126–127, summarising results to date and concluding '... it is to be hoped that the necessary support will be forthcoming to enable the Society to complete the work they have taken in hand'. Letter 4.1 indicates that Lord Bute had given Curle funding in April 1906 after an article in the *Scotsman*, but no newspaper article around November 1906 has been traced to explain the second gift.
[64] In fact a camp kettle inscribed T. LVCANI. He must have mentioned it to Haverfield in a letter that does not survive, as the context implies pre-knowledge. Curle at first saw it as a helmet, but then recognised its character: see Letters 1.21 and 1.24.
[65] Curle 1911a: 168–170, pl. 26 no. 2, pl. 29; Keppie and Arnold 1984: 19–20, no. 54; Manning 2005.
[66] See Letter 1.24 for similar requests to the British Museum.

Letter 3.15[67]

CHRIST CHURCH,
25 Merton St
Oxford

15 July 1907

Dear Curle,

Thank you very much for your letter. We are just back, and have borrowed a colleague's house for July. In August (from the 12th) we occupy Bellingham for a month, as last year.[68] It is very good of you to suggest a move yet further north. I am sure we should like it and I personally want to see your newer finds. But I'm not sure if time will allow.

I have read your paper[69] with real interest and excitement – but with imperfect conviction. I believe in Two Occupations: I believed, indeed, in that before you did. But tho' my beliefs began to grow first, they have gone on slowly. Perhaps the word 'occupation' posts the buds. Thus on page 444, lines 3–23, the evidence proves a reconstruction or alteration of a special building which *might have been* effected without any break in the occupation of the fort as a whole. Someone (some Roman) came over from Germany and desired the German Exercierhalle and built it on. Are you, however, so sure that the vaults at Chesters and Aesica[70] are *additions*? I have heard it *said*, but never understood *why*. And I do not see that your reasons for calling your own vault *later* are conclusive. Why should not a trapdoor with steps be irregular and why should not the *foundations* of a vault go lower than those of the chamber (if the vault is smaller (or larger) than the chamber)? And why should not the *dividing wall* of the Praetorium[71] lie on the disturbed soil of Agricola's occupation. It seems plain that the Praetorium was *altered*. But it is *not* plain that this meant a *new occupation* of the fort – nor do the proofs of the alteration seem to *me* equally conclusive.

Again, with respect to the '4th' occupation; (p. 445) – in line 2 what is the 'large inner ditch'? If it is the *inner* of the three ditches *outside* the later wall, how do you know that it is not also the *outer* ditch of the primary fort? That has 2 ditches on the west: why not also on the *south*?

And, again, why has only the *large* inner ditch nine feet of silt below the cobbles? And *nine* feet means a *lot* of time: one wants to hear more about this deposit.

The question of the gateway at the end of the *via Quintana* I cannot discuss, as it is not marked on your plan, but was the 'bottoming' found on the intervals *between* the triple outer ditches and just outside them? The break in the ditches of the Annexe South might belong as well to the *first occupation* as to any other.

The Reducing Wall is very curious.[72] Did you trace it *over* the ditch of the first period? and how does it (if so) run into the south later wall? It is drawn (like this) ⊣ but is only dotted in

---

[67] Found by Donald Gordon among Curle notebooks in the National Record of the Historic Environment, Edinburgh.
[68] This would be for part of the Corbridge excavation season, 10 July – 12 October.
[69] Curle 1907a, where he argued that the evidence suggested there were four phases of occupation. We have avoided extensive annotation of this letter; it needs to be read and understood in the context of Curle's detailed response (Letter 3.16).
[70] Both on Hadrian's Wall. See Breeze 2006: 201–203, 272–273.
[71] Haverfield used the term for what is better termed the *principia*.
[72] The 2 m-thick masonry Reducing Wall was built across the fort from north to south, cutting off one third of the

as if dubious: one would expect ⌐ . I conjure up a picture of a +/- 15 acre fort built (or rebuilt) for a specially strong garrison for – perhaps – a special campaign or set of campaigns and then, when the need was over and the army withdrawn, reduced in size for occupation by one cohort or ala in the ordinary way.

The general position seems to me this:–

First: an Agricolan fort –? probably soon abandoned – this you do not go into –

Second: a Pian (*Antonine*) fort, built let us say about 140 on Agricola's ruins and held continuously till about 180 but very conceivably held in special strength at the times when we know of special troubles – about 140, about 158–163 and about 180, soon after which it was lost.[73]

Unless evidence emerges of a re-occupation under Sep[timius] Sev[erus], *I* should attribute the alterations in the fort to the dates of these troubles, (or, perhaps, of others not yet known) – But I'm not yet clear as to these alterations?

[The letter breaks off at this point, at the end of a quarto page]

Letter 3.16

PRIORWOOD
MELROSE N.B.

16th July, 1907

Dear Haverfield,

Thanks for your letter. I am glad to have your criticism. I am quite convinced that the history of Newstead fort, between the day on which the Romans entered it and the day they left it divides itself into four distinct periods, though I cannot say whether there was much if any lapse of time between them.[74] You are of opinion that an earlier reconstruction of the fort may have taken place ~~without~~ during a continuous occupation. You naturally, as the Professor of History, approach it with your knowledge of the Antonine occupation in your mind. I approach it knowing little history but knowing also that references are sufficiently scanty to leave room, especially in the South of Scotland, for an unrecorded period of occupation. Of course I can pretend to no special knowledge, but in dealing with this case it seems best to state it solely from an archaeological point of view hoping that some day the combined evidence gathered together from the forts of this Northern road will lead us to a truer state of

Antonine fort, apparently for an industrial area. This was later reversed. See Curle 1911a: 33–35. Hanson (2012: 68–69) and Manning (forthcoming) discuss some of the problems that its interpretation provides.
[73] Haverfield refers to the Antonine invasion, what was then considered to be a revolt among the Brigantes, and an attack on the province recorded by Cassius Dio (see Haverfield and Macdonald 1924: 119–123, which are based on a series of 1907 lectures and thus reflects his views at this time).
[74] In the conclusion to the Report he sustained this four-occupation view, two early (Flavian) and two late (Antonine); Curle 1911a: 340–349. It has retained broad support (e.g. Richmond 1950; Hanson 2012), though Simon Clarke (2012) suggested a more complex phasing. Bill Manning (forthcoming) argues plausibly that the reducing wall represents a reduction of the first Antonine fort before it was fully rebuilt on the lines of the late Flavian one; one might from this argue for five phases of defence construction.

knowledge.[75] If you were digging ~~out~~ a fort where you had no history to guide you and found an entire reconstruction would you not feel inclined to put it down to having been twice-occupied?

Now, as to the Exercierhalle,[76] it must belong to the very last period of occupation of the Praetorium.[77] I infer this from the foundation at Newstead. Agricola had our method of foundation – he founded on red sandstone. The later people founded on river stones. They dug a trench down to solid ground and filled it with cobbles bedded in clay. On this they placed their wall. The cobbles must have been under ground. The N wall of the Praetorium is built in this way. At the point where the W wall of the Exercierhalle breaks off, its cobble foundation begins on a level with the top of the scarcement course of the Praetorium wall.

Now as to the Treasure vault,[78] you have at the W end of the Praetorium a perfectly regular chamber of rectangular form (and into it is set the vault in irregular fashion, something like this).

I have two reasons for supposing it later. If it belonged to the same period as the original chamber the walls would at least have been parallel and they would probably not have been made of old material. 2nd, if it were part of the original plan they would not, in building the E wall, have cut away the earth from the face of the foundation so as to expose the cobblestones which had been sunk in the ground. As regards the crosswall of the Praetorium it was quite entitled to lie on the debris of Agricola's occupation but it did more than that, it lay at a much higher level than the main wall of the Praetorium and the foundations of the pillars behind it. Moreover, it was of inferior masonry. After all, the whole period of occupation cannot have been very long and it is difficult to account for the higher level of the exercise hall without supposing that debris of ruined buildings played a part in it.

---

[75] Curle's confidence in the primacy of archaeological observation is noteworthy, and his response to Haverfield is very strongly founded on arguments from detailed field observations which still pass muster today.
[76] A large building in front of the *principia*, traversing the *via principalis*, which could have acted as an indoor riding school for exercising horses. Curle used the German term, as he did in the publication: Curle 1911a: 44, '*Exercier-Halle*, or Drill-Hall', though he doubted this was its purpose.
[77] The term used incorrectly at this stage for the *principia*. See Letter 1.18 n.97.
[78] Strong room inserted into the central room of the rear range of the *principia*: Curle 1911a: 50–51, pl. 10 no. 3.

The 'large inner ditch' is the ditch immediately beyond the wall.

Nothing is perhaps so unsafe as to adopt the attitude of our Mr Mackie[79] who says this could not be because the Romans wouldn't do it, but I don't believe it was the outer ditch of the early fort because the ditches are too far apart and secondly because it is much wider and deeper than the early inner ditch.

Assuming it was so we have still the outer ditches carried through below the road. The doubling of the ditches in the W is curious but it was really the exposed front of Agricola's camp. We found no double ditches in the E and it is very unlikely that the position of the ditches in the S as regards distances apart, would be much different from what it is on the W.

I confess, however, that the large amount of silt under the road filling is greater than elsewhere, and it rather puzzles me. I can only explain it by supposing that they threw branches into the ditch or some vegetable matter before they put in the stones. I agree that the break in the ditches of the S annexe might be first occupation; the bottoming at the S end of the quintana[80] was got after passing Agricola's ditches. It rose in the centre and tapered off to the sides and could be nothing else but a road. I am not sure that we went deep enough to look for it by the outer ditches.

The reducing wall has not yet been traced to its junction with the main wall on the S. As soon as the hay is cut we shall do it but its character is quite evident.

The baths are turning out well and I think we have at least three distinct levels in one part although stone hunters have ransacked it. I think I shall be able to find more problems for you in it. What I believe about the whole place is that after Agricola, and not long after him, there was an occupation. I believe that the reduction of size of the fort is Antonine. I should say that one-half of our decorated pottery is before Pius and, I imagine, more than half the coins. However, this is all theory. I don't profess to prove it so far. They want me to give the Rhind lectures[81] next year on Newstead and I am considering the question. I am rather diffident about it, especially in this time, which is rather scanty.

I hope you will come and see us, if you can, if only for a weekend.

Believe me,

Yours sincerely,

James Curle

---

[79] The Clerk of Works leading the excavations in the field; see *Dramatis personae*.
[80] *Via quintana*, the transverse street running behind the *principia* and *praetorium*, parallel to the *via principalis*.
[81] Haverfield had delivered this prestigious annual lecture series to the Society of Antiquaries of Scotland in 1906 (see Letter 3.1). Curle did indeed deliver the Rhind lectures for 1908 on 'The Roman station of Newstead'; see Letters 1.41, 1.45, 1.46, and discussion in Chapter 4.

Letter 3.17

PRIORWOOD
MELROSE N.B.

28th July, 1907

My Dear Haverfield,

Thanks for your letter.[82] Of course I quite admit that previous results must not be lightly disregarded or overlooked. At the same time the amount of accumulated evidence of what happened on this Eastern line of route[83] is very scanty and I feel one must approach the problem with a very open mind. From the Border to Cramond[84] the results for comparison are practically nil.

Cappuck[85] produced little or nothing to help us. I don't know about Bremenium.[86] Does any really good account of the excavations exist?

The plan looks complicated and suggests change. The fragmentary state of things at Newstead must leave many points unsolved, but what we have found will be useful for future diggers on the same line of advance.[87] If the same conditions are met with in other halting places it will confirm the theory I hold. After all, in dealing with a question of the kind, you must judge by a combination of circumstances. Other diggers have held Treasure vaults a secondary addition for reasons which they put forward. The mere want of symmetry in construction may not prove that the thing is later, but when you find that irregularity, combined with other circumstances proving an alteration of the building, I hold you are entitled to consider the irregularity as carrying weight.

Quite apart from the Treasure vault you have what in my mind is sufficient proof (1) of a period in which the Praetorium in a post, reduced in size, was entered from the via principalis and (2) of a subsequent period in which the buildings again overpassed the limits of the reducing wall, the Praetorium still being entered from the same street. It would be entirely wrong to say that irregularity in line must be secondary, but when you find two kinds of masonry on an isolated irregularity of construction in a mediaeval building, it is nearly always to be assumed that it is due to alteration, and its history nearly always bears this out.

Irregularity in the lines of the Newstead vault a priori leaves one to suppose it due to a later alteration, because a man building in a cramped position and having to regard the foundations of existing walls is made more likely to lay his foundation askew than a builder who starts fair

---

[82] Not preserved, but clearly a response to Letter 3.16.
[83] The Roman road known now as Dere Street.
[84] Fort on the Firth of Forth, just west of Edinburgh on the river Almond. Unexcavated in Curle's time, though stray finds clearly indicated the presence of a fort. See Rae and Rae 1974, esp. 163–165; Holmes 2003.
[85] A small fort on Dere St, near Jedburgh, 17 km south of Newstead. The 1886 excavations had not revealed much; a fuller story emerged from further work in 1911 and 1949. See Curle 1933; RCAHMS 1956: 381–383.
[86] High Rochester: a large outpost fort north of Hadrian's Wall in Northumberland, at the junction between Dere St and a road leading to the mouth of the Tweed. See Breeze 2006: 100–101.
[87] Curle made this point in the Report (1911a: 8), arguing for work at Cappuck, Pennymuir and Chew Green. The former took place shortly after, inspired by Curle's Newstead work (Stevenson and Miller 1912), and Letter 4.9 strongly implies that Curle was planning further work on the 'Cheviot Camps', which must be Pennymuir and/or Chew Green, in 1913/1914.

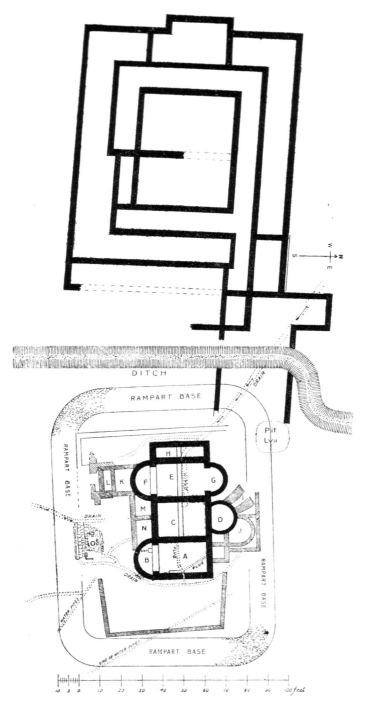

Figure 10.5. Plan of the bath and mansio complex in the west annexe
(Curle 1911a: 93, fig. 7).

from the beginning, but I hold his exposure of the cobble foundation on the E side as being stronger evidence of secondary work than the wall askew.[88]

The baths are, I think, going to confirm our theories, which is satisfactory [Figure 10.5].[89] We appear to have (A) a small building: (B) a widening of that building and great addition to its length: (C) a reduction in size by means of a ditch cut through it, in which the Eastern portion is surrounded by a wide cobble foundation on which possibly a rampart or double wall was placed: (D) a building on top of this foundation, water pipes crossing it and the drain from it crossing the filled-in ditch. The levels of (A) and (B) do not differ very greatly: (C) is undoubtedly higher, and on digging out the reducing ditch the fragments of pottery are few but quite distinct from those in Agricola's ditch. They correspond with types at Birrens.[90] We have found a sinking at one point in the cobble foundation and I have hopes of getting a pit, which may produce some fragments to help us. Perhaps I shall be able to go to see Corbridge.[91] I must see the Carlisle and perhaps the Newcastle museum one of these days. Let me know if you can find time to come here. Meanwhile, excuse this lengthy letter,

Yours sincerely,

James Curle

PS Did the Romans have chimney pots, or exposed ends to flue pots? We have found a fragment in brick, which suggests something of the kind.[92] JC

Letter 3.18

PRIORWOOD
MELROSE N.B.

10th December, 1907

Dear Haverfield,

I am sending you today a box containing two enamelled fibulae.[93] You were good enough to say you would take them to the man at the Ashmolean.[94] I should like them cleaned and if possible repaired, though whether he will be able to repair I am not quite certain. In each of the small boxes he will find not only a fibula but the enamelled collar which was round the loop on the head, also some bits of the spring. The type is one you know well and he will doubtless have others to work from if he can restore the loops. Unfortunately, the bronze is

---

[88] As with Letter 3.16, Curle used strong, detailed arguments from field observation to counter Haverfield's objections.
[89] Curle 1911a: 88–103.
[90] *Blatobulgium*, a Hadrianic and Antonine fort in eastern Dumfriesshire on the main western route into Scotland. Excavated in 1895 (the results Curle drew upon; Christison *et al.* 1896), 1936–1937 and 1962–1967; see Robertson 1975.
[91] A bustling supply base for the Roman army and civilians, just south of Hadrian's Wall, and a focus of Haverfield's excavations at this time (Freeman 2007: 281–298).
[92] This is probably the item subsequently published by Lowther (1936); it does not seem to appear in Curle 1911a.
[93] Safety-pin style of brooch. From the brooches Curle illustrated, these are probably the two enamelled trumpet brooches (Curle 1911a: pl. 86 nos 13–14).
[94] The University of Oxford's Museum of Art and Archaeology. Haverfield's man is probably William Young, who was appointed as plaster art restorer in the museum in 1900, later becoming its Conservator (1905–1937). He appears also in Letter 1.65.

very soft. In Edinburgh we simply paint over with shellac and lay in a glass-topped box with cotton wool. If possible I should like them back soon, as they must be drawn, with others, for slides.

Mr Brook[95] has managed to pull into shape the bronze mask from the baths well.[96] It is going to be fine when finished [Figure 8.11]. I have not got very much of late at Newstead. In fact, we have been busy filling in. The early ditch has produced several very good specimens of early pottery and I can now produce from it parallels for all the decorated vases in the pits containing the armour etc which lay to the S.[97] Among interesting things we have got from it was a little pine tablet for writing on.[98] The wax was gone.

I got an interesting piece of Samian at the mouth of a drain used by the last occupation, where it discharges into the last ditch.

I think it is without doubt a Rheinzabern and probably by Reginus, who is said to have worked in the time of Marcus Aurelius.[99]

I have just started pit-hunting again S of the railway, but funds are running out[100] and I don't know if we shall see much more.

Believe me,

Yours sincerely,

James Curle

Letter 3.19

PRIORWOOD
MELROSE N.B.

8th January, 1908

Dear Haverfield,

I thank you very much for the trouble you have taken about the oar [Figure 10.6]. I am much interested in Mr Balfour's letter.[101]

---

[95] William Brook, of Brook and Son Goldsmiths in Edinburgh, who carried out other restoration work on the Society's collections around this time; see Dalgleish 2022. This is a notable development from Curle's assertion a year earlier that there was no-one in Edinburgh able to do this work (Letter 3.14).
[96] Curle 1911a: 170–171; Keppie and Arnold 1984: 20, no. 55. See Letter 1.41.
[97] An interesting example of Curle's focus on the chronological value of samian in disentangling his sequence.
[98] Curle 1911a: 308, pl. LXXX.6
[99] Centre for samian production in Rheinland-Pfalz; Tyers 1996: 113–114.
[100] Although the Antiquaries put up some of their own funds, continuing the work for so long relied heavily on funds from the wider public, and there were regular appeals (e.g. Letters 3.8, 3.14, 4.1). 'The cost of the excavation has amounted to £2159, 5s 6d., of which £308, 11s. 2d. has been advanced from the Society's funds and £1850, 4s. 4d. has been raised by subscription from Fellows and members of the public' (*Proceedings of the Society of Antiquaries of Scotland* 45 [1910–1911]: 8–9).
[101] Wooden steering oar found in Pit LXV; Curle 1911a: 313, pl. 69 no. 5. Henry Balfour (1863–1939) was curator of the Pitt-Rivers Museum in Oxford, and his note is quoted in full in Curle's publication.

I noted that among the gold oars of the Limavaddy boat[102] one had a hole in the shaft suggesting a steering paddle. What puzzled me was the cut-out in the blade, for which Mr Balfour suggests a good reason.[103] What are we to deduce from this fact? Was the Melrose valley a lake! I suppose really it belonged to a ferry boat. I should like to meet Mr Balfour when we come to you in March and I shall perhaps ask him about another wooden thing which puzzles me, if I may write to him. Yes! my brother is going to be married again.[104] We have known the lady, a Miss Butler, for a good many years, and I think it is in every way satisfactory. My 'occupations' have not altered much.[105] We have 1st the earth fort with curious gateways, which I attribute to Agricola: to this then follows the extension of the size of the fort in which we find a titulus in front of the N, S and W gates. I believe this occupation immediately followed Agricola and perhaps belongs to the period of his recall. My only evidence for this is that we found early pottery in the West gate titulus[106] and also in the part of the large ditch that we excavated. The bowl and **e** s q[107] was found in both and generally the pottery seemed the same as that of the earth fort no.1.

Of course, you must remember that the quantity is not large: but as far as our evidence goes, the 2nd occupation is early. Then, I believe, there came a gap. Then comes a point which is rather interesting; these tituli were filled up. The one on the S gate appears to have been filled up before the reduction in size of the fort and a road carried over it, before the entrance was moved farther E. This suggests to me the beginning of the Antonine advance and the re-occupation for a very short time of the 2nd fort. Then we have the cutting down perhaps corresponding with a permanent frontier line on the vallum.

Lastly, a re-occupation of this earlier area, perhaps in an attempt to hold a line farther S or one of the attempts to recover the lost territory.

What about your potters' marks from Corbridge? I am the more anxious to see them as Walters[108] has asked me to review his catalogue of Roman pottery.[109] Have you seen it? He boldly classifies all his pieces as either Rutenian, Lezoux or German.[110]

I am quite sure or as nearly so as one can be quite certain of such things that some of his Lezoux pieces are Graufesenque. He classifies some 24 pieces as Lezoux bowls of type 29[111]

---

[102] Late Iron Age gold boat model from a hoard found at Broighter (the preferred modern name), Co. Derry. See Raftery 1984: 181–192.

[103] He argued it held a cord that fastened the oar to a boat's gunwale, taking some of the weight and preventing the oar's loss.

[104] A.O. Curle; see *Dramatis personae*.

[105] See the intense discussion in Letters 3.15–3.17, some six months previously. Curle's view here is slightly more developed, with the reducing wall coming after a short Antonine reoccupation of the full area of the late Flavian fort.

[106] Detached section of ditch and embankment placed in front of an entrance as a protection and to prevent a direct frontal assault. In fact Curle found a curved section of ditch extending across the entrance, better termed a *clavicula* (see Jones 2011: 49, in the context of temporary camps). He is referring here to the curved ditch section shown in red outside the west gate on the plan facing Curle 1911a: 38.

[107] Meaning of this apparent abbreviation is obscure.

[108] H.B. Walters (1867–1944) of the British Museum, who had just published the catalogue of their Roman pottery (Walters 1908); see *Dramatis personae*. Curle was a self-taught pottery specialist.

[109] Curle 1909b, reviewing Walters 1908. He offered a much more positive view than Haverfield, who dealt with it in a dismissive footnote (1909: 414 n.2): 'Much of its grouping was obsolete before the book was published'.

[110] Rutenian was a synonym for south Gaulish production centres such as La Graufesenque, common in the literature of the time but now fallen from use (e.g. Oswald and Pryce 1920: 11). Lezoux was the dominant pottery of the central Gaulish tradition. 'German' would now be termed East Gaulish, for instance Rheinzabern.

[111] Typology follows Dragendorff 1895.

found in London. This rather puzzles me as such bowls are supposed to be of the period before AD 75 and are not found in Germany or in Pompeii.

I wonder whether Déchelette is right in putting his 1st period of Lezoux so early. His evidence is not very clear and as regards his second period 75–110 I feel quite convinced that Divixtus whom he puts down as one of his principal potters, was exporting his wares to Scotland in the Antonine period.[112]

With all good wishes for the New Year to Mrs Haverfield and yourself,

Believe me,

Yours very truly,

James Curle

Figure 10.6. The wooden steering oar. © National Museums Scotland (X.FRA 1131).

---

[112] The discussion is continued in Letter 3.21, and Curle's views influenced Haverfield's publication of the Corbridge material (1909: 411). Curle discussed this in some detail with R.A. Smith (Letters 1.39–1.43).

Letter 3.20[113]

20, BRADMORE ROAD,
OXFORD.

24 Febr [1908]

Dear Curle,

I am sending you a parcel, today or tomorrow, of pieces of Samian from the Corbridge Pottery Shop[114] and also your slides.[115] I should be very glad if you could send me your views of the ware.[116] It appears to me incredible that the stamp GENITORF (in particular) could belong to the fourth century and not early in that. Not all the stamps are represented in the collection sent, so I enclose the total list. Would you mind keeping the Corbridge bits a day or two, till I hear where they are to go – whether back to me or to Newcastle.

I have worked further at the Pan Rock[117] things and incline to the middle or 1st half of the 2nd cent. for the wreck. The ivy leaved rims seem, as far as I can gather, to have gone out about then: the straight-sided cup came in rather earlier and the bulging cup, of which one ex.[ample] is assigned to the Pan Rock in the Guildhall Coll.[ection] (Smith says – in error: but that is a priori) went out thereabouts. The shallow bowl (or deep saucer), figured rather badly in Smith's No. 11,[118] and represented by 3 pieces from Corbridge fairly perfect (GENITORF etc) and by many from Pan Rock seems to be a deeper form of Dragendorff[119] 31 but really distinct from it. I don't know if you have any analogies to it.

With our united kind regards to Mrs Curle,

Yours sincerely

F. Haverfield

---

[113] From the 'Home and Abroad' collection.
[114] A building inserted into the corner of Site IV at Corbridge had been used to store pottery: samian, coarse wares, mortaria and Castor ware. See Forster 1908: 247–256. Reappraisal of the archive indicates the published report conflated several phases, and the sequence needs re-examined (Frances McIntosh, pers. comm.).
[115] Most probably for Curle's forthcoming Rhind lectures; see Letters 1.41, 1.45, 1.46.
[116] The first such request in their relationship. There is no trace of Curle's views influencing the publication, but he was quoted on other matters relating to pottery (Haverfield 1909: 419).
[117] The Pudding Pan Rock Roman shipwreck c.2 km north of Herne Bay, Kent, containing samian pottery. See Smith 1907; Walsh 2017; and Letters 1.42–1.43.
[118] Smith 1907.
[119] Dragendorff 1895.

[Appendix of potters' stamps enclosed with the letter][120]

AIISTIVIM	cup Drag.33
ALBILLVUM[121]	cup (5 exx)
GENIALIS FE:	cup
GENITOR F	saucer and bowl
IVNII	do[122]
*MA....I M	do (doubtful if hence)
MACRINUS F	do
MARCI F	do
... NIANI OF	do
PATERCLINI	do (three exx)
PATERNI	do
SATURNINI	do (prob. 2 exx, one a fragment]NI
SEDATIANI	do
... OCI FEC?	?
.... CILIS	?
*VINII	large cup. } I'm not sure if from the spot
*CERIAL: M	fragm. }

Letter 3.21

PRIORWOOD
MELROSE N.B

9 September, 1908

Dear Haverfield,

I am sorry to hear you are leaving so soon[123] as I fear that now I cannot well get away before the 21st. If the weather improves and work is still going on I should like to go over so will you let me have a postcard to say who is in charge. I should like particularly to see the pottery. If one went for the night I suppose the inn at Chollerford would be a good place to stop or is

---

[120] See Forster 1908: 254.
[121] Haverfield drew it reversed, as on the stamp.
[122] Ditto.
[123] The context indicates this relates to Haverfield's excavations at Corbridge, the season running from 7 July to 10 October. The man in charge was probably Robert Forster; Haverfield was the figurehead director, which would explain why he appears to have left the excavations about a month before they officially closed; cf. Bishop 1994.

there a respectable place at Hexham?[124] The masonry at Corbridge must be well worth seeing. I am not sure that I can help you as to the distinction between Lezoux periods ii and iii for the reason that nearly all the pottery here of the 1st and 2nd occupations is Rutenian.[125] By the beginning of the third period I fancy Lezoux iii was in full swing. I expect that the Lezoux pottery of the early years of the 2nd century is absent. In Germany I saw this summer a great many fragments from the ditch of the earth fort at the Saalburg[126] – Trajan and Hadrian period before 139.

The characteristic of these pieces was the coarser execution of early scrolls i.e. bad copies of design from La Graufesenque, but many of these pieces may have come from Trier or Heiligenberg[127] and this phase of things may not be exemplified here.

I find however in the ditch two pieces which must be by the maker of one of our later Newstead bowls.

In one respect I believe Déchelette may be mistaken.

The potter Divixtus whom he places as the leading man of the 2nd period, is a contemporary of Cinnamus.[128] Both have left their names in Scotland and both made bowls of the large medallion type. The bowl 30 by Divixtus in the B M catalogue[129] certainly is in style early, but the execution is not so coarse. That may simply be an example of continuance of earlier forms noted in Germany. Bowl 30 was made by both Cinnamus and Divixtus but the later bowls are easily to be distinguished from those of the Domitian period. The arrow points I have never seen on any of our later fragments here. Bowl 29 does not occur in the early ditches at the Saalburg. A very typical form of the early period here is Hofheim VI,[130] the round platter with a section like this.

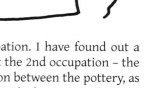

Its occurrence is, I believe, a sure indication of 1st Century occupation. I have found out a little more about Newstead, which is interesting. First, I believe that the 2nd occupation – the extended fort – immediately followed the first. There is no distinction between the pottery, as far as we have seen it. It probably ended in the 1st century, and I believe the large pits, where we made our last best finds, date from the ending of this period.

2nd, along the W front the big ditch, filled up after this period, was never again used.

3rd, On the W front the wall was built by the fourth occupation, as it is partly over the edge of the ditch. It seems very probable that the 2nd period was simply an earth fort (although in this Mackie[131] does not agree with me). As far as I know, most of the early forts in Germany are earth forts. The stone walls come in the 2nd century and later. Can you tell me whether there any examples of stone forts without ditches? Most of such forts in Germany are built on old

---

[124] Respectively a village and a town in Northumberland, close to Corbridge.
[125] South Gaulish. Lezoux was the centre of the later central Gaulish industry.
[126] A fort on the Taunus *limes*, north of Frankfurt; Jacobi 1897. For these travels, see Letter 1.48.
[127] Other East Gaulish potting centres; see Oswald and Pryce 1920: 11.
[128] Déchelette 1904: vol. I, 165, 182, 269.
[129] Walters 1908: 199, M1038.
[130] The samian from Hofheim (another fort in the Taunus area near Frankfurt) was published by Emil Ritterling (1904), who corresponded with Curle, sending him relevant literature; see Letter 3.22.
[131] The Clerk of Works, leading the excavations in the field; see *Dramatis personae*.

sites and when sections are merely cut through ditches the exact period to which they belong may easily be mistaken.

I had hoped that you and Mrs Haverfield would have been able to pay us a visit this autumn. If there is any chance of your doing so please let me know. My wife joins me in kind regards to Mrs Haverfield,

Believe me,

Yours sincerely,

James Curle

Letter 3.22

PRIORWOOD
MELROSE N.B.

21st February, 1909

Dear Haverfield,

Thank you for your letter received last week. I hope my wife will be able to come with me on the 9th but at present she does not think she will be able to travel. She has been generally run down and her nerves upset but I don't think has anything seriously the matter and I am hopeful that ten days hence she may be all right.

I thought we had nearly finished with Newstead. Of course there are more rubbish pits but as they were uncertain and finds scarcer, I determined to stop, after cleaning out a bit of the E annexe ditch and investigating a line of ditches lying further to the E.

I am almost sure now that this last ditch is the boundary of a Great Camp much bigger than the fort[132] – the camp of a marching army – but a new point emerged on Friday.

Mackie[133] was cleaning out a bit of the ditch and in it he found a Roman cist with a grave urn covered with a sandstone lid.[134] The cist is of sandstone but it is just like the coverings of roof tiles one sees on the Rhine. This opens up new possibilities as it is hardly likely to be solitary. It is probably an 'Antonine' cemetery.

Yes! the Antiquaries are odd.[135] Apparently my showing my slides to you at Oxford makes it impossible for them to look at them afterwards.

---

[132] Curle 1911a: 15–20. For the camps around Newstead see Jones 2012; this is Newstead I, now recognised as part of a complex of camps to the east of the fort.
[133] See *Dramatis personae*.
[134] Curle 1911a: 19, pl. IV.
[135] The Society of Antiquaries of London. Curle had hoped to lecture to them on Newstead; see Letter 1.47, written in May of the same year. Presumably he had lectured in Oxford on the topic.

Ritterling has sent me his limes publication on Wiesbaden which is interesting.[136]

Yours sincerely,

James Curle

Letter 3.23[137]

Left hand corner, at an angle, *STATION HASLEMERE*
Right hand corner, *LING COTTAGE, HINDHEAD, SURREY*.

29 March (till April 6) [1914].

Dear Curle,

<u>By all means</u> let us have your paper for the R.S. meetings.[138] I can't fix a date offhand. Baddeley[139] offered us lately a paper, which we agreed to have, but he hasn't yet said when it would be ready – we suggested our June (or July) meeting. Bryce[140] also promised a paper, but that will hardly be ready till the winter.

As to printing, I expect we should demand that, unless you very much objected. But when you say 'decadence as it creeps … to the Rhine', I hope you don't mean to suggest that the Teutons have ruined art there and everywhere – as Reinach[141] said when he once (by a horrid blunder of our Extension Scheme) was asked to lecture in Oxford to a (largely German) audience on German Art. No doubt Teutons aren't artistic in the mass – but more blame perhaps attaches to the wholesale production for export to all over the Western Empire. The worsening of workmanship which that causes destroys artistic ideals also; good art has to be individualist.

Atkinson's[142] present project is a study of the designs etc on certain datable Dragendorff 37 pieces at Pompeii.

We have come here, to a little house lent us by a cousin, to refresh in upland air.[143] But east winds and heavy rain conspire against us. We go back to Oxford for Easter – the house, for one

---

[136] Ritterling 1909.

[137] From the 'Home and Abroad' collection.

[138] The Roman Society. Curle spoke to the Society on 2 March 1915, on a parade helmet from Nijmegen (published as Curle 1915) and on the production and development of Samian ware; see note of meeting in *Journal of Roman Studies* 5 (1915): 250–251.

[139] Welbore St Clair Baddeley (1856–1945) spoke to the Society on 30 June 1914, discussing and exhibiting a sixteenth-century panorama of Rome; *Journal of Roman Studies* 4 (1914): 241–244.

[140] James, 1st Viscount Bryce, OM GCVO PC FRS FBA (1838–1922), academic, jurist, historian and Liberal politician, and ambassador to the USA 1907–1913, who published a comparison of the Roman empire and the British in India at this time (Bryce 1914); see Hingley 2000: 25–26, 49, 50, 53; Freeman 2007: 513, 514, 519. He spoke to the Society on 29 June 1915 (*Journal of Roman Studies* 5 [1915]: 253) on 'Religion as a factor in the history of empires' (published as Bryce 1915).

[141] Salomon Reinach (1858–1932); French classical archaeologist; Director of the Musée des Antiquités Nationales, Saint-Germain-en-Laye.

[142] Donald Atkinson (1886–1963), later Professor of Ancient History at Manchester. This project became Atkinson 1914.

[143] Ling Cottage was owned by Haverfield's distant relatives, the Mackarness family. Haverfield's close friend, the Eton schoolmaster Robert (Bob) Booker married Margot Mackarness in 1907. The couple were living there in April 1910 (perhaps on some sort of grace and favour arrangement?), with Hindhead being just about close enough to Eton. As the letter head reports, Ling Cottage is near Hindhead.

thing, is wanted by its owners and after Easter, if the weather mends and warms, I hope to go and see some excavators now struggling and freezing at Ribchester and Ambleside.[144] I have had a horrid cold or chill or other ailment which has rather laid me out.

I am extremely glad that G. Macdonald[145] has got so well over his late illness. He will now be better than ever and enjoy life more than he has done for some years. He was very uncomfortable at Insch[146] in July and I wondered how it was going to end. His recent wall-work seems to have been very successful.[147]

My wife desires to be very kindly remembered to Mrs Curle and the children (or one of them).

Yours sincerely

F. Haverfield

Letter 3.24[148]

WINSHIELDS,
HEADINGTON HILL,
OXFORD

15 April 1914

Dear Curle,

Many thanks: I have heard from your brother: it seems that Macdonald (or his father) worked the thing out himself.[149] M[acdonald] is supposed to be about to enter Rome; if the railwaymen strike,[150] he will (I suppose) be staying there some time.

June 30 will do admirably for us for a provisional date, and if politics veto it, we must find the next best we can. My wife and I would be very delighted if you and Mrs Curle would come and see us on your way up to or down from town.[151]

I don't know much of Alnmouth,[152] except that it looks nice from a distance! But Alnwick is near and there are interesting things in the Castle,[153] though they are not open to everybody. I could write to the Duke, if you like and bid him shew you them, but I dare say you have other and better introducers, if you don't already know him. I don't fancy he is himself about at

---

[144] Ribchester: Roman fort in Lancashire, which produced a famous cavalry helmet. Ambleside: small Roman fort at head of Windermere. See Bidwell and Hodgson 2009: 99–101, 112–114.
[145] See *Dramatis personae.*
[146] Village in Aberdeenshire where Haverfield and Macdonald stayed (in early July, most likely), while excavating the Roman temporary camp of Glenmailen, it being the nearest railway station to the site. See Macdonald 1916b; *Journal of Roman Studies* 3 (1913): 331–332.
[147] A series of excavations in 1912 and 1913 to trace the line of the Wall are reported in Macdonald 1915; he noted (p.123) that Haverfield visited Mumrills with him in January 1913.
[148] From the 'Home and Abroad' collection, not the Haverfield archives.
[149] The allusion to earlier work remains elusive. George MacDonald's father, James, died in 1900.
[150] The imminent but ultimately suspended Italian rail-workers strike was widely reported in the British press.
[151] London.
[152] Small coastal town in Northumberland.
[153] Seat of the Duke of Northumberland, with a private museum largely of items from the family's extensive estates. For the collection, see Collingwood Bruce 1880.

Alnwick much in June and the Lanx[154] usually goes south with him, I believe. Of Roman 'camps' etc there is nothing near Alnmouth, but if you take your car, you can run into very jolly country Cheviot[155] way and you can search for the (partly very doubtful) 'Devil's Causeway.'[156]

Yours sincerely

F. Haverfield

Letter 3.25[157]

11th December 1914

Dear Curle,

I have written to Hardinge Tyler[158] and said that I believe that the Advocates' Library[159] has a legal right to our Journal and has its eyes on us, that it is more blessed to give than to be commandeered; and that he had better tell the printer to send back numbers at once and the rest as issued – as was actually done in regard to the Bodleian[160] – and that, as the Council sanctioned that for Bodley, we need not go to (or wait for) the Council ~~for it~~ again. Dickson[161] ought, therefore, to get the vols. soon; if he doesn't, may I be told?

I am writing a *third* edition of my 'Romanization'![162] At the moment I am wrestling with a sentence on Castor ware.[163] So far as I can make out it is widely diffused, but not extraordinarily abundant, in Germany; most places shew a little, none (except Köln) much, and no kilns for its making have been found anywhere on the Continent; moreover, the continental stuff is adorned almost wholly with rather stereotyped Jagdszenen.[164] On the other hand, there is enough of the ware, and it differs enough in minutiae from the British, to shew that there *were* kilns somewhere over there. I do not feel clear whether the ware sprang up first in Germany, or not, potting was going on, apparently, at Castor quite early in the Roman period. In any case, the British potters seem to have done more potting, more ambitious potting and more on Late Celtic lines, than their continental rivals. I cannot make out the origin of the ware; barbotine decoration does not seem to occur on any earlier Late Celtic pots and must, I suppose, have come from the Mediterranean. But I don't find anything helpful in my books.

---

[154] 4th-century Roman silver figured dish, now in the British Museum; see Collingwood Bruce 1880: 136–139; Haverfield 1914.

[155] Hills spanning the Scottish-English border.

[156] Roman road running 89km from Corbridge to Berwick-on-Tweed. See Margary 1973: 478-483.

[157] Found by Donald Gordon among Curle notebooks in the National Record of the Historic Environment, Edinburgh.

[158] George Darce Hardinge-Tyler, MA, FSA (1881–1935) of Bathwick, Somerset; sometime Secretary of the Roman Society and editor of its *Journal of Roman Studies*, 1910–1918. The Society was founded in 1910; the letter reflects the need to get the journal into copyright libraries.

[159] The Library of the Faculty of Advocates in Edinburgh was at the time the copyright library for Scotland, with a right to claim a copy of every book published in the British Isles.

[160] The Bodleian Library of the University of Oxford was also a copyright library.

[161] William Kirk Dickson (1860–1949), Scottish advocate and Keeper of the Advocates Library, 1906–1925.

[162] Haverfield 1915.

[163] Colour-coated pottery made in the Nene Valley in eastern England (Tyers 1996: 173–175), a topic that had occupied Curle in preparing his Report; see e.g. Letters 1.19, 1.32–1.34, 1.38, 1.58; Curle 1911a: 254–256.

[164] Hunting scenes.

We had Geo. Macdonald here last weekend. He seemed exceedingly well – better than I have seen him for a long time, and less overworked, which may be a good thing out of this war. – Did you hear that Déchelette[165] has been killed? Salomon Reinach[166] wrote to me he (D), being 53, had been appointed to a garrison officer's work at Lyon, suited to his years. But he insisted on getting an active command, and was killed by a shell at the head of his battalion.

Are you likely to come south any time? If so, let us know. We expect, all being well, to be here most of the Xmas vac. The Coleridges,[167] to whom we not seldom go about now, are staying in London; their son is training in an OTC, in town and they want to be with him.

I was very sorry not to get up north in September. I started and reached Wroxeter, but was so tired that I funked the long journey on and came home again. Between the doctor, and staying quietly here, and (no doubt) the better war news, I am better again.

Please present my wife's and my kindest regards to Mrs. Curle and to Christian.[168]

Yours sincerely,

F. Haverfield

---

[165] See *Dramatis personae*.
[166] Salomon Reinach (1858–1932) was director of the Musée des Antiquités Nationales in St Germain-en-Laye from 1901.
[167] Extended family of the poet Samuel Taylor Coleridge (1772–1834), prominent in society. The Coleridge's ancestral home was The Chanter's House, Ottery St Mary, Exeter, an area where the Haverfields often holidayed. In 1876 Bernard John Seymour Coleridge (1851–1927) married Mary Alethea Mackarness (1851–1940), a family which the Haverfields had married into. The identity of the Coleridge son training in the O(fficer) T(raining) C(orps) is likely the Rt Hon. Lord Geoffrey Duke of Coleridge, 3rd Baron Coleridge (1877–1955). The regiment would have been the 4th Battalion of the Devonshire Regiment that was created in August 1914.
[168] Mrs Blanche Curle (née Nepean) and daughters Christian (the eldest), Pamela and Barbara.

Letter 3.26

Hunter's Inn, N Devon[169]

Sunday, July 29 [1917][170]

Dear Curle,

Macdonald says you want to know about Hahn (resp. Hagn). <u>One</u> Hahn[171] was once at Ch. Ch.[172] and just before the war, had a house close to one end of the Forth Bridge: I heard various news about him, at 2nd and 3rd hand, in the summer of 1914, and later he wrote from abroad (presumably, via a neutral from D[d].)[173] to a Ch.Ch. man whom I didn't know, or barely knew, and who has, I think, been since killed:[174] the letter was printed in some organ or other, which is all I know of it. Personally I would not be very inclined to think that he was addicted to espionage at all and that, having got away in August 1914, he came back again, but all things are possible in this odd world of today. We have been on the seaboard of Exmoor for a month and are due to catch an [*sic*] horribly early train tomorrow (Monday) morning to return to Oxford, where we shall be probably all of August and September. Will you be down south and inclined to come and see us any time? I may at the end of Aug. come up to Carlisle to a Cumberland Antiquarian Soc. meeting, being President. But travelling is a bother nowadays and I can't say; nor is the date yet fixed up. If I did I could run on to Melrose, would you be there and would Mrs Curle like to see me? I don't think my wife will come: she <u>may</u> object to my travelling so far alone just now.

With kind regards

Yours very sincerely

F. Haverfield

---

[169] The Hunter's Inn, now a National Trust property, was a favourite holiday location for the Haverfields.

[170] Based on other Haverfield correspondence. This letter is from the 'Home and Abroad' collection, not the Haverfield archives.

[171] Of all the Curle-Haverfield correspondence published here, this is the most curious, not least because it seems Curle was trawling for information. Hahn is most likely Kurt Hahn (1886–1974), the founder of Gordonstoun School among other educational establishments. Before the War he had been at Haverfield's old college, Christ Church, although they were not contemporaries. Hahn left Britain two days before the outbreak and via a circuitous route arrived back in Germany. He was then seconded to the Zentralstelle für Auslandsdienst and was involved in state intelligence and propaganda. His specialism was analysing the English newspapers. Before he evacuated from Britain, he was known to have enjoyed summer holidays in Moray – hence his later connection with Gordonstoun. We suspect Curle knew some of this but then confused facts, with his interest here in some way linked with the arrests and trials of Peter Hahn and Carl Muller as German spies in February–May 1915, which may explain Haverfield's reference to (?Curle's idea of) Hahn leaving and then coming back. Peter Hahn was later jailed for seven years and Muller executed in June 1915, hence Haverfield's 'dismissing' Curle's enquiry. What is unclear is why Haverfield says Hahn had a house close to one end of the Forth Bridge for it would imply it being closer to Edinburgh. All accounts seem to say that Hahn pre-1914 stayed in Moray. Letter 3.23 describes MacDonald and Haverfield at Ythan Wells in northern Aberdeenshire in 1913. Was Curle originally asking MacDonald about Hahn because he had links with the area, even if Curle got his Hahns wrong?

[172] Christ Church college, University of Oxford.

[173] Expansion of Dd. uncertain. Deutschland seems unlikely in this context.

[174] Haverfield's Christ Church man defies identification.

Chapter 11
From Home and Abroad

Table 11.1. British and continental correspondence to James Curle, 1906–1934

No.	Name	Date
4.1	J. Anderson	21 April, 1906
4.2	O. Almgren	3 Feb, 1907
4.3	J. Mestorf	23 Feb, 1907
4.4	C. Smith	22 April, 1907
4.5	J. Anderson	3 Sept, 1907
4.6	V. Hoffiller	21 Feb, 1910
4.7	P. Hume Brown	1 July, 1910
4.8	H. Dragendorff	23 April, 1912
4.9	A. Mackie	6 Oct, 1913
4.10	L. Frölich	20 Nov, 1913
4.11	B. Salin	16 July, 1914
4.12	G.M. Kam	25 Feb, 1915
4.13	G. Baldwin Brown	30 April, 1916
4.14	E. Fabricius	13 Aug, 1928
4.15	E. Fabricius	2 Sept, 1928
4.16	G.G. Coulton	1 Jan, 1934

Letter 4.1

From Dr Joseph Anderson.[1] Handwritten.

SOCIETY OF ANTIQUARIES OF SCOTLAND
NATIONAL MUSEUM OF ANTIQUITIES
QUEEN STREET; EDINBURGH

April 21st 1906

Dear Sir,

The tale of discovery following discovery, each more varied and interesting than anyone could have expected, is growing so steadily that I begin to wonder whether we can find any means of expanding the Museum so as to give room for the multitude of treasures you will bring to

---

[1] Keeper of the National Museum of Antiquities; see *Dramatis personae*.

light before you are done. The pits are evidently the features of Newstead, and they seem to be abundant. I wonder if there were similar pits at any of the other stations, which we have missed. The swords I suppose must be cavalry weapons, but they are so rarely met with in other places that your finding more than one is most remarkable. The Scandinavian swords to which you refer I think must be a good deal later.[2]

I am glad to hear that you have got such a handsome subscription from Lord Bute.[3] I got two of five pounds each and one of one pound this week – probably due to your article in the Scotsman.[4] It was remarkably well-written, and just the thing wanted.

Yours truly,

J. Anderson

Letter 4.2

From Professor Oscar Almgren.[5] In English, handwritten.

Stockholm

3rd February 1907

Dear Mr Curle,

I thank you very much for your kind and interesting letter about the fibulas and for the nice paper you sent me about your excellent finds at Newstead.[6]

The evolution of these fibulas is not quite easy to understand.[7] In seeing nos I and II with the little ring at the upper end, I thought of a type that I have seen in some samples in the Rhinelands and in Belgium [Figure 11.1]. I send you a copy[8] of a figure in colours that I have found in the *Annalen des Vereins für nassauische Altertumskund und Geschichtsforschung* XII, Taf. I:4, and belonging to a paper by Cohausen[9] on Roman enamelled work [Figure 11.2]. There are three samples of the type at Wiesbaden, 3 I have seen at Mainz, 1 at Speier, 1 at Köln and 2 at Liège, all found in or near the named cities. I think I have seen somewhere a figure of such a fibula found in England, but I have not noted where. I should think it is a proper <u>west</u>-Roman type, a local variety of my group IV.[10]

---

[2] Swords occur in too many periods and contexts of Scandinavian prehistory to hazard a guess as to what Curle was referencing here, although one may suspect it was the finds from bog deposits; he did not quote these in relation to swords, but was aware of the material (e.g. Curle 1911a: 187 n.4, quoting scabbard finds from Thorsberg).
[3] Lord Bute sent a further donation later in the year; see Letter 3.14.
[4] *The Scotsman* 17 April 1906: 5.
[5] Oscar Almgren (1869–1945), authority on brooches (Almgren 1897) and Professor of Scandinavian and Comparative Archaeology at Uppsala University, Sweden. See *Dramatis personae*.
[6] Almgren presumably referred to Curle 1906 or Curle 1907b.
[7] From his description it is certain that 'No. I' is Curle 1911a: pl. 87 no. 26; it is likely that 'No. 2' is no. 27 on the same plate.
[8] No longer extant.
[9] Cohausen 1873. The image shows an enamelled Romano-British trumpet brooch from the collection in Wiesbaden Museum.
[10] Almgren 1897: 34-47, pl. 4 (*kräftig profilierte Fibeln*, strongly profiled brooches, which often have a trumpet-like head and a near-central device on the turning point of the bow).

I do not know any other Roman fibula in the Continent who has this little ring above, and the trumpet-like head of your no. I as well as the shape of the foot seems me also connect this type with that enamelled type from Wiesbaden etc. How the corniform[11] appendices on your fibula are to be declared, I cannot say, but I do not think they can be derived from Hildebrand's[12] fig. 120, where the corresponding appendices are emerging from the head not from the middle of the bow. The last form is nearly only found in Hungary (I know only one from Germany, found at Heddernheim near Frankfurt),[13] so it is not ~~much~~ very likely, that it has been the prototype of an English form.

I think your dating of Fig. I is very probable. Perhaps you can have a nearer dating of the supposed prototype from Wiesbaden by inquiring at Professor Dr. E. Ritterling,[14] Wiesbaden, (the Director of the Museum there), who wrote to me the other day, that they have found now in this town a great quantity of fibulas under circumstances that allow a very good and narrow dating.

Have you seen a very good paper on helmets like yours from Newstead in 'Mittheilungen über Römische Funde in Heddernheim' I, Frankfurt 1894? It is entitled 'Die Heddernheimer Helme, die etruskischen und die griechischen Helm des Frankfurter Historischen Museums in ihrer Bedeutung für die Geschichte antiken Helmformen' von Otto Donner v. Richter.[15]

Prof. Montelius[16] sends you his best greetings.

Believe me,

Yours sincerely,

Oscar Almgren

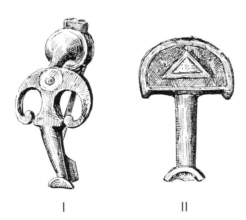

*Figure 11.1. The brooches from Newstead that Curle and Almgren were discussing
(extracted from Curle 1911a: pl. 87).*

[11]   Horn-like.
[12]   Hildebrand 1873: 152, fig. 120.
[13]   Almgren is probably referencing Riese 1898: pl. 2 no. 29.
[14]   Emil Ritterling (1861–1928) German archaeologist and historian. Curle did indeed correspond with Ritterling; see Letter 3.22 and *Dramatis personae*.
[15]   Donner-von Richter 1894.
[16]   Oscar Montelius (1843–1921), Swedish archaeologist renowned in particular for his work on typological schemes; based at the State Historical Museum in Stockholm. See *Dramatis personae*.

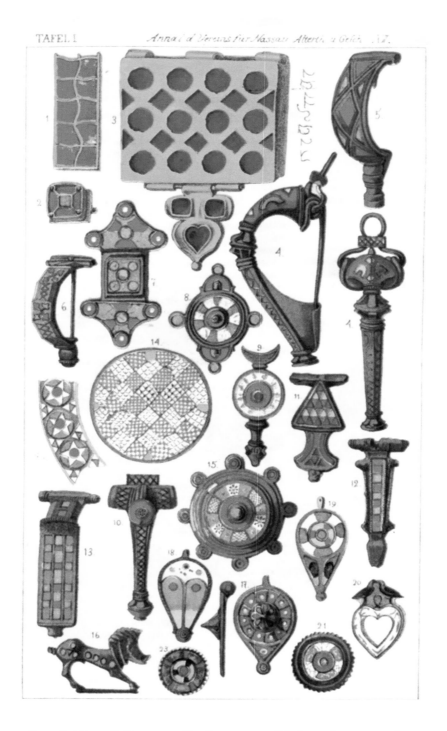

Figure 11.2. Enamelled items quoted by Almgren as parallels, from Cohausen 1873: pl. I:4.

Letter 4.3

From Johanna Mestorf.[17] Handwritten in German.[18]

Schleswig-Holsteinisches Museum Vaterländischer Altertümer[19]
KIEL in Holstein

23 February, 1907

Esteemed colleague,

To my shame my gratitude to you for your kindness in sending me your excellent report on the excavation of the Roman military station at Newstead is overdue.[20] The general conclusion is of great interest to me and I hope no obstacles will be in your way during your continuing research. Amongst the discovered items are several of great importance for our country according to their chronology. These are especially the mask helmet, the leather shoes and the garment fragments with reference to the cut and type of fabric.

The helmet is of interest to me as it supports my understanding I expressed in a paper years ago, that the silver mask from the Torsberg moor finds is in its present form a later construction [Figure 11.3].[21] The frontpiece, possibly a piece of loot, has the hinge at the top and below at the back the stud to attach the neckpiece. The latter is, of course, useless and makes no sense and has no relationship to the attached neckpiece and which resembles in its form remarkably the calotten-shaped Scandinavian helmet.[22]

I take it you are familiar with the leather shoes of our moor bodies.[23] If this is not the case I would send you my short paper published some years ago if I know that these lines reach you under the correct address. I would very much like to know if the woman's shoe (or both shoes) are cut from <u>one</u> piece of leather, and if the upper and sole are connected, or if the latter forms a second part which is joined to the upper by a seam. It is also conceivable that the sole trimmed with nails is a second one and forms a <u>double sole</u> which is joined to the inner sole as is the case with Roman sandals.

Finally, I would like to know if there exist enough remnants of the clothes to be able to make out the pattern / sagum = plaid, or trousers, jacket or others; and if the fabric is made of wool and simple linen = twill fabric or patterned fabric (perhaps diamond shaped).[24]

---

[17] Johanna Mestorf (1828–1909), prehistoric archaeologist and director of the Kiel museum. See *Dramatis personae*.

[18] Translator Mrs Elfriede Mackay.

[19] Museum of Antiquities of the Fatherland.

[20] Presumably Curle 1906 or Curle 1907b.

[21] Mestorf's paper has not been traced among her extensive bibliography, but she made the same point in the caption to a well-illustrated catalogue of the museum's collection on its fiftieth anniversary (Mestorf 1885: 29 no. 553, pl. 46). For the find, see Engelhardt 1863; Matešić 2015: 196–207, who offers a new reconstruction of the mask and skull cap as Germanic versions of Roman parade helmets.

[22] Skullcap-shaped. The reference is probably to Migration-period helmets from sites such as Ultuna and Vendel.

[23] For a brief overview of Mestorf's pioneering work on bog bodies, see van der Sanden 2002.

[24] Mestorf's orthography is hard to follow here.

Dear Sir, please excuse the many questions. It is quite important for me to collect confirmation for my dating of the bog bodies and that the Romans in the northern countries without doubt adapted some things from the German style of dress (2nd century AD sagum). Our moor finds have given us extremely precious information and enlightened us on the history of the art of spinning and weaving.

Yours sincerely,

J. Mestorf

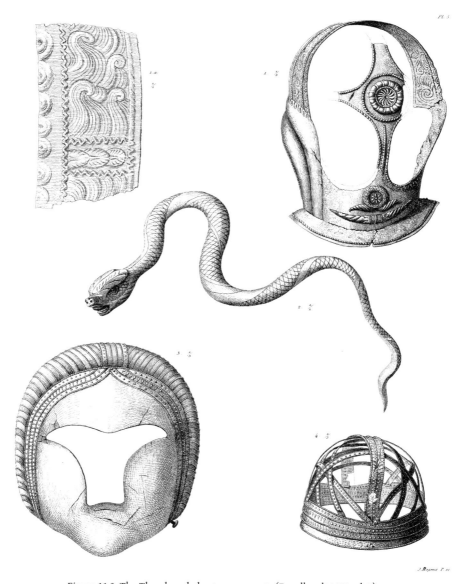

Figure 11.3. The Thorsberg helmet components (Engelhardt 1863: pl. 5).

Letter 4.4

From Cecil Smith.[25]

Department of Greek and Roman Antiquities
London: W.C.

22 April 1907

Dear Mr Curle,

The object is a vase in form of a foot, on the sole of which is the inscription.[26]

It is published by Heuzey in the Mém. de la Soc. des antiquaries de France VIII (1877) p 94.[27]

Yours very truly

Cecil Smith

Letter 4.5

From Joseph Anderson.[28]

SOCIETY OF ANTIQUARIES OF SCOTLAND
NATIONAL MUSEUM OF ANTIQUITIES
QUEEN STREET, EDINBURGH

Sept 3rd 1907

Dear Sir,

I have given some consideration to the various points indicated in yours of 29th ult. I quite agree that it is most desirable that the record of Newstead should be produced in a manner worthy of the subject and creditable to the Society, and I need not say that your proposal to surrender the profits of your lectures[29] for that purpose will, l have no doubt, be appreciated by the Council. I infer that you have in your mind a volume to be sold to those who may

---

[25] Sir Cecil Harcourt Smith (1859–1944) was Keeper of Greek and Roman Antiquities at the British Museum from 1904 to 1909; see *Dramatis personae*. For Curle's acknowledgement, see Letter 2.3.
[26] ΑΚΟΛΟΥΘΙ, from the verb 'to follow': 'he, she, it follows'.
[27] Heuzey 1877 (volume 8 in the fourth series). Curle's interest in this vase may have been stimulated by the patterns formed by hobnails on some shoes he found at Newstead (Curle 1911a: 152), though his treatment is quite summary and he does not quote this work.
[28] See *Dramatis personae*.
[29] His 1908 Rhind lecture series; see pp33–34 and Letters 1.41, 1.45, 3.1, 3.16.

choose to buy it – not to be distributed gratis to the Fellows and to foreign exchanges like the Proceedings. This would mean an impression of about 500 I fancy. The present impression of the Proceedings is 930. Of course it might be for consideration whether the Society could afford to issue it to all the Fellows. But in order to be able to judge of this and to understand approximately what is implied by a separate publication, whether for sale, or for distribution to the Fellows, it would be necessary to have some practical data to put before the Council when the proposal is considered.[30] If you tell me the size of paper and of type you prefer I could easily get an estimate for the letterpress from Neill and Co[31] for an amount of matter of the average size of the published Rhind Lectures. The illustrations cannot be estimated beforehand, but this would be something to go upon.

As to the other matter – proceeding with the preparation of the illustrations – the first thing to be found is the size of the page. Then you can arrange the fibulae say, by roughly sketching them as you desire them to be placed in order on the plate, and send me plate by plate, and I will get them drawn from the originals as you have them arranged. The same thing can be done with the other small objects. I fancy the best way to do would be to affix to each figure a number, and to have opposite each plate a page with the descriptive headings under each number. The larger things probably would come best as blocks in the text.

As to the slides, Inglis's charge,[32] when we give him drawings, photos, or any kind of engraving to copy, is 1/- for the negative,[33] and 1/- for the slide, so that each slide costs at least 2/-. When he has to come here and make photos, each photo costs 7/6.

I regret that the worst of the iron things are sweating, but I do not know that there is any process which can stop the chemical action in the interior of those pieces in which there is none of the iron left.[34] I remember the keeper of the Reading Museum[35] told me that they had tried everything but found nothing effective. The things that are going wrong are those from the soil near the surface, which have all their metallic character destroyed by oxidation and chlorination.

Yours very truly,

J. Anderson

[30] For discussion of the publication process, see D. Clarke 2012: 30–32. Curle was able to argue for a much grander volume than Anderson was proposing here.
[31] Printers for the Society of Antiquaries from 1856.
[32] We are grateful to David Clarke for the following information. Alexander Adam Inglis was born in Aberdeen in the late 1840s and died c. 1916. He was a professional photographer, specialising it seems in landscape and architectural photography, from 1881 based at Rock House, Calton Hill. Rock House already had an impressive photographic pedigree by this time, having been home to D.O. Hill and Robert Adamson, John and Thomas Annan, and Archibald Burns. Members of the Inglis family continued to work from Rock House until the mid-20th century. Alexander Adam Inglis was a Royal Warrant Photographer to both Edward VII and George V.
[33] One shilling, two shillings, seven shillings and sixpence in pre-decimal currency.
[34] Curle's notebooks show that he corresponded widely to find ways to conserve ironwork. Other correspondence shows his dissatisfaction with the techniques available at NMAS, e.g. Letters 1.65, 3.14, 3.18.
[35] Where the large collection of Roman ironwork from Silchester was held.

Letter 4.6

From Viktor Hoffiller.[36] Handwritten, in German.

Rome

21.2.1910

My dear Sir,

Occupied as I am with my work on Roman weapons,[37] I learn with great pleasure that your excavations in Newstead have delivered rich material in this area. Actually I have only read Haverfield's news about it in the Archaeologischer Jahresbericht[38] and in the Kurze Notiz by Domaszewski. I haven't seen the reports published by the Society of Antiquaries of Scotland. The day after tomorrow I will leave here and will be in Paris until around the middle of March. I would very much hope you to be so good as to send me a card to the address noted below as to when I might expect publication. Perhaps it might also be possible that I be sent the pages relating to the weapons, If, perhaps, Herr Reinach[39] has the papers, then there would be no point in having them sent to me, since Herr Reinach may possibly be so friendly as to make these available to me.

Thanking you in advance for all your work, I remain, yours faithfully, ready for any reciprocal service.

V. Hoffiller

Custos of the Croatian National Museum, Agram[40]

Letter 4.7

From Peter Hume Brown.[41] Handwritten.

20 Corrennie Gardens,
Edinburgh

July 1, 1910

Dear Mr Curle,

Very many thanks for your most interesting communication regarding the excavations at Newstead. It gives me sincerely the information I wanted and will be a valuable addition to my

---

[36] Viktor Hoffiller (1877–1954), curator at the National Museum of Croatia. See *Dramatis personae*. Translated by Dr C. Martin.
[37] Published as Hoffiller 1911; 1912.
[38] Haverfield published regular reviews of recent British work in *Archäologischer Anzeiger*; we have not traced the Domaszewski reference.
[39] Salomon Reinach (1858–1932), director of the Musée des Antiquités Nationales in St-Germain-en-Laye.
[40] Hoffiller wrote in German; Agram was the historical German name for Zagreb.
[41] Peter Hume Brown (1849–1918), first Professor of Scottish History, Edinburgh University (1901–1918). See *Dramatis personae*.

book.[42] Perhaps, when the note is printed, on your return, you will do me the further kindness of revising it. The results of your work seem to be far and away the most interesting and important that have yet been reached in Scotland. We shall all look forward to the appearance of your book in the autumn.

As you kindly suggest, I shall apply to Dr Anderson[43] about illustrations.

Again thanking you for the trouble you have taken for me.

I am,

Yours very truly,

P. Hume Brown

Letter 4.8

From Hans Dragendorff.[44] Printed proforma in German, with Curle's details entered by hand.[45]

THE GERMAN IMPERIAL ARCHAEOLOGICAL INSTITUTE
Berlin, W. 50, Ansbacherstr 46

23 April, 1912

J.-No 128[46]

The Central Board of the Imperial Archaeological Institute at its Annual General Meeting elected you, dear Sir, to be a Corresponding Member of the Institute and would ask for a kind word of acceptance of the election, so that the Diploma can be sent to you.

In order to issue the Diploma and then to forward it to you, your main first name and correct address is respectfully requested.

The General Secretary

Dragendorff

---

[42] Curle is thanked for assistance in the preface to Hume Brown 1911, an expanded edition of an earlier work. This is reflected in an appended note to the first chapter, summarising the results, and a series of photos of finds, poorly integrated with the text, it must be said: the bronze face mask, the brass helmet, two leather shoes, two iron blacksmith's tongs, a series of iron tools, and three bronze camp kettles (Hume Brown 1911: 6–7, pls 1–4). The revised version of the same author's school history of Scotland includes an image of the iron face-mask helmet (Hume Brown 1910: 11).

[43] Keeper at NMAS, where the Newstead finds were held. See *Dramatis personae*.

[44] See *Dramatis personae*. Dragendorff was secretary of the Imperial Archaeological Institute. He was a Roman specialist; Curle had used his foundational work on samian (Dragendorff 1895), while Dragendorff reviewed Curle's 1911a publication very favourably in the *Journal of Roman Studies* (Dragendorff 1911). This probably prompted this prestigious invitation.

[45] Translator Mrs Elfriede Mackay.

[46] Perhaps *Jahresnummer*, Year-number, the running tally of invitations that year.

Letter 4.9

From Alexander Mackie.[47] Handwritten.

Balmuildy

6th Oct, 1913

Dear Mr Curle,

In reply to your kind enquiry, the bath building[48] seems to have belonged to the first occupation as it fills the space of the missing ditch at south-east, provided that the wall and ditches are contemporary, also the sewer replacing the ditch enters the north-east corner of building; another finely built drain emerges from the east side near south corner trending eastwards. While on the western side the one previously found and supposed to be connected with the first mentioned we find starts from northern apse encircling the one on S. and also trends in an easterly direction.

The drain through the wall appears to have had no connection with the baths as the hypocaust adjacent is far deeper and is served by the drain running to the ditch on east, this in turn connects with one of the short small sewers and could only take the water from the wall or small space between it and the baths.

There is also a suspicion of a second occupation or enlarging, as a small chamber has been inset between the two apses and a small branch drain taken from the other enters this structure.

The style of heating is mixed brick pillars and built blocks but we have not found any hewn pillars or jambs; unfortunately the site is under several large trees which, of course, cannot be removed.

We have also been stripping a portion for barracks and find the remains of supposed post holes in remarkably regular sequence.[49]

We also have your kind remarks about your pleasant trip to the Cheviot Camps and starting something in that direction;[50] as you are probably aware the Glasgow Committee[51] are going to suspend operations here for an indefinite period in about three weeks – 25th – owing to lack of funds.

Mr Miller[52] says they expect to get a sum from the Carnegie[53] folks, but it will be next April before the application can be made and the autumn before it could be made available, although

---

[47] Curle's Clerk of Works from Newstead. See *Dramatis personae*. The Letter is important in giving a voice to a man who is otherwise silent in the published reports, and it shows him as a methodical observer of the field data, though at this stage of the excavation it is clear with hindsight that the sequence he proposes of bathhouse and ditches is incorrect.
[48] The discussion is around the annexe bathhouse; a second one lies within the fort. Mackie was mistaken at this stage; the annexe bathhouse is clearly secondary as it overlies the fort defences, as the report notes (Miller 1922: 47–55, esp. 52, and fig.10; see also Bailey 1994: 303). Curle is acknowledged for his assistance in the report (Miller 1922: vi); Letter 1.66 shows he visited the site.
[49] Only one barrack (Block IX) could be investigated before the First World War intervened (Miller 1922: 32–41).
[50] The implication of this and Mackie's final line is that Curle was considering further fieldwork. In the Report, Curle noted the need for 'more excavation of the forts in the hill-country, Cappuck, Pennymuir, Chew Green' (Curle 1911a: 8). Miller had excavated at the small fort of Cappuck, on Dere Street south of Newstead, in 1911 and 1912 as 'a natural sequel to the excavation by Mr James Curle of the fort at Newstead on the Tweed' (Stevenson and Miller 1912: 476); Mackie was his Clerk of Works, while Curle and George Macdonald are thanked for visiting and assisting with pottery and coin research respectively (Stevenson and Miller 1912: 448). The 'Cheviot camps' must thus be the temporary camps at Pennymuir in Roxburghshire (RCAHMS 1956: 375–377; Jones 2011: 293–294) and/or the military complex of Chew Green, just over the Border in Northumberland (Frere and St Joseph 1983: 140–142).
[51] The Excavation Committee of the Glasgow Archaeological Society: see Miller 1922: v–vi.
[52] Steuart Napier Miller, lecturer in Roman history and antiquities at Glasgow University and excavator of the site on behalf of the Glasgow Archaeological Society. See Miller 1922.
[53] The Carnegie Trust (founded by Andrew Carnegie in 1901) provides grants for improving and extending

they may restart earlier on a definite promise, so if you have anything in diem[54] would be pleased to assist after we finish here.

Yours very faithfully

A. Mackie

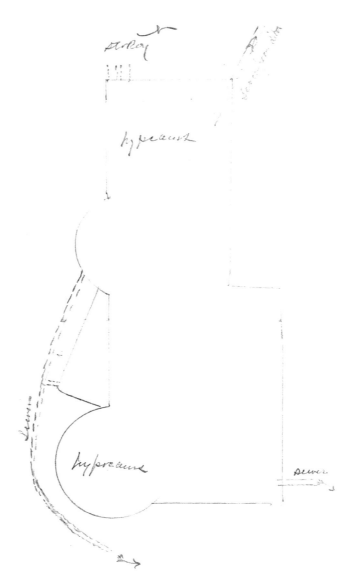

[This sketch of the building, showing its outline but no internal details, came with the letter. Annotations note two hypocausts and three sewers. The annotation at top left is illegible.]

---

opportunities for scientific study and research in Scottish Universities. They funded both the excavation and the publication (Miller 1922: v).
[54] Paid by the day.

Letter 4.10

From Leopold Frölich.[55] Handwritten in German.[56]

HEIL- & PFLEGEANSTALT KÖNIGSFELDEN
(Kt. AARGAU)
DIREKTION

20.XI.1913

Dear Mr Curle!

Kindly forgive that I reply to your letter of 20 October only today. I have been ill for some time and my work had been impeded by an eye ailment. I am really unsure as to what kind of photograph you would like to have and so I thought it would be better for your lecture if I would let you have a few samples of our collection of crockery.[57] I will send you therefore, by post, a box of terra sigillata undecorated, and more decorated. The decorated ones correspond to the types 29, 30 and 37 according to Dragendorff.[58] The sherds came from our 'rubbish heap' but have been imported from Graufesenque[59] in Gaul and are dated from the second half of the 1st century AD.

I hope to give you a little pleasure with these.

We are still busy researching in our rich terrain and we are filling up our small Museum more and more with treasure.

Hopefully you will find time again for a visit to Switzerland. It would give me much pleasure to see you again.

If I can be of any more help to you I would be at your disposal and greet you with high esteem.

Yours sincerely,

Dr Frölich

---

[55] Leopold Frölich (1860–1933), who excavated around the legionary fortress of *Vindonissa* (Windisch), especially on the rubbish heap (*Schutthügel*). See *Dramatis personae*.
[56] Translated by Mrs Elfriede Mackay.
[57] Letter 1.71 indicates the context was a lecture on samian to students in Glasgow. Curle donated the sherds to NMAS in 1935; *Proceedings of the Society of Antiquaries of Scotland* 70 (1935–1936): 19.
[58] Dragendorff 1895.
[59] Centre for production of *terra sigillata*/samian in southern France, near Narbonne.

Letter 4.11

From Bernhard Salin.[60] Handwritten.

RIKSANTIKVARIEN
Stockholm, Sweden

16 July 1914

Dear Sir,

I send you today the clichées[61] and hope you will get them in good condition, I mean of course that the clichées will come undamaged into your hands.[62]

You write 'Månadsbladet 7th årgång 1871, figs 17 or 18 and 19' and there must be something wrong here, because the first year of Månadsbladet is 1872, but we suppose you may have thought on other illustrations we have sent [Figure 11.4].[63] If wrong, write again.

I am always glad to hear something from you.

Believe me

Yours very truly

Bernhard Salin

Figure 11.4. Parallels for oval brooches that Curle sought but was not able to obtain,
from Montelius 1877: figs 17–18.

---

[60] Bernhard Salin, (1861–1931), State Antiquary for Sweden; see *Dramatis personae*. Curle clearly knew him well; see Letter 1.7.
[61] Printing blocks.
[62] The context was Curle's study of Viking-period oval brooches; the Royal Academy of History and Antiquities, Stockholm is thanked for permission to use blocks (Curle 1914: figs 12–18).
[63] Curle was referring to Montelius 1877, it seems, as figs 17–19 show three relevant brooches. Salin sent a series of blocks, mostly from this paper but only one of the three Curle requested! Montelius 1877: figs 13, 19, 26–28, covering Curle's figs 12 (right) and 15–18; the other illustrations are from a different source.

Letter 4.12

From G.M. Kam.[64] Handwritten.

Nijmegen

25th Feb 1915

My dear Sir!

Your kind letter of the 4th Jan came duly to hand. You ask me if I know the bronze mask from Nijmegen in the Gildemeester collection, Amsterdam.[65] I never saw it but as far as I know it is not a mask but a bronze helmet and I have not Lipperheide.[66] To get a photograph of it I think it will be very difficult because that Gentleman is rather a queer man and I am with him on bad terms because I bought away under his nose the bronze shield at Köln [Cologne] and now the helmet with silvered visor mask [Figure 11.5].[67] I went up very early in the morning to the man who had to sell it and while I was dealing about the affair there came Gildemeester. His wife who opened the door said to G. 'The master of the house, my husband, is not at home' and I saw parting [?] G on his back and I bought the object for £420,-[68] – while he had been asking in May last to G. for £500,- which at that time he would not pay and I was in Swiss. In Amsterdam G has locked up in his house his collection in Schranks[69] and nobody can get to see it.

My bronze shield is not from the Waal river but has been discovered in Blerik near to Venlo.[70] The place was named Blaricum by the Romans. I have still a couple of printings 'das Medusenhaupt von Blaricum von R Gaedechens Professor in Jena. Fest-Programm zu Winkelman's[71] Geburtstage am 9 Dec 1874', which is exhausted.[72] I will send you an exemplar by book post.

It will wonder you that yesterday I got in my museum still another helmet bronze silvered digged up with the gravel at Pannerden on the German frontier.[73] Close here where the Rhine is dividing itself in two branches, the Waal who comes to Nijmegen and the Rhine who goes to Arnhem. It is a beautiful piece and most interesting because it is Etruscan dated about 5–4 centuries before Christ. Die Alterthümer unser Heidnisches Vorzeit Dr L. Lindenschmit. Band I Heft III No 2, Altitalische Helme B Erz periode? wie L. sagt.[74] The exempel there is found in Apulien and L[indenschmidt] Band IV, Etruskische Bronzehelme Tafel 55 N 1 but without decoration on the rim and the front part.[75]

---

[64] Gerard Marius Kam (1836–1922) amassed a large private collection which became the Rijksmuseum G.M. Kam in 1922. See *Dramatis personae*. Our grateful thanks to Louis Swinkels, Marenne Zandstra and Stefanie Hoss for assistance with various aspects of this letter.

[65] This is the iron face mask with bronze coating and white metal plating, probably from the Waal, recorded by Garbsch (1978: 63, O5, pl. 18.1) as coming from the Gildemeester collection; it is now in the Rijksmuseum van Oudheden in Leiden.

[66] Kam did not have a copy of Lipperheide 1896, where the mask was published.

[67] On which Curle published an article (Curle 1915). Garbsch 1978: 63, O6, pl. 19.1.

[68] Kam does indeed seem to have converted what he paid into British pounds; he had worked in England, so would have been familiar with the currency.

[69] Cupboards.

[70] Garbsch 1978: 84, R9, pl. 43.

[71] J.J. Winkelmann (1717–1768), famous German art historian and archaeologist. The reference is Gaedechens 1874.

[72] This seems to be 'exhausted', sold out, rather than 'exhaustive'.

[73] Kam 1915: 260–261, where he gives the context as 'dredged from the Waal close to the Dutch border'. Although ultimately from the Etruscan tradition, this is a late Republican or Augustan helmet of Type Buggenum (Schaaff 1988: 325–326). For this helmet, see Klumbach 1974, no. 8, pl. 8; Robinson 1975, 21, pls 16-17; 28, fig. 23.

[74] Lindenschmit 1864: 3rd part, pl. 2. no. 2 is from Apulia.

[75] Lindenschmit 1900: pl. 55 no. 1, from Italy.

Occassionly [*sic*][76] I will send you a photo. Also from a silver bar springly [*sic*][77] by the silver thread twisted from one pommel to the other, digged up in the same place where the helmet-with-visor-mask came to daylight.[78] I do not know any parallel of this piece but I suppose it was a bar who the Lady or Gentleman had in her hands to command the slaves and opportunely to knock them on their hands. The weight is 60 grams.

Since three weeks I had an attaque of the gout so that I could not move. Now I am recovering.

Meanwhile I remain,

Dear Sir,

Yours truly,

G. M. Kam

[The two following sketches came with this letter. One has the legend 'a bronze can, also digged up where the helmet-with-visor-mask is discovered'.[79] The other is of the decorative terminals described in the letter. Dimensions are in metres.]

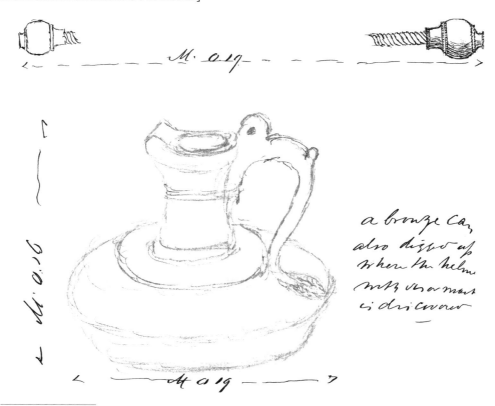

---

[76] Probably 'On occasion', i.e. in due course.
[77] Probably intended as like a spring or spiral.
[78] The accompanying sketch shows two globular decorative pommels with a twisted rod between them; they are not apparently preserved in the Museum het Valkhof collection. Dr Swinkels makes the plausible suggestion that they may be the ends of an ornate spindle, by comparison with amber examples of similar size (Koster 2013: 181–183).
[79] Den Boesterd 1956: 71, no. 258, pl. 11, where no locality is given, but the dimensions match precisely and it is the only such jug in the collections at that date.

Figure 11.5. Face-mask helmet from the river Waal near Nijmegen, formerly in the collection of G.M. Kam; published by Curle. © Museum het Valkhof.

Letter 4.13

From Gerard Baldwin Brown.[80] Handwritten.

25 Coates Gardens
Edinburgh

30 April [1916][81]

My dear Curle,

I do not know if I ever answered your kind query about the Nijmegen helmet.[82] I should like to have a note about it if you will kindly send it to me. I suppose it is not the same as a fine Roman helmet from North Brabant I saw and photographed in the Museum at Leiden a few years ago?[83]

The Burlington Magazine[84] have written to me about the Lewis objects[85] and I have seen your brother on the subject. He is quite willing that the Magazine should publish the find, even before your paper appears in the Society's 'Proceedings',[86] and I am sending to the Magazine the print from Inglis's[87] negative of the objects. Your brother also favoured that the drawing of the detail on one of the objects should be sent to the Magazine as soon as the engravers, who have it in hand for reproduction, have finished with it.

I have told them that you have kindly agreed to furnish a note about the objects, and they will be very glad to have this M.S.[88] as soon as you are able to send it to them. (The Burlington Magazine, 17 Old Burlington St, W.)[89]

I am assuming that you have the material by you and will not need the illustrations. If you <u>do</u> need them by you, there must be a little delay.

Yours sincerely,

G. Baldwin Brown

A.O.[90] is anxious that there should be <u>no information given as to where the objects are at present</u>.[91]

---

[80] Gerard Baldwin Brown (1849–1932), at the time Watson-Gordon Professor of Fine Art, Edinburgh University. See *Dramatis personae*.
[81] The envelope is postmarked 1916.
[82] Curle 1915; Letter 4.12.
[83] The Deurne helmet, a 4th-century gilded and inscribed silver helmet found in 1910 by peat diggers in De Peel, North Brabant, Netherlands. See Braat 1973.
[84] The world's leading monthly journal on art and its history, founded 1903.
[85] Viking burial assemblage from Bhaltos; see Letter 1.77.
[86] *Proceedings of the Society of Antiquaries of Scotland*, where it appeared as Macleod *et al.* 1916. A.O. Curle, as Director of the Museum, would have been involved in the reporting of the find.
[87] A freelance photographer used by the museum; see Letter 4.5.
[88] Manuscript.
[89] Published as Curle 1916.
[90] A.O. Curle, James Curle's brother, mentioned earlier in the letter.
[91] In Letter 1.77, Curle commented unfavourably on the whereabouts of the finds, in the Nicolson Institute in Stornoway.

Letter 4.14

From Ernst Fabricius.[92] Handwritten in German.[93]

Freiburg i. Br[esgau]
Goethestrasse 44

13 August 1928

My esteemed Mr Curle,

I am very sorry that I missed the friendly visit of your daughter today. It would have given me the greatest pleasure to have seen Miss Curle again and to have been able to instruct her to send my greetings to you because I always think with heartfelt gratitude of the beautiful days spent with you in Melrose which were the high point of my whole trip to Great Britain.[94] But it does please me that Miss Curle has got to know my wife and my daughter Sophie and, equally that my wife and my daughter have made the acquaintance of your daughter, because I have indeed talked so much about Priorwood from the delightful welcome I found at your house, from the flowers from Mrs Curle and from the Abbey[95] which you were so kind to show me, from the valley of the Tweed, from the delightful trip to Chew Green and the beautiful journey to Bremenium.[96] How vividly all those visits remain in my memory.

My journey right to the end was most enjoyable and interesting.

I was able to spend a further few days in Gilsland and to take part in Mr Simpson's[97] excavation at Birdoswald. The beginnings of an old fort were coming to light at the time I had to leave and I am eager to learn of the further successes of the excavation. Above all I feel myself now so much more in touch with the scientific work in Roman Britain and I view it as an advantage to have met the researchers who have carried out this work in your country and continue to do so.

If I had had the good fortune to see your daughter I would have sent my good wishes and best regards to you and Mrs Curle. So I have to do this in writing and include a special greeting to Miss Curle.

Be assured of my sincere gratitude and esteem.

Ernst Fabricius

---

[92] Ernst Fabricius (1857–1942), German historian, archaeologist and classical scholar: excavated in Greece and Asia Minor: President of the Reichslimeskommission, the state organisation overseeing the investigation of the Roman frontier (*limes*) in Germany. See *Dramatis personae*.

[93] Translated by Mrs Ishbel Gordon and Dr Connie Martin, assisted by Mr Brian Martin.

[94] In 1928 Fabricius was invited by the Society of Antiquaries of Newcastle, the Society of Antiquaries of Scotland, the Cumberland and Westmorland Antiquarian and Archaeological Society and the University of Durham to visit northern England, the Antonine Wall and the Borders. As part of his tour of the Roman remains, on 8 July he stayed with JC, visiting Newstead and other sites on Dere Street, including Chew Green in Northumberland, and on to High Rochester (*Bremenium*), accompanied by A.O. Curle and Miss Curle; cf. Reception Committee's report of Professor Fabricius' visit, *Proceedings of the Society of Antiquaries of Newcastle* (4th series) 3 (1928): 280–286.

[95] Melrose Abbey.

[96] High Rochester outpost fort.

[97] Frank G. Simpson (1882–1955), archaeologist who excavated at Birdoswald and elsewhere on Hadrian's Wall (Birley 1961: 190–191).

Letter 4.15

From Ernst Fabricius. Handwritten in German.[98]

Freiburg i. Br.[esgau]

2 September 1928

Esteemed Mr Curle!

When I returned yesterday from Donaueschingen[99] where I have been visiting the excavation of the Roman fort of Hüfingen[100] I found here the issue of The Scotsman with the unveiling of the monument at the site in Newstead [Figures 11.6–11.7].[101] The two good reports and the superb pictures in which I recognised you, Sir George Macdonald and (if I'm not mistaken) your esteemed brother, gave me the greatest pleasure. I could picture myself there and could imagine hearing the speeches which seem to be well rendered in the reports. It is a lovely idea by way of such a memorial to make the many people, who might otherwise hurry away thoughtlessly, aware of the historical meaning of the site, just as your work has made us, the archaeologists of the world, so intensely aware.

I have, frankly thanks to your kindness, both the knowledge of the locality, and the view from the Cheviots of The Three Hills,[102] and of the results of your labours.

I give hearty thanks for your friendly letter.

In the fort at Hüfingen we have, both mixed together and on top of one another, the remains of at least five periods, all from the time of Tiberius to the 1st year of Vespasian. No coins beyond the years 73/74, no fragments of more recent sigillata! But a lot of overlapping graves, large barrack buildings burnt but reconstructed over the older defensive ditches, also here flattened by the plough, 'a wide and fairly level plateau on a bluff above a stream'[103] in the middle of natural communications zones not far from the source of the Danube.

With best wishes to your esteemed family.

Your grateful servant,

Ernst Fabricius

---

[98] Translated by Mrs Ishbel Gordon and Dr Connie Martin, assisted by Mr Brian Martin.
[99] A small German town near the sources of the river Danube.
[100] In Baden-Württemberg. For the excavations, see Revellio 1937 (which Fabricius edited).
[101] A memorial in the form of an altar mirroring that of one found by Curle at the site (RIB I: 2123, erected by G. Arrius Domitianus), made of Swedish granite, was erected at the north-west corner of the site beside the road by the Edinburgh Border Counties Association. It was unveiled by Curle in a ceremony on 28 August 1928 (*The Scotsman* 29 August 1928: 8, 9). *The Scotsman* for 17 August 1928 records that Bailie George Hope Tait (see *Dramatis personae*) suggested the idea and proposed a Roman altar with a steel pillar rising from it, surmounted by a Roman eagle and the letters SPQR, but this was felt to be 'savouring too much in the glorification of a Roman triumph which, after all, was but a transitory incident in the development of the country'. The final monument was designed by the architect W.H. Johnson of Menzies, Cockburn and Johnson, Edinburgh, and sculpted by George Sutherland, Galashiels.
[102] The three Eildon hills which dominate the town of Melrose and give rise to the name *Trimontium*.
[103] Fabricius gave this quote in English; they are the words of George Macdonald, quoted in *The Scotsman* article about the unveiling (29 August 1928: 9).

A group after the unveiling at Newstead including Sir George Macdonald, Bailie Hope Tait, Dr James Curle, Sir George Douglas, Mr A. Eddington, the Earl of Home, and (seated) Col. Douglas Elliott and Mr J. Sutherland.

Figure 11.6. Unveiling of the Trimontium monument on 28 August 1928. It was made of Swedish granite, and took the form of the altar to Jupiter dedicated by Gaius Arrius Domitianus which Curle had found in his excavations. Present, from the left, are: George Macdonald; Bailie George Hope Tait (who proposed the idea); Alexander Mackie (Clerk of Works at the excavations); James Curle; Sir George Douglas (Kelso); Alexander Eddington (Edinburgh); the Earl of Home (President of the Border Counties Association); seated, from left, Col. Douglas Elliott (Secretary of the Association); Mr George Paterson Sutherland (of Sutherland Sculptors, Galashiels, who made the monument). The image is from the Border Telegraph, 29 August 1928; our thanks to the Old Gala Club for locating it. It is seemingly not the photo that Fabricius saw in The Scotsman, as A.O. Curle is not present.

Figure 11.7. Erecting the Trimontium stone, 1928. Mason William Hunter on the left with nine-year-old George S. Sutherland; mason George Steel on the right with six-year-old John McD. Sutherland, grandsons of the firm's founder..

Letter 4.16

From George Gordon Coulton.[104] Handwritten on embossed St John's College, Cambridge notepaper.

1 Jan 1934

Dear Dr Curle

On the face of it your <u>mesnil</u>[105] seems to me the best conjecture, considering the infiltration of French into Scottish at that time. If at any time I can think of any other, I will let you know; but, for myself, I should not hesitate to print <u>mesnil</u> as a conjecture.

I am very glad to hear that excavations are going on well.[106] You will be amused to find that <u>Scot. Abbeys</u>[107] has been put (with due reservations) in Abp.[108] Hayes's 'White List' for the faithful in America.[109] The Soc. Antiqs. might care to see the booklet, in view of that Bute – Fort Augustus – memorial[110] to them in protest against my appointment. I have another copy.

My wife joins me in all good wishes for 1934 to you and yours. I am still plodding at vol 3 of <u>5. cent</u>[111] – faint but pursuing. Poor Maclean,[112] as you probably know, was very ill for a week or so, but I hear much better accounts of him now.

Yours sincerely,

G.G. Coulton

---

[104] George Gordon Coulton (1858–1947), Fellow of St John's College, medieval historian and controversialist (Summerson 2018). See *Dramatis personae*.

[105] *Mesnil* (little house) suggested by Professor Lawrence Keppie and confirmed by Brian Martin (pers. comm.) from French *mansionile* (diminutive of 'mansio'). In his attempt to define the precinct wall of the monastery and town of Melrose from charter evidence, Curle had sought Coulton's assistance with a 1779 entry in the Sasines for Roxburghshire which mentioned 'that house and yard for the Manel of Melrose'. He conjectured that 'Manel' was either a rendering of the French 'mesnil' or a corruption of the Scots 'Girnel' or tithe barn (Curle 1935: 17).

[106] This seems to be a general reference to excavation work in Scotland; Curle was not undertaking any himself at this stage.

[107] Coulton 1933.

[108] Archbishop.

[109] Joseph Patrick Hayes (1867–1938), Archbishop of New York from 1919, then Cardinal from 1924.

[110] We have not pursued this reference, but suspect it was a protest against his appointment as Rhind lecturer in 1931, most likely based on a religious dispute: Coulton was known for getting embroiled in arguments, especially religious ones, and Summerson (2018) noted his 'recurrent conflicts with a group of Roman Catholic historians'. The Butes were a prominent Catholic family in Scotland; Fort Augustus was a Benedictine Abbey at the time.

[111] His *magnum opus*: volume 3 of *Five centuries of religion* (Cambridge: CUP, 1923–1950).

[112] There is too little information to contextualise this reference securely, but it may be Lauchlan Maclean Watt, minister of Glasgow Cathedral 1923–1924, Moderator of the General Assembly, poet, author and critic.

Chapter 12
Miscellanea

Letter 5.1[1]

G.H. Leith-Buchanan to Curle. Handwritten.

The New Club,
Edinburgh

Febr. 26th 1896

Dear Mr Curle,

In reply to yours of the 21st, the Roman altar you mention, belongs, of course, to Lady Leith Buchanan, who seems averse to part with it, so that I regret I cannot comply with your request. It is at Ross, in the entrance hall, where it has been seen and admired by a good many people [Figure 12.1].[2]

Sincerely yours,

George H. Leith-Buchanan

Figure 12.1. Altar to Silvanus from Newstead which was once at Ross Priory in Dunbartonshire. © National Museums Scotland (L.1951.42).

---

[1] NMS Library: SAS Ms. UC 17/266. Ink heading (applied in museum, not in Curle's hand): 'Altar from Newstead'.
[2] The altar to Silvanus found at Newstead in 1830. It was originally at Drygrange, the estate on which the bulk of the fort lay, before passing to Lady Leith-Buchanan at Ross Priory, Dunbartonshire. It finally came to NMAS on loan in 1951 (RIB I: 2124). Curle was presumably seeking to acquire it for the museum; the letter is from the collection of the Society of Antiquaries of Scotland, indicating Curle was acting officially. At the time he was Librarian.

Letter 5.2

Curle to H. St George Gray,[3] between October 1905 and March 1906.

The original letter has not been traced; it is quoted in a footnote to Gray 1906: 136, discussing the Newstead scale armour as a parallel to a find from Ham Hill, Somerset.[4]

Mr James Curle, jun,. F.S.A., has kindly sent me an outline of a scale which is of the same general form as the Ham Hill ones, with two holes on either side near the top for joining the scales together, but with one hole only at the top for attachment to the tunic ... The Newstead scales are 1⅛ inch long (28.3 mm) by ½ inch wide (12.5 mm), of 'bright brass and very thin'. Mr Curle says that 'many of them were fastened together by wires almost square in section. The largest number of scales fastened together was 15. I have handed over 337 of the scales to the museum at Edinburgh. The find was made on September 21st, 1905, near the bottom of a great pit in the courtyard of the praetorium, along with a number of other objects. A human skull was found at the same level. Coming up in the mud some of the scales may have had the appearance of being rolled together, but it would be a mistake to describe them as being found in bundles. I have not as yet formed any definite theory as to this pit, but I must say that at 13 feet deep it contained a coin of Hadrian, and from the silt of the bottom we recovered a coin of Titus or Vespasian (somewhat defaced).'[5]

Letter 5.3

Extract from a 1907 appeal for funds from the Society of Antiquaries of Scotland.[6]

But much remains to be done, and it would be disappointing to have to discontinue work which has been so fruitful until the whole site has been examined. The funds already subscribed have been applied most carefully under the personal supervision of Mr James Curle, who, fortunately for the interests of archaeology, resides close to the spot.

But these funds are well-nigh exhausted, and part of the camp itself has not been opened; the northern and western defences are untouched; the eastern annexe has not been fully excavated; and the western annex contains buildings which it is very desirable to examine, as being likely to yield dates of occupation. The cemetery has not yet been discovered, nor has the foundation of the bridge across the Tweed.

In these circumstances, I venture to make a strong appeal to Fellows of the Society and others interested in the early history of our country to contribute to the completion of the work so well begun and carried on. Subscriptions of any amount, however small, ...'

---

[3] Harold St George Gray (1872–1963) was an antiquary based in Somerset; perhaps his most striking achievements were the excavation and publication of the Iron Age lake villages at Meare and Glastonbury. See *Dramatis personae*.
[4] Gray noted that he became aware of this find from Curle's notes on the work in *Scottish Historical Review* 3 (1906), 126–127, the relevant part appearing in October 1905.
[5] For this discovery see Letters 1.18, 3.6–3.9; Curle 1911a: 158–159.
[6] This is a foreword dated 9 January 1907 by Herbert Maxwell, President of the Society, to a report by Curle (1907b) on progress to date, issued as a pamphlet by the Society.

Letter 5.4

James Curle to Thomas Hardy. Handwritten.[7]

Priorwood,
Melrose N.B.

27 January 1913,

Dear Mr Hardy,

I have hesitated to write to you but my neighbour and friend Sir George Douglas[8] has encouraged me to do so.

I have lately been re-reading your words with renewed pleasure and as I read I cannot help noting how in your Wessex the remains of older civilisations, ancient tracks, barrows, and Roman earthmounds, with all their suggestiveness, come into the landscape.

I don't know if you have heard of the excavation of the site of the Roman fort at Newstead, near here, carried out in 1905–10. The earthworks had long been levelled, indeed every trace of works on the surface had vanished when we began operations, but still we had the good fortune to recover a harvest of things illustrative of Roman military life such as rarely falls to an excavation in this country. I hope and believe that the record of the digging operations would be of interest to you and I have therefore ventured to send you a copy of my book 'A Roman Frontier Post'. I shall feel honoured if you will accept it. May I send with the book an expression of gratitude for all the pleasure I have had from your work.

Believe me,

Yours very truly,

James Curle

---

[7] This letter to the renowned author and poet Thomas Hardy (1840–1928), discovered by Provost William Windram of Melrose, forms part of the collection of Dorset County Museum and was included in an article in the *Trimontium Trumpet* of 2010.

[8] Sir George Douglas (1856–1935) of Springwood Park, Kelso; poet and writer; long-standing acquaintance of Hardy from Douglas's brother's land-agency training days at Wimborne in Dorset. He hosted Hardy and his wife in September 1891 in the Borders and escorted them to Abbotsford, Melrose Abbey etc. Douglas was present at the unveiling of the Trimontium Stone in 1928 (see Figure 11.6 and notes to Letter 4.15).

Letter 5.5

Thomas Hardy to James Curle. Handwritten.[9]

Max. Gate

30.1.1913

Dear Mr Curle,

I really do not deserve this gift of a beautiful book you send me. There was certainly no need for you to hesitate in writing on such a subject – one which has always interested me, though, alas, I am very ignorant of the real condition of things in Britain during the Roman period.

The allusions in my books to the remains from that day, and earlier, are of a casual superficial kind. Since you allude to the novels I may be allowed to say that, to myself, my impressions, such as they are, of these remains and remote times, are perhaps more directly expressed in some of the poems. However, I won't be sure.

I shall value 'A Roman Frontier Post'; and with thanks believe me

Yours very truly,

Thomas Hardy

Letter 5.6

James Curle to J.G. Callander.[10] Typewritten.

Melrose

25th April, 1921

Dear Callander,

I have a note from Mr Maxwell Scott[11] this morning, who sends me an extract from Sotheby's Catalogue, giving particulars of Lot 333, the Antique Celtic Bronze Mask from Abbotsford [Figure 12.2].[12] I see that it is to be sold on Tuesday 24th May. They have obviously printed this note in order to send it out to America, and attract as much attention as possible. I hope the

---

[9] We are indebted again to Provost Windram for the information that this letter is now in the manuscript collection of Yale University and was published in Purdy and Millgate 1984.

[10] Keeper of NMAS, 1919–1938; see *Dramatis personae*.

[11] Major General Sir Walter Constable Maxwell-Scott, Bt, CB DSO (1875–1954), great-great-grandson of Sir Walter.

[12] The Torrs horns and pony cap, long termed a 'chamfron' or horse-mask but in fact more plausibly a cap; the horns, though ancient, were suspected to have been attached after its discovery, but a contemporary newspaper account makes it clear that this is indeed how it was found (Atkinson and Piggott 1955; Briggs 2014). It is unique, but its art style is typical of the so-called 'Torrs-Witham-Wandsworth' style of the third century BC (Megaw and Megaw 2001: 192–200; Harding 2002; Hunter 2009). It was found in 1812 during drainage of Torrs Loch near Castle Douglas in the county of Kirkcudbright, given to Sir Walter Scott, and exhibited at Abbotsford until it was purchased by the National Museum of Antiquities of Scotland at the Sotheby's sale.

Society will take it up and do what we can to buy it. I'm afraid we shall have to pay a good deal for it, but, as you know, it is quite unique, and we must get it.[13]

Yours very truly,

James Curle

Figure 12.2. Pony cap and horns, dating to the 3rd century BC, found in a moss at Torrs, Kirkcudbrightshire. Photo by Neil McLean, © National Museums Scotland (X.FA 72).

[13] Curle was acting here in his role as one of the Honorary Curators of the museum, with responsibility for guiding acquisitions; see discussion on p.25. See also Letter A5 for negotiations with the British Museum. It was successfully acquired for £305. See *Proceedings of the Society of Antiquaries of Scotland* 56 (1921–1922): 8, 21–22; Stevenson 1981: 188.

Letter 5.7

James Curle to Sir Herbert Maxwell.[14] Handwritten.

Priorwood,
Melrose,
Scotland

31st December, 1931

My dear Sir Herbert,

It was very kind of you to send me these two versions of Galatian Rhymes,[15] both of which I return.

I can see that the text I printed[16] was extremely 'corrupt'. I should like to know what mediaeval romances lie embedded in the play The Black Knight. The great King Alexander, Billy Heaton and all the rest of them have a long ancestry.

I suppose Billy in the context is an endearing or familiar epithet just as the minister speaks of 'Billy Jonah' in the Scotch Presbyterian Eloquence.[17]

In your Galloway version[18] I have no doubt King George was originally St George of Cappadocia who, I believe, was slain by a Galatian.

In Dr Selby's version[19] taken from the Newstead boys I am sure 'prove kind' is a misreading for 'propine',[20] a word I always remember in this connection and which came back to me at Vichy a year or two ago when reading the baths regulations in Spanish. I saw that one was to give 'nullas propinas'. I am afraid, notwithstanding, we did 'propine'.

With kind regards,

Believe me

Yours very sincerely,

James Curle

---

[14] Sir Herbert Maxwell (1845–1937), MP, author, amateur artist and antiquary, among many other interests, who would have been well known to Curle from his Presidency of the Society of Antiquaries of Scotland while Curle was excavating *Trimontium*. See Behan and Hutchinson 2011, and *Dramatis personae*.

[15] Known in Scots more commonly as *Galoshins*, performed by guisers and involving the resurrection of someone after a duel; performed at Halloween or New Year. For the topic see Hayward 1992 (but note the critical review of Chandler 1994); Lyle 2011.

[16] *Times Literary Supplement* 26 November 1931: 960, col. 2, 'The guisers'; Hayward 1992: 245–247, one of four versions he recorded from Newstead.

[17] Crokatt 1786.

[18] For Galoshins in Galloway see J. Hunter 2008: 121–122.

[19] William McDowell Selby (1873–1933), the doctor in Port William, Wigtownshire, was a noted local antiquary. His collection is now in Stranraer Museum, and includes some finds from Newstead, suggesting he visited the site (or visited Curle); see Murray 2005, and *Dramatis personae*.

[20] Chambers Dictionary (1993) notes this as an archaic, chiefly Scottish term, giving the meaning as: 'to pledge in drinking; to present or offer'. The former context is most likely here; the version of Galoshins Curle recorded included the line 'Perhaps you will propine with some whisky or some beer'.

Letter 5.8

James Curle to Thomas Scott.[21] Handwritten.

Priorwood, Melrose, Scotland

15 January, 1936

Dear Mr Scott,

I saw Sir George Macdonald on Monday and I asked him for a copy of his paper on the remains of the Roman Statue found at Milsington which I thought you might like to have [Figure 12.3].[22] I am sending it on to you with the note he added later, showing Sir Walter's interest in the find.[23] One always wonders how a piece of a great equestrian statue found its way out into the hill country. The statue itself was not the sort of monument you would find in a fort in a military zone such as Caledonia and we have always thought it must have come from some great centre like York.

On Saturday after I left you I was going round some fences at Hoscote[24] with Matthew Rodger and I noticed a bit of a broad road coming down to the Borthwick at the side of the Muselee. When I asked him what it was he said it was the old drove road by which in older days men could drive cattle from Falkirk tryst to York. Now that road is running between Milsington and Hoscote and I have little doubt that it represents a very ancient prehistoric highway and that the people, who carried off the pieces of the statue from the sack of York or wherever it came from, must have travelled along it. Is your Pot Syke (where the money is!) far from this track?[25]

Many thanks for your letter. I have given 'xxxxx' an offer of the farm but I don't know if he will accept it. I shall keep in view what you tell me. I have also to thank you for your help and for your kindness on Saturday.

Believe me,

Yours very truly,

James Curle

[21] This letter was kindly shown to us by Mrs Kathleen W. Stewart of Milsington. It was sent to her grandfather after he had met Curle and expressed an interest in the find discussed.
[22] Gilt bronze lower right leg from an over-life-sized equestrian statue, found in draining a bog around 1820 along with an inscribed bronze barrel-shaped cylinder, perhaps a weight casing or statue base. Published by Sir George Macdonald (1926: 7–14). Curle also included with this letter a signed offprint of his own summary of the find for one of the local antiquarian societies (Curle 1936).
[23] Macdonald 1927, recording a letter of Sir Walter Scott's concerning the leg.
[24] The neighbouring farm to Milsington; Mrs Stewart tells us that Curle acted as factor for this farm.
[25] Pot Sike (the form on current maps) is a tributary of the Dean Burn some 1 km west of Milsington; '... there is still a tradition of treasure waiting to be found in the Pot Syke' (Curle 1936: 193).

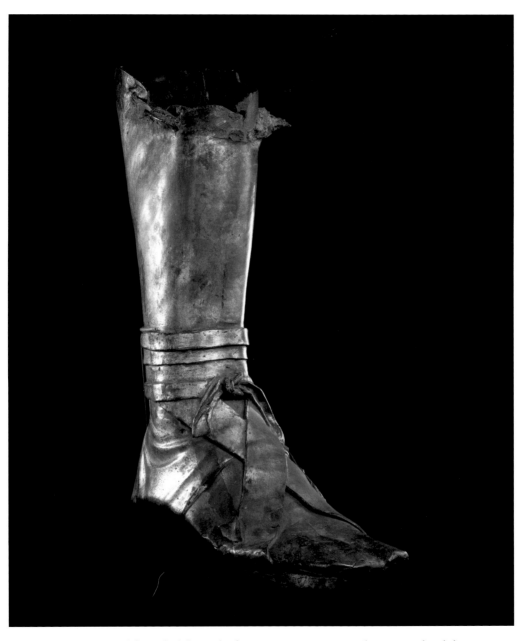

Figure 12.3. Over-life-sized gilt bronze leg from an equestrian statue, Milsington, Roxburghshire.
© National Museums Scotland (X.FT 140).

Letter 5.9

James Curle to George Macdonald.[26] Handwritten.

ST. CUTHBERT'S[27]
MELROSE
ROXBURGHSHIRE

15th April, 1939

My dear Macdonald,

Here is a rough sketch of the fort in Roumania [*sic*] on the Limes by the Aluta[28] 'Castrele de la Sepata de jos'.

I only have a slide. It is evidently a small fort with an independent outwork covering the gate – a form of clavicula but I feel sure there is an example of ditches being arranged in this way nearer home and that I have taken the Roumanian example as an illustration, but I can't remember where I saw it.

Yours ever,

James Curle

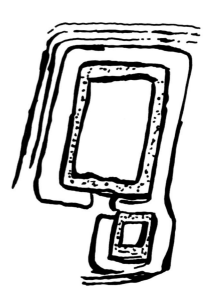

---

[26] Glasgow University Library, Museum Records MR.55/27; drawn to our attention by Prof. L. Keppie. For Macdonald, see *Dramatis personae*.

[27] The widowed Curle, whose tombstone mentions both Priorwood and St Cuthbert's, moved to the smaller 18th-century house just west of the Abbey as World War 2 approached and moves began to requisition Priorwood as a military hospital. St Cuthbert's later reverted to the name of Harmony, the West Indies plantation of its original owner.

[28] The two adjacent (indeed contiguous) *numeri* forts of Săpata-de-Jos lie by the Cotmeana river, some 40km east of the valley of the *Aluta* or Olt, and are part of the so-called *limes Transalutanus* on the south-eastern frontier of the province (Haynes and Hanson 2004: 26, fig. 1.2). Christescu (1936) published a plan in his report on his 1929–1930 excavations, but this does not show the features Curle recorded; indeed, it shows no means of accessing the gates at all, as the ditch is depicted as continuous! There has been no subsequent work (Cătăniciu 1981: 36, fig. 65; Gudea 1997, 76–78).

Letter 5.10

James Curle to M.V. Taylor.[29] Handwritten.

ST. CUTHBERT'S
MELROSE
ROXBURGHSHIRE

15th February 1941

My dear Miss Taylor,

I send you the short Memoir of Sir George Macdonald I have written for the Antiquaries.[30] When I think of his own Memoir of Haverfield[31] I know how imperfect it is but at least it records the work he did for the Society. I am grateful for the help you gave me.

I hope you have escaped bombs in Oxford, it is horrible how many landmarks are being demolished through the evil rage of these demented Huns. I have still one of my daughters with two small children in Malta where raids are endemic. The other one who was in Haifa has I am glad to say been evacuated to South Africa.[32]

With kind regards,

Believe me,

Yours very sincerely,

James Curle

---

[29] Margerie Venables Taylor (1881–1963), who served as Haverfield's assistant for several years, and was subsequently Secretary of the Roman Society (1923–1954) and editor of its *Journal of Roman Studies* (1923–1960); she had an impressive publication pedigree on Roman Britain. See Freeman 2007: 379–381.
[30] Curle 1940.
[31] Macdonald 1924.
[32] Such family details indicate Curle and Taylor knew one another well, presumably from Curle's acquaintance with Haverfield and references in the Letters to trips to Oxford, as well as his connections with the Roman Society (Chapter 4).

Appendix
Letters between the British Museum and A.O. Curle

We have selected here some of the correspondence to A.O. Curle from the British Museum that casts light on topics explored elsewhere in the volume or that serves to make a contrast in the way the two brothers were being treated by Hercules Read and his contemporaries. We have avoided material related to the Traprain Treasure, which is treated elsewhere,[1] and have not included some letters that are of only passing significance.

Letter A1

NATIONAL MUSEUM OF ANTIQUITIES
Queen Street
EDINBURGH

4th February, 1914

Dear Sir Hercules,

As you expressed a desire to have them, I send herewith a few casts in wax from the more important pieces of moulds which I found in my excavation of the Vitrified Fort at Rockcliffe[2] in the Stewartry of Kirkcudbright last Autumn, some of which I showed you when I was last in town.

With kind regards,

Yours very truly,

Alexr O. Curle

P.S. My brother James is writing a paper on the Viking brooches[3] found in Scotland, and would be much obliged if you would allow Mr Oldland[4] to take a photograph for him of the pair from Barra in your charge.

A.O.C.

---

[1] Painter 2022.
[2] The Mote of Mark, a hill overlooking the Solway Firth near the village of Rockcliffe in Dumfries and Galloway. On the hilltop is a fort occupied in the 6th and 7th centuries which was destroyed by fire, vitrifying the rampart. The site had been used for large-scale high-quality metal working – gold, silver, iron and copper alloy (A.O. Curle 1914; Laing and Longley 2006).
[3] See Letter 1.75 for background.
[4] An assistant in Read's department who appears regularly in the Letters as a facilitator of practical requests. See *Dramatis personae.*

Letter A2

The British Museum
London WC

5th September, 1917

My dear Curle,

I have had a curious interview with a certain Lady Hunter who has an Indian idol and a couple of bronze plaques in the form of winged beasts.

She brought them to Reginald Smith[5] during my absence and I understood that she wanted to give them to the Museum and I wrote to thank her. She has just been in to say that Smith made a mistake and that her purpose is to sell them for some war fund, that she had taken them to you, and that you had said that you would like to buy them, but would like my opinion first! This is all very complicated and I don't know what to do.

In the first place, I thought that you, like the rest of us, had no money to buy.[6] Is this so? It is convenient for me to know on general principles. In the second place and specifically, what *can* be the interest to you of these curious bronzes? I myself should not have thought for a moment that you would take any interest in them, or that you had a place or series where they would fit.[7]

Lady Hunter tells me that she had made no promises to you, and that, as a matter of fact, she would prefer that the things were here, but you may well have understood something different, so I told her that I had better write to you so that at any rate there should be no misunderstanding between you and me on the matter.

Yours very truly,

C.H. Read

Letter A3

The British Museum
London WC

13th October, 1917

My dear Curle,

I did not answer your letter about Lady Hunter's things at once, as I had not finished the business. As I told you she wanted to sell the things and give the money to the Red Cross, and on my asking her how much she wanted, she said she would like £5.

---

[5] A curator in Read's department and an extensive correspondent with James Curle; see *Dramatis personae*.
[6] No official purchase funds.
[7] Read's condescending tone is even stronger in Letter A4: 'any more limited Museum'.

It was plenty of money for some rather unsaleable goods, but they amused me and I considered that, after all, I should be contributing to the Red Cross. So I bought them out of my own pocket. I have no official money.

The Indian lady is South Indian, of a well-known type, but a good specimen. The two human-headed winged bulls are very odd. I am sure they are perfectly good genuine pieces, but of what age or where made I really don't know at present. King, our Assyrian man,[8] is very interested in them and wants me to publish them somewhere.

Yours very truly,

C.H. Read

Greetings to James

Letter A4

The British Museum
London WC

16th October, 1917

My dear Curle,

I am glad you are not inclined to be a Joseph Anderson[9] with me over Lady Hunter's specimens.

I really think they are much more use here than in any more limited Museum.[10]

Yours very truly,

C. H. Read

---

[8] Leonard William King (1869–1919), Assistant Keeper in the Egyptian and Assyrian Antiquities department (1892–1919); Caygill 2002: 387; Wilson 2002: 199, 201, 220.
[9] See *Dramatis personae* and, for Read's antagonism towards Anderson, Letter A5.
[10] A strikingly arrogant phrase which would have been guaranteed to rouse Joseph Anderson's ire.

Letter A5

The British Museum
London WC

24th May, 1921

My dear Curle

I am much interested in your letter on my address for the Antiquaries.[11]

I am not altogether surprised that you find my strictures on the Edinburgh methods rather severe, but in my case it is not amiss at some times to see ourselves as others see us.[12]

As I have one half of me Scottish and about in all two-thirds Celtic (i.e. extreme West of England) no one can say that I am unlikely to be sympathetic to the aspirations of the North.

As I pointed out, however, the matter is a much wider one than merely England versus Scotland. Carried to its logical end, it is speedily found to be an absurd proposition that strikes at the root of all science.

You say that today there is a change in method since Anderson's time.

I cannot see it. A few days ago a letter came here from Callander[13] practically forbidding the Museum to bid for the horse mask to be sold at Sotheby's tomorrow.[14] It struck me as wanting in tact for, after all, it cannot be otherwise than impertinent to forbid the British Museum to bid for British Antiquities. A request would have been just as efficacious and far more polite.

I don't say that Callander was *quite* as rude as Anderson used to be. I shall never forget Franks[15] writing to Anderson telling him about a lot of the Lewis chessmen (I think the Londesborough Collection) that were coming up for sale, and offering to help secure them for Edinburgh. Franks got no reply until just before the sale, when he received a formal official letter, making no reference to his proposal, but curtly ordering him not to bid against Edinburgh.[16]

That was Anderson at his very best, of course, and no doubt Callander is more civil.

The matter of unusual relics that I referred to were the Culbin Sands flints, of which Anderson had tens of thousands and wouldn't cede one.[17] They may have disappeared by this time. But the one action that made me see that Anderson would stop at nothing was the case of the Melfort cist burial, where Franks bought from the owner the whole of the remains

---

[11] Read's Presidential address at the Anniversary Meeting of the Society of Antiquaries of London on 28 April 1921; published as Read 1921. He was making a plea for the British Museum as a 'world museum' and lamenting divergent views elsewhere (Read 1921: 180): 'The claim made for the national Scottish museum is that it has a vested right to everything Scottish, and in addition may secure anything else that it can get. That was the principle laid down by its late director, Dr. Joseph Anderson, a distinguished antiquary, and probably a man of wide views on other subjects. Yet he seriously maintained that nothing that could claim a Scottish origin should ever leave the country.'
[12] Evoking Robert Burns, *To a Louse* : 'O wad some Pow'r the giftie gie us / To see oursels as others see us!' (Kinsley 1971: 157).
[13] J. Graham Callander, Director of NMAS; see *Dramatis personae*. Extracts of the letter, and the context, are given in Foster and Jones 2008: 247.
[14] The Torrs pony cap. See Letter 5.6.
[15] A.W. Franks (1826–1897), Director of the British Museum before Read; see *Dramatis personae*.
[16] The chesspieces were successfully acquired for NMAS. See *Proceedings of the Society of Antiquaries of Scotland* 23 (1888–1889): 9–14.
[17] To the British Museum.

and Anderson declined to surrender the two bronze armlets that are (doubtless) still in the Museum. There could be no legal or other ground[18] but his sheer greed for his retaining them. This was too much for me to stand so I resigned from the Scottish Antiquaries, as not liking their ideas of honesty.[19] Poor Herbert Maxwell, the President, was thoroughly ashamed but no one dared to contradict Anderson. Either Anderson wasn't a real Scot, or you are quite wrong in saying that if the Scot is approached in the right way he is not difficult to deal with.

You see, my dear Curle, all these things really did happen to me and frankly I resent them even now. To you they are either ancient history or you know nothing about them and you regard them as Academic matters.

In the matter of the Cadboll Stone[20] I consider the only people who come out of the business with untarnished reputations were the Trustees of *this* Museum. I hold that the Scottish Secretary[21] behaved in a most unjustifiable way in attacking poor Macleod at a moment when he had almost bled to death in order to get material advantage from him. I wouldn't have done such a thing for twenty Cadboll stones.

Forget this long tirade, if you can, and try to remember that I am looking at the thing as dispassionately as possible, but not from your side of the business.

Yours very truly,

C.H. Read

Letter A6

11th June, 1926 (copy unsigned)[22]

[As regards an ivory plaque sent to be appraised].

I find it hard to believe in its authenticity. The figure of the King has an expression of almost cinema-like intensity, not characteristic of 10th century Kings.

His crown is rather Drury Lane,[23] his sword unusually slender; his belt is oddly arranged to make room for the sword hilt.

The chalice is not of the right form; the hands and feet of the figures are badly done; the arms are strangely flat; the undercutting shelves immediately away from the edges; and the shape is unusual, unless my memory fails me.

---

[18] In fact, under the Scottish law of Treasure Trove, the purchase of the material by the British Museum was illegal. See Stevenson 1981: 181.
[19] Read vanishes from the list of Fellows published annually in the *Proceedings of the Society of Antiquaries of Scotland* in 1904.
[20] Pictish cross-slab, dated *c.* AD 800, with the cross face removed and a later (1676) funerary epitaph added. In the 1860s the stone was removed from the chapel of Cadboll by the MacLeods of Cadboll to Invergordon Castle. The stone was subsequently given in 1921 to the BM by Captain Macleod when he sold the estate, but this engendered enormous controversy, and it was returned to Scotland and deposited in NMAS. For full discussion, see Foster and Jones 2008: 238–251.
[21] Robert Munro; the correspondence discussed by Foster and Jones (2008: 245) gives a less dramatic sense of the events.
[22] The tone is that of Read.
[23] The theatre area of London.

Letter A7

20th March, 1928

[As regards a candlestick sent to be appraised].[24]

I'm afraid it has met with adverse criticism on all sides. Forsdyke[25] does not accept the feet as Roman and in this Department Smith and I do not feel confident about the rest.

Again thanking you for letting me look at it.

ABT,[26] Assistant Keeper

---

[24] A.O. Curle was a candlestick collector. See A.O. Curle 1926; Ritchie 2002: 31–32.
[25] (Sir) Edgar John Forsdyke (1883–1979), then a curator in the Department of Greek and Roman Antiquities, subsequently its Keeper, and then Director of the British Museum 1936–1950 (Caygill 2002: 385).
[26] Alec Bain Tonnochy (1889–1963), Assistant Keeper and later Keeper of the Dept of British and Medieval Antiquities; Caygill 2002: 392.

Bibliography

Abbreviations

CIL   *Corpus Inscriptionum Latinarum.* Berlin: Georg Reimer

NOTS   Hartley, B, and B.M. Dickinson 2008-2012. *Names on* terra sigillata. *An index of makers' stamps and signatures on Gallo-Roman* terra sigillata *(samian ware)*, vols 1–9. London: Institute of Classical Studies.

RIB I   Collingwood, R.C. and R.P. Wright (eds) 1965. *The Roman Inscriptions of Britain I. Inscriptions on stone.* Oxford. Clarendon Press.

RIB II   Frere, S.S. and R.S.O. Tomlin (eds) 1990. *The Roman Inscriptions of Britain II: Instrumentum Domesticum* (in eight fascicules), Gloucester: Alan Sutton Publishing.

References

Abercromby, J. 1912. *A study of the Bronze Age pottery of Great Britain and Ireland.* Oxford: Clarendon Press.

Ackerman, J.Y. 1855. *Remains of pagan Saxondom.* London: John Russell Smith.

Aldred, C. 1947. A gold beaker from Peru, *The Scottish Art Review* 2.2: 25–26.

Allen, J.R. 1904. *Celtic art in pagan and Christian times.* London: Methuen & Co.

Allen, J.R.L. 2016. A whetstone from south-east England at Newstead, Melrose (*Trimontium*): the reach of a major Roman stone industry, *Proceedings of the Society of Antiquaries of Scotland* 146: 113–119.

Almgren, O. 1897. *Studien über nordeuropäische Fibelformen der ersten nachchristlichen Jahrhunderte.* Stockholm: I. Haeggström.

Anderson, J. 1874. Notice of the excavation of the brochs of Yarhouse, Brounaben, Bowermadden, Old Stirkoke, and Dunbeath, in Caithness, with remarks on the period of the brochs; and an Appendix, containing a collected list of the brochs of Scotland, and early notices of many of them, *Archaeologia Scotica* 5.1: 131–198.

Anderson, J, 1881a. *Scotland in early Christian times. The Rhind Lectures in archaeology - 1879.* Edinburgh: David Douglas.

Anderson, J, 1881b. *Scotland in early Christian times (second series). The Rhind Lectures in archaeology for 1880.* Edinburgh: David Douglas.

Anderson, J, 1883. *Scotland in pagan times: the Iron Age. The Rhind Lectures in archaeology for 1881.* Edinburgh: David Douglas.

Anderson, J, 1886. *Scotland in pagan times: the Bronze and Stone Ages. The Rhind Lectures in archaeology for 1882.* Edinburgh: David Douglas.

Anon. 1892. *Catalogue of the National Museum of Antiquities of Scotland.* New and enlarged edition with illustrations. Edinburgh: Society of Antiquaries of Scotland.

Anon. 1912. *Illustrated catalogue of casts of representative examples of Romano-British sculpture.* London: Society for the Promotion of Roman Studies.

Anon. 1938. *Report on the Royal Scottish Museum for the year 1937.* Edinburgh: Scottish Education Department.

Armit, I. 2003. *Towers in the north: the brochs of Scotland.* Stroud: Tempus.

Arts Council England 2012. *Acceptance in Lieu: Report 2010-12.* London: Arts Council England.

Atkinson, D. 1914. A hoard of Samian ware from Pompeii, *Journal of Roman Studies* 4, 27–64.

Atkinson, D. 1916. *The Romano-British site on Lowbury Hill in Berkshire.* Reading: University College Reading.

Atkinson, R.J.C. and S. Piggott 1955. The Torrs chamfrein, *Archaeologia* 96: 197–235.

Axboe, M. 2007. *Brakteatstudier.* Copenhagen: Det Kongelige Nordiske Oldskriftselskab (Nordiske Fortidsminder B25).

Bailey, G. 1994. The provision of fort-annexes on the Antonine Wall, *Proceedings of the Society of Antiquaries of Scotland* 124: 299–314.

Beck, F. and H. Chew. 1991. *Masques de fer. Un officier romain du temps de Caligula.* Paris: Édition de le Réunion des musées nationaux.

Behan, P.O. and S. Hutchinson 2011. Sir Herbert Maxwell (1845–1937) – a great Victorian and Edwardian amateur naturalist and antiquarian, *The Scottish Naturalist* 123: 5–134.

Benndorf. O. 1878. *Antike Gesichtshelme und Sepulcralmasken.* Vienna: Karl Gerold's Sohn (separately printed from original in *Denkschriften der philosophisch-historischen Classe der kaiserlichen Akademie der Wissenschaften* 28).

Bidwell, P. and N. Hodgson 2009. *The Roman army in northern England.* Kendal: Arbeia Society.

Birley, A.R. 2012. The inscriptions, in F. Hunter and L. Keppie (eds) 2012: 137–151.

Birley, E. 1961. *Research on Hadrian's Wall.* Kendal: Titus Wilson and Son.

Birley, E., I.A. Richmond and J.A. Stanfield 1936. Excavations at Chesterholm-Vindolanda: third report, *Archaeologia Aeliana* (4th series) 13: 218–257.

Bishop, M.C. 1994. *Corstopitum. An Edwardian excavation.* London: English Heritage.

Bishop, M.C. 1998. Military equipment, in H.E.M. Cool and C. Philo (eds), *Roman Castleford. Excavations 1974-85. Volume I. The small finds*: 61–81. Wakefield: West Yorkshire Archaeology Service.

Bishop, M.C. 1999. The Newstead 'lorica segmentata', *Journal of Roman Military Equipment Studies* 10: 27–43.

Bishop, M.C. 2004. *Inveresk Gate: excavations in the Roman civil settlement at Inveresk, East Lothian, 1996-2000.* Loanhead: Scottish Trust for Archaeological Research.

Bishop, M.C. 2011. Weaponry and military equipment, in L. Allason-Jones (ed.), *Artefacts in Roman Britain. Their purpose and use*: 114–132. Cambridge: CUP.

Bishop, M.C. 2012a. *Tracht und Bewaffnung.* James Curle and the Newstead military equipment, in F. Hunter and L. Keppie (eds) 2012: 169–179.

Bishop, M.C. 2012b. *Handbook to Roman legionary fortresses.* Barnsley: Pen and Sword.

Black, G.F. 1893. Scottish charms and amulets, *Proceedings of the Society of Antiquaries of Scotland* 27 (1892–1893): 433–526.

Blackwell, A. 2018. *A reassessment of the Anglo-Saxon artefacts from Scotland: material interactions and identities in early medieval northern Britain.* PhD thesis, University of Glasgow. https://theses.gla.ac.uk/30708/ (accessed 8 August 2022)

Boesterd, M.H.P. den 1956. *Descriptions of the collections in the Rijksmuseum G.M. Kam at Nijmegen V. The bronze vessels.* Nijmegen: Department of Education, Arts and Sciences.

Bosanquet, R.C. and F. King 1963. Excavations at Caerleon 1909, *The Monmouthshire Antiquary* 1: 1–10.

Bottini, A., M. Egg, F.-W. von Hase, H. Pflug, U. Schaaf, P. Schauer and G. Waurick 1988. *Antike Helme. Sammlung Lipperheide und andere Bestände des Antikenmuseums Berlin.* Mainz: Römisch-Germanisches Zentralmuseum.

Boyd Dawkins, W. 1874. *Cave hunting, researches on the evidence of caves respecting the early inhabitants of Europe*. London: Macmillan and Co.

Braat, W.C. 1973. Der Funde von Deurne, Holland, in H. Klumbach (ed.), *Spätrömische Gardehelme*: 51–83. Munich: C.H. Beck (Münchner Beiträge zur Vor- und Frühgeschichte 15).

Brailsford, J.W. 1975. The Polden Hill hoard, Somerset, *Proceedings of the Prehistoric Society* 41: 222–234.

Branigan, K. and M.J. Dearne 1991. *A gazetteer of Romano-British cave sites and their finds*. Sheffield: Department of Archaeology and Prehistory, University of Sheffield.

Breeze, D.J. 2001. Gerard Baldwin Brown (1849–1932): the recording and preservation of monuments, *Proceedings of the Society of Antiquaries of Scotland* 131: 41–55.

Breeze, D.J. 2006. *J. Collingwood Bruce's Handbook to the Roman wall*, 14th edition. Newcastle-upon-Tyne: Society of Antiquaries of Newcastle-upon-Tyne.

Breeze, D.J. 2012. The end of Roman Newstead, in F. Hunter and L. Keppie (eds) 2012: 117–121.

Breeze, D.J. 2020. *The Pilgrimages of Hadrian's Wall, 1849–2019: a history*. Kendal: Cumberland and Westmorland Antiquarian and Archaeological Society / Society of Antiquaries of Newcastle.

Briggs, S. 2014. The Torrs *chamfrein* or head-piece: restoring 'a very curious relic of antiquity', in C. Gosden, S. Crawford and K. Ulmschneider (eds), *Celtic art in Europe: making connections. Essays in honour of Vincent Megaw on his 80th birthday*: 341–355. Oxford: Oxbow.

Brown, I.G. (ed.) 2003. *Abbotsford and Sir Walter Scott: the image and the influence*. Edinburgh: Society of Antiquaries of Scotland.

Brünnow, R.E. and A. von Domaszewski. 1904. *Die Provincia Arabia: auf Grund zweier in den Jahren 1897 und 1898 unternommenen Reisen und der Berichte früherer Reisender 1. Die Römerstraße von Mâdebâ über Petra und Oḏruḥ bis el-ʿAḳaba*. Strasbourg: Trübner.

Brünnow, R.E. and A. von Domaszewski. 1905. *Die Provincia Arabia: auf Grund zweier in den Jahren 1897 und 1898 unternommenen Reisen und der Berichte früherer Reisender 2. Der äußere Limes und die Römerstrassen von el-Maʿân bis Boṣra*. Strasbourg: Trübner.

Brünnow, R.E. and A. von Domaszewski 1909. *Die Provincia Arabia : auf Grund zweier in den Jahren 1897 und 1898 unternommenen Reisen und der Berichte früherer Reisender 3. Der westliche Ḥauran von Boṣrâ bis eš-Šuhba und die Gegend um die Damaskener Wiesenseen bis eḍ-Ḍumêr*. Strasbourg: Trübner.

Bryce, J. 1914. *The ancient Roman empire and the British empire in India: the diffusion of Roman and English law throughout the world*. Oxford: OUP.

Bryce, J. 1915. Religion as a factor in the history of empires, *Journal of Roman Studies* 5: 1–22.

Buchanan, M., D. Christison and J. Anderson 1905. Report on the Society's excavations of Rough Castle on the Antonine Vallum, *Proceedings of the Society of Antiquaries of Scotland* 39 (1904–1905): 442–499.

Cătăniciu, I.B. 1981. *Evolution of the system of defence works in Roman Dacia*. Oxford: BAR (International Series 116).

Caygill, M. 2002. Curatorial staff 1756–May 2002, in Wilson 2002: 380–393.

Chaffers, W., W.A. Nicholls and A.W. Franks. 1871. *Catalogue of the collection of glass formed by Felix Slade*. London: privately printed (not seen; details from British Library catalogue).

Chandler, K. 1994. Review of Hayward 1992, *Folk Music Journal* 6 no. 5: 669–671.

Childe, V.G. 1935. *The prehistory of Scotland*. London: Kegan Paul, Trench, Trubner & Co.

Childe, V.G. 1944. Arthur J.H. Edwards, Director of the Museum, 1938–1944. *Proceedings of the Society of Antiquaries of Scotland* 78 (1943–1944): 150–151.

Christescu, V. 1936. Le 'castellum' romain de Săpata-de-Jos, *Dacia* 5–6 (1935–1936): 435–447.

Christison, D. 1898. *Early fortifications in Scotland. Motes, camps and forts. (The Rhind lectures in archaeology for 1894).* Edinburgh: William Blackwood.

Christison, D. 1900. The forts, 'camps,' and other field-works of Perth, Forfar, and Kincardine, *Proceedings of the Society of Antiquaries of Scotland* 34 (1899–1900): 43–120.

Christison, D. and J. Anderson. 1901. Excavation of the Roman camp at Lyne, Peeblesshire, undertaken by the Society of Antiquaries of Scotland in 1901, *Proceedings of the Society of Antiquaries of Scotland* 35 (1900–1901): 154–186.

Christison, D., J. Barbour, J. Macdonald, G. Baldwin Brown and J. Anderson. 1896. Account of the excavation of Birrens, a Roman station in Annandale, undertaken by the Society of Antiquaries of Scotland in 1895. *Proceedings of the Society of Antiquaries of Scotland* 30 (1895–1896): 81–199.

Christison, D., M. Buchanan and J. Anderson 1901. Account of the excavation of the Roman station of Camelon, near Falkirk, undertaken by the Society in 1900, *Proceedings of the Society of Antiquaries of Scotland* 35 (1900–1901): 329–417.

Christison, D., M. Buchanan and J. Anderson 1903. Excavation of Castlecary fort on the Antonine Vallum, *Proceedings of the Society of Antiquaries of Scotland* 37 (1902–1903): 271–346.

Church, A.H. 1905. *Corinium Museum. A guide to the museum of Roman remains at Cirencester* (9th edition). Cirencester: Corinium Museum.

Clarke, D.V. 1990. The National Museums' stained-glass window, *Proceedings of the Society of Antiquaries of Scotland* 120: 201–224.

Clarke, D.V. 2002. 'The foremost figure in all matters relating to Scottish archaeology': aspects of the work of Joseph Anderson (1832–1916), *Proceedings of the Society of Antiquaries of Scotland* 132: 1–18.

Clarke, D.V. 2012. James Curle and Newstead, in F. Hunter and L. Keppie (eds) 2012: 23–33.

Clarke, S. 2000. The west annexe at Newstead (Trimontium), Roxburghshire, *Proceedings of the Society of Antiquaries of Scotland* 130: 457–467.

Clarke, S. 2012. Roman Dere Street and the road network around Newstead fort, in F. Hunter and L. Keppie (eds) 2012: 93–104.

Clarke, S. and R. Jones 1994. The Newstead pits, *Journal of Roman Military Equipment Studies* 5: 109–124.

Clarke, S. and A. Wise 1999. Evidence for extramural settlement north of the Roman fort at Newstead (Trimontium), Roxburghshire, *Proceedings of the Society of Antiquaries of Scotland* 129: 373–391.

Coffey, G. 1910. *Royal Irish Academy Collection. Guide to the Celtic Antiquities of the Christian period preserved in the National Museum, Dublin* (second edition). Dublin: Hodges, Figgis and Co.

Coffey, G. and E.C.R. Armstrong 1910. Scandinavian objects found at Island-bridge and Kilmainham, *Proceedings of the Royal Irish Academy* 28C, 107–122.

Cohausen, A. von 1873. Römischer Schmelzschmuck, *Annalen des Vereins für Nassauische Alterthumskunde und Geschichtsforschung* 12: 211–240.

Collingwood, W.G. 1927. *Northumbrian crosses of the pre-Norman age.* London: Faber and Guyer.

Collingwood Bruce, J. 1851. *The Roman wall. A description of the mural barrier of the north of England.* London: Russell Smith.

Collingwood Bruce, J. 1867. *The wallet-book of the Roman Wall, a guide to pilgrims journeying along the barrier of the lower isthmus.* London and Newcastle-upon-Tyne: Longman / D.H. Wilson.

Collingwood Bruce, J. (ed.) 1880. *A descriptive catalogue of antiquities, chiefly British, at Alnwick castle.* Newcastle-upon-Tyne: privately published.

Collingwood Bruce, J. 1885. *Lapidarium septentrionale: or, a description of the monuments of Roman rule in the north of England.* London and Newcastle-upon-Tyne: Society of Antiquaries of Newcastle-upon-Tyne

Collingwood Bruce, J. 1907. *The hand-book to the Roman Wall* (5th edition, edited by R. Blair). London / Newcastle-upon-Tyne: Longmans, Green and Co. / Andrew Reid and Co.

Connolly, P. and C. van Driel-Murray. 1991. The Roman cavalry saddle, *Britannia* 22: 33–50.

Coulton, G.G. 1933. *Scottish abbeys and social life.* Cambridge: CUP.

Craw J.H. 1924. On two bronze spoons from an early Iron Age grave near Burnmouth, Berwickshire, *Proceedings of the Society of Antiquaries of Scotland* 58 (1923–1924): 143–160.

Cree, J.E. 1909. Notice of the excavation of two caves, with remains of early Iron Age occupation, on the estate of Archerfield, Dirleton, *Proceedings of the Society of Antiquaries of Scotland* (1908–1909), 243–268.

Crokatt, G. 1786. *Scotch Presbyterian eloquence display'd: or, the folly of their teaching discover'd, from their books, sermons, and prayers, &c. with considerable additions, taken from scarce and valuable MSS. &c.* London: printed for and sold by the booksellers.

Curle, A. 1975. Richard Curle, *The Joseph Conrad Society (U.K.) Newsletter* 1, no. 6: 12–14. https://www.jstor.org/stable/20870293 (accessed 17 June 2022).

Curle, A.O. 1914. Report on the excavation, in September 1913, of a vitrified fort at Rockcliffe, Dalbeattie, known as the Mote of Mark, *Proceedings of the Society of Antiquaries of Scotland* 48 (1913–1914): 125–168.

Curle, A.O. 1923. *The Treasure of Traprain. A Scottish hoard of Roman silver plate.* Glasgow: Maclehose, Jackson and Co.

Curle, A.O. 1926. Domestic candlesticks from the fourteenth to the end of the eighteenth century, *Proceedings of the Society of Antiquaries of Scotland* 60 (1925–1926): 183–214.

Curle, A.O. and L.J.F. Keppie 2004. Macdonald, Sir George (1862–1940), *Oxford Dictionary of National Biography* (revised entry). https://doi-org.nls.idm.oclc.org/10.1093/ref:odnb/34700 (accessed 12 July 2022).

Curle, A.T. 1937a. The ruined towns of Somaliland, *Antiquity* 11: 315–327.

Curle, A.T. 1937b. Carved stones, British Somaliland, *Antiquity* 11: 352–354.

Curle, C. (ed.) 2008. *Letters from the Horn of Africa 1923-1942. Sandy Curle, soldier and diplomat extraordinary.* Barnsley: Pen and Sword Military.

Curle, C.L. 1940. The chronology of the early Christian monuments of Scotland, *Proceedings of the Society of Antiquaries of Scotland* 74 (1939–1940): 60–116.

Curle, C.L. 1982. *Pictish and Norse finds from the Brough of Birsay 1934-74.* Edinburgh: Society of Antiquaries of Scotland.

Curle, J. 1892. Notes on two brochs recently discovered at Bow, Midlothian, and Torwoodlee, Selkirkshire, *Proceedings of the Society of Antiquaries of Scotland* 26 (1891–1892): 68–84.

Curle, J. 1895. Notes upon three early Iron Age brooches from the island of Gotland, Sweden, *Proceedings of the Society of Antiquaries of Scotland* 29 (1894–1895): 292–301.

Curle, J. 1906. Excavations at Newstead fort: notes on some recent finds, *Scottish Historical Review* 3 no. 12 (1905–1906): 471–474.

Curle, J. 1907a. The Roman fort at Newstead: traces of successive occupations, *Scottish Historical Review* 4 no. 16 (1906–1907): 443–450.

Curle, J, 1907b. *The Roman military station at Newstead, near Melrose.* Edinburgh: Society of Antiquaries of Scotland (pamphlet issued by the Society with an appeal for subscriptions; copy held in National Library of Scotland, HP4.88.12).

Curle, J. 1909a. Notes on the pottery, in F.A. Bruton (ed.), *The Roman fort at Manchester*: 95–125. Manchester: Manchester University Press.

Curle, J. 1909b. Review of Walters 1908, *The Classical Review* 23 no. 7: 229–231.

Curle, J. 1911a. *A Roman frontier post and its people: the fort of Newstead in the parish of Melrose*. Glasgow: Maclehose.

Curle, J. 1911b. The pottery, in F.A. Bruton, *Excavation of the Roman forts at Castleshaw (near Delph, West Riding)*, 44–52. Manchester: Manchester University Press.

Curle, J. 1913a. Notes on some undescribed objects from the Roman fort at Newstead, Melrose, *Proceedings of the Society of Antiquaries of Scotland* 47 (1912–1913): 384–405.

Curle, J. 1913b. Roman and native remains in Caledonia, *Journal of Roman Studies* 3: 99–115.

Curle, J. 1913c. The Romans in Scotland, *Classical Association of Scotland: Proceedings 1912-13*: 36–60.

Curle, J. 1913d. Address delivered to the Berwickshire Naturalists' Club at Berwick, 9th October 1913, *History of the Berwickshire Naturalists' Club* 22.2: 47–64.

Curle, J. 1914. On recent Scandinavian grave-finds from the island of Oronsay, and from Reay, Caithness, with notes on the development and chronology of the oval brooch of the Viking time, *Proceedings of the Society of Antiquaries of Scotland* 48 (1913–1914): 292–315.

Curle, J. 1915. On a Roman visor helmet recently discovered near Nijmegen, Holland, *Journal of Roman Studies* 5: 81–86.

Curle, J. 1916. A find of Viking relics in the Hebrides, *The Burlington Magazine* issue 29, no. 152, September 1916: 241–243.

Curle, J. 1917a. Terra sigillata: some typical decorated bowls, *Proceedings of the Society of Antiquaries of Scotland* 51 (1916–1917): 130–176.

Curle, J. 1917b. Note on additional objects of bronze and iron from Newstead, *Proceedings of the Society of Antiquaries of Scotland* 51 (1916–1917): 231–233.

Curle, J. 1923. The Roman fort at Balmuildy, *Scottish Historical Review* 20, no. 79: 173–180.

Curle, J. 1925. Note on a primitive weapon or tool, fashioned by fixing a stone in a wooden shaft, found in a moss at Bogancloch, parish of Rhynie, Aberdeenshire, *Proceedings of the Society of Antiquaries of Scotland* 59 (1924–1925): 18–20.

Curle, J. 1929. The coming of the Romans, in T. Gowland and J.E. Fairbairn (eds), *Melrose and fair Tweedside*: 11–12. Galashiels: A. Walker and Son.

Curle, J. 1932a. An inventory of objects of Roman and provincial Roman origin found on sites in Scotland not definitely associated with Roman constructions, *Proceedings of the Society of Antiquaries of Scotland* 66 (1931–1932): 277–397.

Curle, J. 1932b. Roman drift in Caledonia, *Journal of Roman Studies* 22: 73–77.

Curle, J. 1933. Cappuck, *History of the Berwickshire Naturalists' Club* 28.2: 155–158.

Curle, J. 1935. *A little book about Melrose*. Edinburgh: Neill and Co. (reprinted from papers in the *History of the Berwickshire Naturalist's Club* 29.1 [1935]: 29–70; the booklet is not dated, but the copy in the NMS library is annotated 1935).

Curle, J. 1936. The leg from a Roman bronze statue found at Milsington, *History of the Berwickshire Naturalists' Club* 29.2: 193–195.

Curle, J. 1940. Sir George Macdonald, K.C.B.: 1862–1940. A memoir, *Proceedings of the Society of Antiquaries of Scotland* 74 (1939–1940): 123–132.

Curle, J.H. 1922. *The shadow-show* (eleventh edition). London: Methuen.

Dalgleish, G.R. 2022. 'Buckets of silver': the Traprain Treasure and its replicas, in Hunter *et al.* (eds): 37–47.

Dalgleish, G. and H.S. Fothringham. 2008. *Silver: made in Scotland*. Edinburgh: National Museums Scotland.

Déchelette, J. 1903. La sépulture de Chassenard et les coins monétaires de Paray-le-Monial, *Revue archéologique* (fourth series) 1: 235–258.

Déchelette, J. 1904. *Les vases céramiques ornés de la Gaule romaine (Narbonnaise, Aquitaine et Lyonnaise)*. Paris: Alphonse Picard & Sons.

Dent, J.S. 2012. The Newstead Environs Project and the Iron Age in the Borders, in F. Hunter and L. Keppie (eds) 2012: 213–227.

Diamond, H.W. 1847. Account of wells or pits, containing Roman remains, discovered at Ewell in Surrey, *Archaeologia* 32: 451–455.

Dix, B. 2004. Hartshorne, Albert (1839–1910), *Oxford Dictionary of National Biography*. https://doi-org.nls.idm.oclc.org/10.1093/ref:odnb/33745 (accessed 14 June 2022).

Doggett, N. 2004. Peers, Sir Charles Read (1868–1952), *Oxford Dictionary of National Biography*. https://doi-org.nls.idm.oclc.org/10.1093/ref:odnb/35454 (accessed 11 July 2022).

Donner-von Richter, O. 1894. Die Heddernheimer Helme, die etruskischen und der griechische Helm des Frankfurter Historischen Museums in ihrer Bedeutung für die Geschichte antiker Helmformen, *Mittheilungen über römische Funde in Heddernheim* 1: 21–49.

Dore, J.N. 2007. Coarseware, in W.S. Hanson, *Elginhaugh: a Flavian fort and its annexe*: 270–325. London: Society for the Promotion of Roman Studies (Britannia monograph 23).

Dragendorff, H. 1895. Terra sigillata. Ein Beitrag zur Geschichte der griechischen und römischen Keramik, *Bonner Jahrbücher* 96–97: 18-155.

Dragendorff, H. 1896. Verzeichniss der Stempel auf Terra sigillata-Gefässen, *Bonner Jahrbücher* 99: 54-163

Dragendorff, H. 1911. Review of Curle 1911a, *Journal of Roman Studies* 1: 134–137.

Dudley, D.R. and G. Webster. 1965. *The Roman conquest of Britain A.D. 43-57*. London: Batsford.

Elliot, S.D. 1929. Trimontium memorial, *History of the Berwickshire Naturalists' Club* 27/1: 69.

Elliot, W. and F. Hunter 2012. Gleaned from the soil: fieldwalking Trimontium, in F. Hunter and L. Keppie (eds) 2012: 181–211.

Ellis, R.H. 1978. *Catalogue of seals in the Public Record Office. Personal seals: volume 1*. London: HMSO.

Engelhardt, C. 1863. *Thorsbjerg mosefund*. Copenhagen: G.E.C. Gad.

Evison, V. I. 2008. *Catalogue of Anglo-Saxon glass in the British Museum*. London: British Museum (Research Publication 167).

Ewart, J.C. 1911. Animal remains, in Curle 1911a: 362–377.

ffoulkes, C. and C. Blair 2004. Dillon, Harold Arthur Lee-, seventeenth Viscount Dillon (1844–1932). *Oxford Dictionary of National Biography*. https://doi-org.nls.idm.oclc.org/10.1093/ref:odnb/32830 (accessed 14 June 2022).

Fischer, S. 2019. 'Et ego in Arcadia' – a quinquennial 'Concordia' from Viggeby, Norrsunda parish, Uppland, Sweden, in C. Ekström, K. Holmberg, M. Wijk and B. Gunnarsson (eds), *Samlad glädje 2019. Numismatiska klubben i Uppsala 1969-2019*: 95–101. Uppsala: Numismatiska klubben i Uppsala.

Fitzpatrick, A.P. 2007. Druids: towards an archaeology, in C. Gosden, H. Hamerow, P. de Jersey and G. Lock (eds), *Communities and connections: essays in honour of Barry Cunliffe*, 287–315. Oxford: OUP.

Forster, R.H. (ed.) 1908. Corstopitum: report of the excavations in 1907, *Archaeologia Aeliana* (third series) 4: 205–303.

Foster, S.M. and S. Jones 2008. Recovering the biography of the Hilton of Cadboll Pictish cross-slab, in H.F. James, I. Henderson, S.M. Foster and S. Jones, *A fragmented masterpiece.*

Recovering the biography of the Hilton of Cadboll Pictish cross-slab, 205–284. Edinburgh: Society of Antiquaries of Scotland.

Fox, C. 1939. The Capel Garmon firedog, *Antiquaries Journal* 19: 446–448.

Franks, A.W. 1863. Description of the plates, in Kemble 1863: 123–217.

Freeman, P.W.M. 2007 *The best training-ground for archaeologists. Francis Haverfield and the invention of Romano-British archaeology*. Oxford: Oxbow.

Frere, S.S. and J.K. St Joseph 1983. *Roman Britain from the air*. Cambridge: CUP.

Froehner, W. 1879. *La verrerie antique. Description de la collection Charvet*. Le Pecq: J. Charvet.

Fulford, M. 2021. *Silchester revealed. The Iron Age and Roman town of Calleva*. Oxford: Windgather Press.

Gaedechens, R. 1874. *Das Medusenhaupt von Blariacum* (Fest-Programm zu Winckelmanns Geburtstage am 9. December 1874). Bonn: Verein von Alterthumsfreunden im Rheinlande.

Garbsch, J. 1978. *Römische Paraderüstungen*. Munich: C.H. Beck.

Gillam, J.P. 1957. Types of Roman coarse pottery vessels in northern Britain, *Archaeologia Aeliana* (fourth series) 35: 180–251.

Gillam, J.P. 1970. *Types of Roman coarse pottery vessels in northern Britain* (third edition). Newcastle upon Tyne: Oriel Press.

Gillam, J.P. 1976. Coarse fumed ware in north Britain and beyond, *Glasgow Archaeological Journal* 4: 57–80.

Gordon, D. (ed.) 2005. *'My Dear Haverfield': the Curle correspondence (1905-1909) (and letters from and to Sir George Macdonald) with Professor Haverfield, as contained in the Haverfield Archive in the Sackler Library, Oxford*. Melrose: Trimontium Trust.

Gordon. D. (ed.) 2008. *Letters to Hercules: the Curle/British Museum correspondence (1891-1931)*. Melrose: Trimontium Trust.

Gordon, D. 2012a. The Trimontium Trust, in F. Hunter and L. Keppie (eds) 2012: 239–243.

Gordon, D. 2012b. The James Curle letters, in F. Hunter and L. Keppie (eds) 2012: 35–39.

Gordon, D. 2012c. Writing about Trimontium, in F. Hunter and L. Keppie (eds) 2012: 229–237.

Gräslund, B. 1987. G. Oscar A. Montelius, *Svenskt biografiskt lexikon* 25 (195-1987): 679. https://sok.riksarkivet.se/sbl/artikel/9465 (accessed 12 July 2022).

Gray, H. St G. 1906. Notes on some antiquities found at Hamdon or Ham Hill, Somerset, and in the neighbourhood, *Proceedings of the Society of Antiquaries of London* (second series) 21 (1905–1907): 128-139.

Gray, H. St G. 1907. Excavations near Forglen House on the borders of Aberdeenshire and Banffshire, *Proceedings of the Society of Antiquaries of Scotland* 41 (1906–1907): 275–285.

Greenshields-Leadbetter, T. 1919. Border bookplates, *History of the Berwickshire Naturalists' Club* 24.1: 39–80.

Greep, S. and M. Marshall 2014. Brigantian immigrants to Londinium? New finds of perforated bone 'spoons', *Lucerna* 47: 2–7.

Grieg, S. 1940. *Viking antiquities in Scotland* (Viking antiquities in Great Britain and Ireland part II). Oslo: Aschehoug.

Groller, M. von 1901. Römische Waffen, *Der römische Limes in Österreich* II: 85–132. Vienna: Alfred Hölder.

Gudea, N. 1997. Der dakische Limes – Materialien zu seiner Geschichte, *Jahrbuch des Römisch-Germanisches Zentralmuseums Mainz* 44,2: 1–113.

Hanson, W.S. 2012. Newstead and Roman Scotland: the Flavian to Antonine periods, in F. Hunter and L. Keppie (eds) 2012: 63–75.

Harden, D.B., H. Hellenkemper, K. Painter and D. Whitehouse. 1987. *Glass of the Caesars*. Milan: Olivetti.

Harding, D.W. 2002. Torrs and the early La Tène ornamental style in Britain and Ireland, in B. Ballin Smith and I. Banks (eds), *In the shadow of the brochs: the Iron Age in Scotland*: 191–204. Stroud: Tempus.

Harrison, S.H. and R. Ó Floinn 2014. *Viking graves and grave-goods in Ireland* (Medieval Dublin Excavations 1962–81, series B, volume 11). Dublin: National Museum of Ireland.

Hartley, B.R. 1972. The Roman occupation of Scotland: the evidence of samian ware, *Britannia* 3: 1–55.

Harvey, P.D.A. 1980. Review of Ellis 1978, *Archives* 14 no. 63: 196.

Haverfield, F. 1893. Romano-British inscriptions, 1892–1893, *Archaeological Journal* 50: 279–307.

Haverfield, F. 1899. Notes on samian ware, *Transactions of the Cumberland and Westmorland Antiquarian and Archaeological Society* 15: 191–196.

Haverfield, F. 1909. Notes on the smaller objects, in W.H. Knowles and R.H. Forster, Corstopitum: report on the excavations in 1908, *Archaeologia Aeliana* (third series) 5: 305–424 (400–423).

Haverfield, F. 1914. Roman silver in Northumberland, *Journal of Roman Studies* 4: 1–12.

Haverfield, F. 1915. *The Romanization of Roman Britain* (third edition). Oxford: British Academy.

Haverfield. F and H.S. Jones. 1912. Some representative examples of Romano-British sculpture, *Journal of Roman Studies* 2: 121–152.

Haverfield, F. and G. Macdonald. 1924. *The Roman occupation of Britain*. Oxford: Clarendon Press.

Haynes, I.P. and W.S. Hanson. 2004. An introduction to Roman Dacia, in W.S. Hanson and I.P. Haynes (eds), *Roman Dacia: the making of a provincial society*: 12–31. Portsmouth, Rhode Island: Journal of Roman Archaeology (Supplementary Series 56).

Hayward B. 1992. *Galoshins. The Scottish folk play*. Edinburgh: EUP.

Henig, M. 2007. *A corpus of Roman engraved gemstones from British sites* (3rd edition). Oxford: Archaeopress (BAR British Series 8).

Henig, M. 2012. Newstead and the art of the Roman frontier, in F. Hunter and L. Keppie (eds) 2012: 153–167.

Héron de Villefosse, A. 1899. *Le Trésor de Boscoreale* (Fondation Eugène Piot, Monuments et Mémoires 5). Paris: Académie des Inscriptions et Belles-Lettres.

Heuberger, S. 1909. Die Grabungsarbeiten, *Gesellschaft Pro Vindonissa. Jahresbericht 1908/09*: 3–11.

Heuzey, L. 1877. Une chaussure antique à inscription grecque, *Mémoires de la Société Nationale des Antiquaries de France* 38, 85–97.

Hildebrand, B. 1973. Hans O.H. Hildebrand, *Svenskt biografisk lexikon* 19 (1971–1973): 43. https://sok.riksarkivet.se/sbl/artikel/13584 (accessed 12.7.22).

Hildebrand, H. 1873. Studier i jämförande fornforskning. I. Bidrag till spännets historia, *Antiqvarisk Tidskrift för Sverige* 4: 15–288.

Hingley, R. 2000. *Roman officers and English gentleman. The imperial origins of Roman archaeology*. London: Routledge.

Hjelmqvist, T. 1902. Sven Söderberg, *Arkiv för nordisk filologi* 14: 298–304.

Hodgson, J.C. 1918. Memoir of the Rev. William Greenwell, D.C.L., F.R.S., F.S.A., a vice-president, *Archaeologia Aeliana* (third series) 15: 1–21.

Hoffiller, V. 1911. Oprema rimskoga vojnika u prvo dova carstva, *Vjesnik Hrvatskoga Arheološkoga Društva* 11: 145–240.

Hoffiller, V. 1912. Oprema rimskoga vojnika u prvo dova carstva, *Vjesnik Hrvatskoga Arheološkoga Društva* 12: 16–123.

Hoffmann, B. in prep. *The Roman glass from Trimontium*.

Hofmann, K., S. Schröer and K. Rösler 2020. 150 Jahre Hans Dragendorff – Gründungsdirektor der RGK. https://www.dainst.blog/crossing-borders/2020/10/15/150-jahre-hans-dragendorff-gruendungsdirektor-der-rgk/ (accessed 12 July 2022).

Holmes, N. 2003. *Excavation of Roman sites at Cramond, Edinburgh*. Edinburgh: Society of Antiquaries of Scotland.

Home, G. 1926. *Roman London*. London: Ernest Benn.

Hume Brown, P. 1910. *A short history of Scotland* (enlarged edition). Edinburgh/London: Oliver and Boyd.

Hume Brown, P. 1911. *History of Scotland to the present time. Volume I: to the accession of Mary Stewart*. Cambridge: CUP.

Hunter, F. 2009. A cap for a pony. Pony cap from Torrs, about 200 BC, in F. Müller, *Art of the Celts 700 BC to AD 700*: 230–231. Brussels/Bern: Historisches Museum Bern.

Hunter, F., A. Kaufmann-Heinimann and K. Painter (eds) 2022. *The late Roman silver treasure from Traprain Law*. Edinburgh: National Museums Scotland.

Hunter, F. and L. Keppie (eds) 2012. *A Roman frontier post and its people: Newstead 1911–2011*. Edinburgh: National Museums Scotland/Trimontium Trust.

Hunter, J. 2008. *Galloway byways* (second edition). Dumfries: Dumfries and Galloway Council.

Huskinson, J. 1994. *Corpus of sculpture of the Roman world. Great Britain, volume I, fascicule 8. Roman sculpture from eastern England*. Oxford: British Academy.

Jacobi, L. 1897. *Das Römerkastell Saalburg bei Homburg vor der Höhe*. Homburg vor der Höhe: privately published.

Johnson, A. 1993. *Roman forts of the 1st and 2nd centuries AD in Britain and the German provinces*. London: Adam and Charles Black.

Jones, R.H. 2011. *Roman camps in Scotland*. Edinburgh: Society of Antiquaries of Scotland.

Jones, R.H. 2012. The Roman camps at Newstead and their context, in F. Hunter and L. Keppie (eds) 2012: 51–61.

Joyce, T.A. 1913. Note on a gold beaker from Lambayeque, Peru, *Man* 13, no. 37: 65–66.

Kam, G.M. 1915. Antieke Helmen in het Museum 'Kam', *Bulletin van den Nederlandschen Oudheidkundigen Bond* (second series) 8: 258–266.

Kelly, S. 2011. *Scott-land: the man who invented a nation*. Edinburgh: Birlinn.

Kemble, J.M. 1863. *Horae ferales; or, studies in the archaeology of the northern nations*. London: Lovell Reeve & Co.

Keppie, L.J.F. 2002. New light on the excavations at Bar Hill fort on the Antonine Wall, 1902–1905. *Scottish Archaeological Journal* 24: 21–48.

Keppie, L. 2012. The search for Trimontium, in F. Hunter and L. Keppie (eds) 2012: 11–21.

Keppie, L.J.F. and B.J. Arnold. 1984. *Corpus of sculpture of the Roman world. Great Britain, volume I, fascicule 4: Scotland*. Oxford: British Academy.

Kidd, D. 1994. The Gotlandic collection of James Curle of Melrose (1862–1944), *Journal of the History of Collections* 6.1: 87–101.

Kidd, D. and L. Thunmark-Nylén 1990. James Curle of Melrose and his collection of Gotlandic antiquities, *Fornvännen* 85: 153–173.

Kilbride-Jones, H.E. 1938. Glass armlets in Britain, *Proceedings of the Society of Antiquaries of Scotland* 72 (1937–1938): 366–369.

Kinnes, I.A. and I.H. Longworth. 1985. *Catalogue of the excavated prehistoric and Romano-British material in the Greenwell Collection*. London: British Museum.

Kinsley, J. 1971. *Burns: poems and songs* (paperback edition). Oxford: OUP.

Klumbach, H. 1962. Römischer Gesichtshelm aus Stuttgart-Bad Cannstatt, *Fundberichte aus Schwaben* (neu Folge) 16: 163–167.

Klumbach, H. 1974. *Römische Helme aus Niedergermanien*. Cologne: Rheinland-Verlag.

Koch, J.K. and E.-M. Mertens (eds) 2002. *Eine Dame zwischen 500 Herren. Johanna Mestorf – Werk und Wirkung*. Münster: Waxmann Verlag.

Koepp, F., F. Drexel and M. Bersu. 1924–1930. *Germania Romana: ein Bilder-Atlas*. Bamburg: C.C. Buchner.

Koster, A. 2013. *The cemetery of Noviomagus and the wealthy burials of the municipal elite*. Nijmegen: Museum Het Valkhof.

Krier, J. and F. Reinert 1993. *Das Reitergrab von Heilingen*. Luxemburg: Musée National d'Histoire et d'Art.

Kruse, F. 1842. *Necrolivonica oder Alterthümer Liv-, Esth- und Curlands bis zur Einführung der Christlichen Religion in den Kaiserlich Russischen Ostsee-Gouvernements*. Dorpat: privately published.

Kruse, F. 1859. *Necrolivonica oder Geschichte und Alterthümer Liv-, Esth- und Curlands Griechischen, Römischen, Byzantinischen, Nortmannischen oder Waräger-Russischen, Fränkischen, Angelsächischen, Anglodänischen Ursprungs* (expanded edition of Kruse 1842). Leipzig: Dyk.

Kuttner, A.L. 1995. *Dynasty and empire in the age of Augustus. The case of the Boscoreale cups*. Berkeley: University of California Press.

Laing, L. and D. Longley. 2006. *The Mote of Mark. A Dark Age hillfort in south-west Scotland*. Oxford: Oxbow.

Lee, B.N. and I. Campbell. 2006. *Scottish bookplates*. London: The Bookplate Society.

Lehner, H. 1904. Die Einzelfunde von Novaesium, *Bonner Jahrbücher* 111/112: 243–418.

Lindenschmidt, L. (the elder) 1864. *Die Alterthümer unserer heidnischen Vorzeit* 1. Mainz: von Zabern.

Lindenschmidt, L. (the elder) 1870. *Die Alterthümer unserer heidnischen Vorzeit* 2. Mainz: von Zabern.

Lindenschmidt, L. (the elder) 1882. *Tracht und Bewaffnung des römischen Heeres während der Kaiserzeit*. Braunschweig: Friedrich Vieweg & Son.

Lindenschmidt, L. (the younger) 1900. *Die Alterthümer unserer heidnischen Vorzeit* 4. Mainz: von Zabern.

Lipperheide, F. von. 1896. *Antike Helme*. Munich: E. Mühlthaler.

Ljungkvist, J. 2006. Ultuna, *Reallexikon der Germanischen Altertumskunde* (2nd edition) 31: 420–422.

Loeschke, S. 1909. *Keramische Funde in Haltern. Ein Beitrag zur Geschichte der augusteischen Kultur in Deutschland*. Münster: Aschendorffschen Buchdruckerei (separate publication of article in *Mitteilungen der Altertumskommission für Westfalen* 5: 103–318).

Lowther, A.W.G. 1936. A Roman 'votive lantern' from Newstead, *Proceedings of the Society of Antiquaries of Scotland* 70 (1935–1936): 387–391.

Lyle, E. (ed.) 2011. *Galoshins remembered*. Edinburgh: National Museums Scotland / European Ethnological Research Centre.

Macdonald, G. 1908. Relics of a Roman holiday: glimpse of Tweedside in the second century, *The Scotsman* 26 February 1908: 9.

Macdonald, G. 1911. *The Roman wall in Scotland*. Glasgow: Maclehose.

Macdonald, G. 1915. Some recent discoveries on the line of the Antonine Wall, *Proceedings of the Society of Antiquaries of Scotland* 49 (1914–1915): 93–138.

Macdonald, G. 1916a. *The evolution of coinage*. Cambridge: CUP.

Macdonald, G. 1916b. The Roman camps at Raedykes and Glenmailen, *Proceedings of the Society of Antiquaries of Scotland* 50 (1915–1916): 317–359.

Macdonald, G. 1924. Biographical notice, in Haverfield and Macdonald 1924: 15–38.

Macdonald, G. 1926. Note on some fragments of imperial statues and of a statuette of Victory, *Journal of Roman Studies* 16: 1–16.

Macdonald, G. 1927. Note on some fragments of imperial statues. A postscript, *Journal of Roman Studies* 17: 107.

Macdonald, G. 1934. *The Roman wall in Scotland* (second edition). Oxford: Clarendon Press.

Macdonald, G. and A. Park. 1906. *The Roman forts on the Bar Hill, Dumbartonshire*. Glasgow: Maclehose.

MacGregor, M. 1962. The early Iron Age metalwork hoard from Stanwick, N.R. Yorks., *Proceedings of the Prehistoric Society* 28: 17–57.

MacGregor, M. 1976. *Early Celtic art in north Britain*. Leicester: Leicester University Press.

Macinnes, L. 1984. Brochs and the Roman occupation of lowland Scotland, *Proceedings of the Society of Antiquaries of Scotland* 114: 235–249.

MacKie, E.W. 2002. *The roundhouses, brochs and wheelhouses of Atlantic Scotland c. 700 BC – AD 500. Architecture and material culture. Part 1: the Orkney and Shetland Isles*. Oxford: BAR (British Series 342).

Macleod, D.J., W.J. Gibson and J. Curle 1916. An account of a find of ornaments of the Viking time from Valtos, Uig, in the island of Lewis, *Proceedings of the Society of Antiquaries of Scotland* 50 (1915–1916): 181–189.

McLeod, S. 2015. 'Ardvonrig', Isle of Barra: an appraisal of the location of a Scandinavian accompanied burial, *Proceedings of the Society of Antiquaries of Scotland* 145: 299–305.

Maldonado, A. 2021. *Crucible of nations. Scotland from Viking age to medieval kingdom*. Edinburgh: National Museums Scotland.

Manning, W.H. 2005. The Newstead parade helmet, in N. Crummy (ed.) *Image, craft and the classical world. Essays in honour of Donald Bailey and Catherine Johns*: 119–141. Montagnac: Monique Mergoil (Monographies Instrumentum 29).

Manning, W.H. 2006a. The Roman fort at Newstead: the weapons and the garrisons, in R.J.A. Wilson (ed.) *Romanitas. Essays on Roman archaeology in honour of Sheppard Frere on the occasion of his ninetieth birthday*: 73–94. Oxford: Oxbow.

Manning, W.H. 2006b. The Roman ironwork deposits from the fort at Newstead, *Bayerische Vorgeschichtsblätter* 71: 15–32.

Manning, W.H. forthcoming. *The iron artefacts from Trimontium, the Roman fort at Newstead*. Edinburgh: Society of Antiquaries of Scotland.

Margary, I.D. 1973. *Roman roads in Britain* (third edition). London: John Baker.

Matešić, S. 2015. *Das Thorsberger Moor 3. Die militärischen Ausrüstungen*. Schleswig: Zentrum für Baltische und Skandinavische Archäologie.

Maxfield, V.A. 1981. *The military decorations of the Roman army*. London: Batsford.

May, T. and E.H. Linnaeus. 1917. *Catalogue of the Roman pottery in the museum, Tullie House, Carlisle*. Kendal: Titus Wilson and Son.

Megaw, R. and V. Megaw 2001. *Celtic art from its beginnings to the Book of Kells* (revised and expanded edition). London: Thames and Hudson.

Meikle, H.W. and H.C.G. Matthew 2008. Maxwell, Sir Herbert Eustace, seventh baronet (1845–1937), *Oxford Dictionary of National Biography*. https://doi-org.nls.idm.oclc.org/10.1093/ref:odnb/34960 (accessed 12 July 2022).

Mestorf, J. (ed.) 1885. *Vorgeschichtliche Alterthümer aus Schleswig-Holstein. Zum Gedächtniss des fünfzigjährigen Bestehens des Museums vaterländischer Alterthümer in Kiel.* Hamburg: Otto Meissner.

Miks, C. 2007. *Studien zur römischen Schwertbewaffnung in der Kaiserzeit* (Kölner Studien zur Archäologie der römischen Provinzen 8). Rahden/Westfalia: Verlag Marie Leidorf.

Miller, S.N. 1922. *The Roman fort at Balmuildy (Summerston, near Glasgow) on the Antonine Wall.* Glasgow: Maclehose, Jackson and Co.

Milne, A. 1769. *A description of the parish of Melrose: in answer to Mr Maitland's quiries, sent to each parish of the kingdom.* Edinburgh: Alexander McCaslan / John Martin.

Minnitt, S. and J. Coles 2006. *The lake villages of Somerset.* Taunton: Glastonbury Antiquarian Society.

Monaghan, J. 1987. *Upchurch and Thameside Roman pottery. A ceramic typology for northern Kent, first to third centuries A.D.* Oxford: BAR (British Series 173).

Montelius, O. 1877. On de ovala spännbucklorna 2, *Konglige Vitterhets Historie och Antiquitets Akademiens Månadsblad* 2 (1875–1877), nos 64–66: 461–484.

Mortimer, J.R. 1905. *Forty years' researches in the British and Saxon burial mounds of East Yorkshire.* London: A. Brown and Sons.

Mowbray, C.L. 1936a. Excavations at the Ness of Burgi, Shetland, *Proceedings of the Society of Antiquaries of Scotland* 70 (1935–1936): 381–387.

Mowbray, C. 1936b. Eastern influence on carvings at St Andrews and Nigg, Scotland, *Antiquity* 10: 428–440.

Munro, R. 1882. *Ancient Scottish lake-dwellings or crannogs.* Edinburgh: David Douglas.

Munro, R. 1890. *The lake-dwellings of Europe: being the Rhind lectures in Archaeology for 1888.* London: Cassell.

Murray, J. 2005. The William McDowall Selby Collection, *Transactions of the Dumfriesshire and Galloway Natural History and Antiquarian Society* (third series) 79: 147–171.

Oddy, W.A. 1993. The history of and prospects for the conservation of metals in Europe, *Current problems in conservation of metal antiquities*: 1–37. Tokyo: Tokyo National Research Institute of Cultural Properties.

Östergren, S. 2002. C. Bernhard Salin, *Svenskt biografiskt lexikon* 31 (2000–2002): 291. https://sok.riksarkivet.se/sbl/artikel/6323 (accessed 12 July 2022).

Oswald, F. and T.D. Pryce 1920. *An introduction to the study of terra sigillata treated from a chronological standpoint.* London: Longmans, Green and Co.

Owen. O.A. 1992. Eildon Hill North, Roxburgh, Borders, in J.S. Rideout, O.A. Owen and E. Halpin, *Hillforts of southern Scotland,* 21–71. Edinburgh: STAR.

Painter, K. 2022. Alexander Curle's scholarly networks, in Hunter *et al.* (eds) 2022: 21–24.

Panke-Schneider, T. 2009. Lebenswerk und Lebensaufgabe: Das Römisch-Germanische Central-Museum, in A. Frey (ed.), *Ludwig Lindenschmidt d. Ä.*: 45–48. Mainz: RGZM.

Péré-Noguès, S. (ed.) 2014. *Joseph Déchelette: un précurseur de l'archéologie européenne.* Arles: Editions Errance.

Petrie, G. 1874. Notice of the brochs or large round towers of Orkney, *Archaeologia Scotica* 5.1: 71–94.

Pflug, H. 1988. Die Helmsammlung der Berliner Museen, in Bottini *et al.* 1988: 8–10.

Piggott, S. 1948. Fire-dogs again, *Antiquity* 22: 21–28.

Piggott, S. 1971. Firedogs in Iron Age Britain and beyond, in J. Boardman, M.A. Brown and T.G.E. Powell (eds), *The European community in later prehistory. Studies in honour of C.F.C. Hawkes*: 245–270. London: Routledge and Kegan Paul.

Piggott, S. and M. Robertson 1977. *Three centuries of Scottish archaeology. George Buchanan to Lord Abercromby*. Edinburgh: EUP.

Purdy, R.L. and M. Millgate (eds) 1984. *The collected letters of Thomas Hardy, vol. 4 (1909–1913)*. Oxford: Clarendon Press.

Rae, A. and V. Rae 1974. The Roman fort at Cramond, Edinburgh. Excavations 1954–1966, *Britannia* 5: 163–224.

Raftery, B. 1984. *La Tène in Ireland. Problems of origin and chronology*. Marburg: Veröffentlichungen des Vorgeschichtlichen Seminars Marburg (Sonderband 2).

RCAHMS 1909. *First report and inventory of monuments and constructions in the county of Berwick*. Edinburgh: HMSO.

RCAHMS 1915. *Sixth report and inventory of monuments and constructions in the county of Berwick (revised issue)*. Edinburgh: HMSO.

RCAHMS 1956. *An inventory of the ancient and historical monuments of Roxburghshire*. Edinburgh: HMSO.

Read, H. 1921. Museums in the present and future, *Antiquaries Journal* 1: 167–182.

Reinach, S. 1895. *Pierres gravées des collections Marlborough et d'Orléans: des recueils d'Eckhel, Gori, Lévesque de Gravelle, Mariette, Millin, Stosch*. Paris: Firmin-Didot.

Revellio, P. 1937. *Das Kastell Hüfingen* (Die Obergermanische-Raetische Limes B V 2, 62a). Berlin and Leipzig: Otto Petters.

Rhodes, M. 2004. Smith, Charles Roach (1806–1890), *Oxford Dictionary of National Biography*. https://doi-org.nls.idm.oclc.org/10.1093/ref:odnb/25789 (accessed 11 July 2022).

Richmond, I.A. 1944. Memoir – James Curle, *Proceedings of the Society of Antiquaries of Scotland* 78 (1943–1944): 145–149.

Richmond, I.A. 1950. Excavations at the Roman fort of Newstead, 1947, *Proceedings of the Society of Antiquaries of Scotland* 84 (1949–1950): 1–38.

Rieckhoff, S. and S. Fichtl 2011. *Keltenstädte aus der Luft*. Stuttgart: Theiss.

Riese, A. 1898. Römische Fibeln aus Heddernheim, *Mittheilungen über römische Funde in Heddernheim* 2: 31–41.

Ritchie, A. 2012. From Colonsay to Whithorn: the work of a 19th-century antiquary, William Galloway, *Proceedings of the Society of Antiquaries of Scotland* 142: 435–465.

Ritchie, J.N.G. 2002. James Curle (1862–1944) and Alexander Ormiston Curle (1866–1955): pillars of the establishment, *Proceedings of the Society of Antiquaries of Scotland* 132: 19–41.

Ritterling, E. 1904. *Das frührömische Lager bei Hofheim im Taunus* (Annalen des Vereins für nassauische Altertumskunde 40). Wiesbaden: Verein für nassauische Altertumskunde.

Ritterling, E. 1909. *Das Kastell Wiesbaden* (Die Obergermanische-Raetische Limes B II 3, 31). Heidelberg: Otto Petters.

Roach Smith, C. 1850. *The antiquities of Richborough, Reculver, and Lymne, in Kent*. London: John Russell Smith.

Roach Smith, C. 1859. *Illustrations of Roman London*. London: privately printed.

Robertson, A.S. 1975. *Birrens (Blatobulgium)*. Edinburgh: T. and A. Constable.

Robertson, A.S., M. Scott and L. Keppie 1975. *Bar Hill: a Roman fort and its finds*. Oxford: BAR (British Series 16).

Robinson, H.R. 1975. *The armour of Imperial Rome*. London: Arms and Armour Press.

Robinson, J. 2008. *Masterpieces of medieval art*. London: British Museum.

Romanes, R. and J. Curle 1898. Letter to the Secretary, presenting the silver chain known as 'Midside Maggie's Girdle' to the National Museum of Antiquities; with notes upon the story of the girdle and its owners, *Proceedings of the Society of Antiquaries of Scotland* 32 (1897–1898): 195–204.

Ross, A. and R. Feachem 1976. Ritual rubbish? The Newstead pits, in J.V.S. Megaw (ed.), *To illustrate the monuments*: 230–237. London: Thames and Hudson.

Roy, W. 1793. *The military antiquities of the Romans in Britain*. London: Society of Antiquaries of London.

Rygh, O. 1885. *Norske Oldsager*. Christiania: Albert Cammermeyer.

Sanden, W. van der 2002. Bog body research since Johanna Mestorf, in Koch and Mertens 2002 (eds): 195–196.

Saria, B. 1960. Viktor Hoffiller (1877–1954), *Südost Forschungen* 19: 395.

Schaaff, U. 1988. Etruskisch-Römische Helme, in Bottini *et al.* 1988: 318–326.

Schönfelder, M. 2002. *Das spätkeltische Wagengrab von Boé. Studien zu Wagen und Wagengraben der jüngeren Latènezeit*. Mainz: Römisch-Germanisches Zentralmuseum (Monograph 54).

Schröder, B. 1905. Die Freiherrlich von Lipperheidische Helmsammlung in den Königl. Museen zu Berlin, *Archäologischer Anzeiger: Beiblatt zum Jahrbuch des Archäologischen Instituts* 20, 15–30.

Schröer, S. 2020. *Mehr als nur Scherben … Hans Dragendorff als Forscher und Wissenschaftsorganisator*. Frankfurt: Römisch-Germanische Kommission.

Schulz, W. 1953. *Leuna. Ein Germanischer Bestattungsplatz der spätrömischen Kaiserzeit*. Berlin: Akademie-Verlag.

Smith, J.A. 1854. Roman antiquities found at Newstead, Roxburghshire, *Proceedings of the Society of Antiquaries of Scotland* 1 (1851–1854): 28–33.

Smith, J.A. 1857. Notices of various discoveries of Roman remains at the Red Abbeystead, near the village of Newstead, Roxburghshire (with an endeavour to localize the site of the Roman station of Trimontium in the neighbourhood of the Eildon Hills), *Archaeologia Scotica* 4.3: 422–427.

Smith, J.A. 1864. Note of fragments of Roman pottery, lead, iron, brass, coins of Hadrian, &c., recently found near Newstead, Roxburghshire, *Proceedings of the Society of Antiquaries of Scotland* 5 (1863–1864): 360–362.

Smith, R.A. 1905. *A guide to the antiquities of the early Iron Age of central and western Europe (including the British late-Keltic tradition) in the Department of British and Mediæval Antiquities*. Oxford: British Museum.

Smith, R.A. 1907. Wreck on Pudding-pan Rock, Herne Bay, Kent, *Proceedings of the Society of Antiquaries of London* 21: 268–292.

Smith, R.A. 1909a. The diving operations on Pudding-pan Rock, Herne Bay, Kent, and the Gallo-Roman red ware recently recovered from the Rock, *Proceedings of the Society of Antiquaries of London* 22: 395-414.

Smith, R.A. 1909b. A hoard of metal found at Santon Downham, Suffolk, *Proceedings of the Cambridge Antiquarian Society* 13: 146–163.

Smith, R.A. 1912. On late-Celtic antiquities discovered at Welwyn, Herts, *Archaeologia* 63: 1–30.

Smith, R.A. 1918. Specimens from the Layton Collection in Brentford Public Library, *Archaeologia* 69: 1–30.

Smith, R.A. 1923. *A guide to the Anglo-Saxon and foreign Teutonic antiquities in the Department of British and Mediaeval Antiquities*. Oxford: British Museum.

Smith, R.A. 1925. *A guide to the antiquities of the early Iron Age in the Department of British and Mediaeval Antiquities* (2nd edition). London: British Museum.

Smyth, W.H. 1831. Account of an ancient bath, in the island of Lipari, *Archaeologia* 23: 98–102.

Stade, K. 1942. Ernst Fabricius zum Gedächtnis, *Bericht der Römisch-Germanisch Kommission* 32: 225–228.

Stanley, W.O. 1876. Notices of sepulchral deposits with cinerary urns found at Porth Dafarch, in Holyhead island, in 1848; and of recent excavations in the sand mounds adjacent in 1875–6, *Archaeological Journal* 33: 129–143.

Stead, I.M. 1968. An Iron Age hill-fort at Grimthorpe, Yorkshire, England, *Proceedings of the Prehistoric Society* 34: 148–190.

Stead, I.M. 1985. *The Battersea shield*. London: British Museum.

Stead, I.M. 2006. *British Iron Age swords and scabbards*. London: British Museum.

Stevenson, G.H. and S.N. Miller 1912. Report on the excavations at the Roman fort of Cappuck, Roxburghshire, *Proceedings of the Society of Antiquaries of Scotland* 46 (1911–1912): 446–483.

Stevenson, R.B.K. 1981. The Museum, its origins and development. Part II: the National Museum to 1954, in A.S. Bell (ed.), *The Scottish antiquarian tradition*: 142–211. Edinburgh: John Donald.

Stuart J. 1864. *Memoir of Alexander Henry Rhind of Sibster*. Edinburgh: Neil and Co.

Summerson, H. 2018. Coulton, George Gordon (1858–1947), *Oxford Dictionary of National Biography* (2004, revised 2018). https://doi-org.nls.idm.oclc.org/10.1093/ref:odnb/32583 (accessed 11 July 2022).

Swinkels, L.J.F. 2000. Gerard Kam, in J.A.E. Kuys, R.M. Kemperink, E. Pelzers and P.W. van Wissing (eds), *Biografisch dictionary Gelderland* 2: 46–48. Hilversum: Verloren. http://www. biografischwoordenboekgelderland.nl/bio/2_Gerard_Kam (accessed 31 August 2022).

Symonds, R.P. 1992. *Rhenish wares. Fine dark coloured pottery from Gaul and Germany*. Oxford: Oxford University Committee for Archaeology (Monograph 23).

Tait, G.H. 1941. *Poems of the Borderland. Historic – romantic – martial*. Galashiels: A. Walker and Son.

Tait, H. 1976. *Jewellery through 7000 years*. London: British Museum.

Thompson, A.H.A. and B. Nurse. 2004. Hope, Sir William Henry St John (1854–1919). *Oxford Dictionary of National Biography*. https://doi-org.nls.idm.oclc.org/10.1093/ref:odnb/33975 (accessed 14 June 2022).

Tomber, R. and J. Dore. 1998. *The National Roman Fabric Reference Collection: a handbook*. London: Museum of London Archaeology Service.

Tomlin, R.S.O. 2018. *Britannia Romana. Roman inscriptions and Roman Britain*. Oxford: Oxbow.

Townley, C. 1815. Account of antiquities recently discovered at Ribchester, *Vetusta Monumenta* 4: 1–12.

Tyers, P. 1996. *Roman pottery in Britain*. London: Routledge.

Vaufrey, R. and M.A. Maurer. 1929. Nécrologie: Louis Capitan, *Journal de la société des americanistes de Paris* 21.2: 401–409.

Vetch, R.H. and M.G.M. Jones 2008. Crossman, Sir William (1830–1901), *Oxford Dictionary of National Biography*. https://doi-org.nls.idm.oclc.org/10.1093/ref:odnb/32645 (accessed 14 June 2022).

Walsh, M. 2017. *Pudding Pan: a Roman shipwreck and its cargo in context*. London: British Museum (Research Publication 202).

Walters, H.B. 1908. *Catalogue of the Roman pottery in the Departments of Antiquities, British Museum*. London: British Museum.

Watt, M. 2009. Gold-foil figures, in C. Adamsen, U. Lund Hansen, F. Ole Nielsen and M. Watt (eds), *Sorte Muld: wealth, power and religion at an Iron Age central settlement on Bornholm*: 43–53. Rønne: Bornholms Museum.

Webster, P. 1996. *Roman samian pottery in Britain*. York: CBA (Practical handbook in archaeology 13).

Wild, J.P. 1970. Button-and-loop fasteners in the Roman provinces, *Britannia* 1: 137–155.

Wilson, D. 1851. *The archaeology and prehistoric annals of Scotland*. Edinburgh: Sutherland and Knox.

Wilson, D.M. 1973. The treasure, in A. Small, C. Thomas and D.M. Wilson, *St. Ninian's Isle and its treasure*: 45–143. Oxford: University of Aberdeen.

Wilson, D.M. 1984. *The forgotten collector. Augustus Wollaston Franks of the British Museum* (Walter Neurath Memorial Lecture 16). London: Thames and Hudson.

Wilson, D.M. 2002. *The British Museum: a history*. London: British Museum Press.

Wilson, D.M. 2004a. Franks, Sir (Augustus) Wollaston (1826–1897), *Oxford Dictionary of National Biography*. https://doi-org.nls.idm.oclc.org/10.1093/ref:odnb/10093 (accessed 11 July 2022).

Wilson, D.M. 2004b, Read, Sir (Charles) Hercules (1857–1929), *Oxford Dictionary of National Biography*. https://doi-org.nls.idm.oclc.org/10.1093/ref:odnb/35693 (accessed 11 July 2022).

Woolliscroft, D. and B. Hoffmann 2006. *Rome's first frontier. The Flavian occupation of northern Scotland*. Stroud: Tempus.

Youngs, S.M. (ed.) 1989. *'The work of angels'. Masterpieces of Celtic metalwork, 6th-9th centuries AD*. London: British Museum.

Index

Entries are in the following order: page references in Chapters 1–7; tables; Letters; Figures.

Epigraphic index

Name	RIB	This volume
Aprilis	II.2: 2492.6	1.61
Atticus, Dometius	II.3: 2427.4–12	3.14
Avitus		1.34
Cinnamus		1.20, 1.21, 1.39–1.43
Cintuginus		1.20–1.23, 1.32
Divixtus		1.39–1.43, 3.19, 3.21
Domitianus, G. Arrius	I: 2123	3.4, 3.5, 4.15 n.101
Favonius, M.	I:200	1.35
Gaetulicus, L. Maximius	I: 2120	1.63
Lucanus	II.2: 2415.65	1.21, 1.24
Probus		1.34, 3.6, 3.7
Senecio	II.3: 2427.21–24	3.12
Uffus	II.3: 2425.5	3.12